Rome

Cities of the Imagination

Rome

A cultural and literary companion

Jonathan Boardman

INTERLINK BOOKS
An imprint of Interlink Publishing Group, Inc.
New York • Northampton

First published 2001 by
INTERLINK BOOKS
An imprint of Interlink Publishing Group, Inc.
99 Seventh Avenue, Broolyn, NY 11215 and
46 Crosby Street, Northampton, Massachusetts 01060
www.interlinkbooks.com

Library of Congress Cataloging-in-Publication Data
Boardman, Jonathan.
  Rome: a cultural and literary companion / Jonathan Boardman.
    p. cm. -- (Cities of the imagination)
  Includes bibliographical references and index.
  ISBN 1-56656-361-5
  1. Rome (Italy)--History--Miscellanea. 2. Rome (Italy)--Description and travel.
  3. Rome (Italy)--Social life and customs. 4. Popular culture--Italy--Rome.
  5. Rome (Italy)--In literature. I. Title. II. Series.
DG809 .B63 2000
945'.632--dc21   00-040725

Design: Baseline Arts Typesetting: WorldView Publishing Services
Cover images: Catriona Davidson; Pictorial Press Ltd.; The National Portrait Gallery
Photo credits: Catriona Davidson (pages
22,29,37,51,55,64,66,72,81,99,107,120,154,178,180,184),
Marco Magni (pages 8,10,16,32,41,61,75,85,91,147,169,193,198,215,223)

Printed and bound in Canada

Contents

CHAPTER FIVE
THE MIDDLE AGES (1: THE PAPACY): CASTEL SANT'ANGELO

CHAPTER SIX
THE MIDDLE AGES (2: THE CITY): STATUE OF RIENZO, THE CAPITOL

CHAPTER SEVEN
THE POPES (1: IN THE WORLD): THE FILARETE BRONZES

CHAPTER EIGHT
THE POPES (2: IN AUDIENCE): THE BORGIA STANZE

CHAPTER NINE
THE POPES (3: IN PRIVATE): VELÁZQUEZ'S PORTRAIT OF INNOCENT X

CHAPTER TEN
SEVENTEENTH- AND EIGHTEENTH-CENTURY VISITORS: CANOVA'S STUART MONUMENT

CHAPTER ELEVEN
Nineteenth-Century Visitors: Babington's Tea Rooms

CHAPTER TWELVE
Unified Italy: Palazzo della Rinascente

CHAPTER THIRTEEN
The Fascist Era: EUR

CHAPTER FOURTEEN
Timeless Rome: Trattoria dell'Omo Gino

EPILOGUE
Leaving Rome

Foreword

My first introduction to Rome was through the Reverend Augustus Hare's *Walks in Rome*: two volumes of intense Victorian scholarship dispensed along forced marches of that indefatigable author's devising. Although the sheer density and pace left me reeling, I was also left with a yearning to see the treasures and antiquities of Rome. Then, in my teens, I was introduced to Fellini's films, hotly followed by several months spent actually exploring the Eternal City.

Since then, I have read dozens of the hundreds of books written about Rome, be they entirely scholarly, social commentary or straightforward guide books. Rarely do they successfully combine all three categories. It has been done. Henry James has done it with consummate brilliance and left the gate open for those coming after him to beat the same path by stating, "...I hold any writer sufficiently justified who is himself in love with his theme."

What makes this study by Jonathan Boardman particularly stand out is the way it stretches across so many fields, rolling scholarship, tourist guide, social history and politics into a cohesive companion. And here is an author so in love with his theme he can see into its heart. This book, like true love as opposed to infatuation, can bear to see its beloved warts-and-all.

If ever a city was built for effect, to stir emotions, then Rome is that place. For over two thousand years she has been playing havoc with people's feelings. Edward Gibbon records, "My temper is not very susceptible of enthusiasm, and the enthusiasm which I do not feel I have ever scorned to affect. But at the distance of twenty-five years, I can neither forget nor express the strong emotions which agitated my mind as I first approached and entered the Eternal City."

And Macaulay had "no idea that an excitement so powerful and agreeable still untried was to be found in this world." For Ibsen, Rome was "beautiful, wonderful, magical." Goethe, on first beholding the city declared, "all the dreams of my youth I now behold realized before me." It was not to every visitor's taste; Lady Morgan was more overwhelmed by the fact that "the senses are everywhere assailed; and the pavements, sprinkled with blood and filth, exhibit the entrails of pigs or piles of stale fish..." And Harry Crosby in the 1920s in his extensive diary dedicates only eleven lines to the city, stating, "Rome. To St. Peter's (ugly, a dreary interior, no mysteriousness and a dwarf woman dressed in black)" and ending, "...and there was the Fontana Trevi into which we threw the littlest gold coin but I don't really know whether I ever want to return to Rome."

Despite all its splendor and its occasional squalor, its pre-eminence as one of the world's great museums, Rome has a life, is a living city with an almost arrogant indifference to its visitors. This book is aptly named a companion since it is a good companion to any armchair traveler, historian or Italophile, and an invaluable companion to any visitor to Rome. The city is both dissected and embraced, observed and analyzed and the writer's knowledge, research and curiosity bring not only a new voice to the already existing and very substantial choir, but often, a new view, particularly of contemporary Rome with an eye both for the mainstream and the off-beat, the obvious splendor and the often forgotten miscellany.

Unlike the Rev. Augustus Hare, whose meticulously learned *Walks in Rome* is hampered by his dour absence of humor and obtrusive distaste for Catholicism, the Rev. Jonathan Boardman, from his unique position as the Anglican vicar of Rome, is both broadminded and witty. His church and vicarage on the Via del Babuino must once have been a haven for all the Anglican pilgrims on their Grand Tours. His position gives him access to the city itself and to the corridors of power in a very privileged way. The gems the author has gathered are shared very generously with the reader.

When Dr. Johnson said "a man who has never been to Italy is always conscious of an inferiority" it was perhaps too early to observe that a man who has been to Italy is often conscious of a superiority. For it is easy to fall into the trap of thinking you know a place so well you almost know it all. By reading the following book, I learned so much about Rome that I didn't know, that I feel thoroughly indebted to its author.

Lisa St Aubin de Terán

In memory of Leslie Boardman

"nec multo opus est nec diu" – Seneca

Requiescat in pace

Preface

I have written something about the acknowledgements in books about Rome within the following text, which itself purports to be one of them. My comments there necessitate that these words of thanks be simple and brief.

Thanks are due to Michael Dwyer for suggesting that I write this and to James Ferguson for trusting me to do so. They enabled me to fulfill a dream; I hope the result is not the material for too many people's nightmares. I am grateful to the Bishop of Woolwich, the Archdeacon of Lewisham and the District Church Council of St. John the Baptist, Southend, for their agreeing my study leave, and I owe a great deal to my colleagues in the Team Parish of Catford (Southend) and Downham, and more widely in the Deanery of East Lewisham, for covering my ministerial absence during the writing; special thanks to Peter Allen, Paul Butler, Grant Homes, Naomi Whittle, and Susan Woolley.

Professor Heinrich Pfeiffer, SJ, of the Gregorian University in Rome was the origin of much of my thinking about Christian art in the city, and Professore Salvatore Valastro offered some useful pointers in the direction of contemporary studies on Rome. Erina Russo de Caro and Anna Risi gave me enjoyable insights into Roman society, artistic and intellectual life. Staff and fellow students at the *Venerabile Collegio Inglese*, particularly Father Pat Kilgariff and Father John McLoughlin, each contributed significantly to my approach to Rome, as did Professor Michael Dewar of the University of Toronto. Worshippers at All Saints' Anglican Church also contributed much to the final moments of the writing, particularly Paul and Nicola Cannock ("Grazie Roma"), Oliver Vordeman ("Forza Lazio") and Ingrid Hammond. I owe large debts of gratitude to my parents, Yvonne and Les Boardman, and Dr. Clive Marsland, who have given me constant encouragement and practical help. Last, but not least, I must thank Ruby Doe; I trust that wherever she is, she knows what she's done to deserve it.

Jonathan Thomas Boardman
La Verna, Umbria

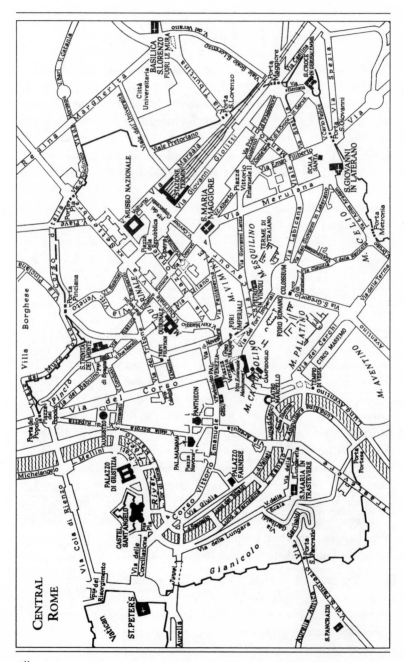

CENTRAL ROME

INTRODUCTION

Caput Mundi

Writing about Rome puts me in mind of one of Monty Python's slightest, but most enduring, characters: Ann Elk; *Miss* Ann Elk, that is. You may recall that her theory of dinosaurs, "all" her "own work," heralded by much throat clearing, ran thus: they are thin at one end, thick in the middle, and thin again at the other end. Reading about cities other than Rome has given me a theory about the *caput mundi*, the World's Head, itself: Rome is thick all the way through. This theory is not *all my own work*, I admit; I have acquired it from multiple sources, and I dedicate it to the genius of the most influential of my literary inspirations, Henry James. He often includes a Roman interlude in his books and, like some of his characters, considers the town to be "inexhaustible." He grants that London might possess "thick detail" looming "large and rich," but it is Rome that confesses "to the psychological moment" of which nothing can be thicker or deeper. No other place on earth has acquired so much continuous living, with the opportunities for both tragedy and comedy that life affords. This is what makes me want to write about Rome, as much as re-visit it, time and again.

I write this as we make our descent toward Ciampino, the smaller of Rome's two current airports (there are very fresh rumors of Perugia being designated the third). We are flying directly over the urban miracle of the ancient world (the first city to achieve one million inhabitants, 2,000 years ago), which is now transformed, sometimes agonizingly, into a twenty-first-century European capital.

Forty years ago, H.V. Morton opened his unrivaled portrait of the city with a reflection upon the strange wonder generated by air travel, still "novel" even in 1960, contrasting it with the laborious journeys of the pilgrims, conquerors and tourists of the past. Even earlier, in 1950, Christopher Kininmonth felt that he needed to describe to his Rome-hungry audience what an aircraft seat actually looked like ("classy dentists' chairs"). Passing through storm clouds today, with uncomfortable pressure in both ears, I can be both more dismissive and more resigned about the sensation of flight than either, while still appreciative of the majestic panoramic views it provides.

Seeing Rome in its entirety, capturing the place as a whole, has been a longed-for, but ever-receding, Holy Grail. The fragments of the great city plan *(forma urbis)* which once graced a custom-built hall in the ancient forum's Temple of Peace illustrate an early pride in what was being attempted. Turner tried to catch it with a fanciful period reconstruction of a cityscape; his vista is taken from the Raphael *Stanze* of the Vatican palace during its decoration by the Master, anachronistically including Bernini's colonnade and Piazza San Pietro. My favorite literary attempt at a foreshortening of Rome is G. M. Trevelyan's in the Introduction to his *Garibaldi's Defence of the Roman Republic.* More novel than history, the portrait has an epic tone:

> *There it all lies beneath us, the heart of Europe and the living chronicle of (the) march to civilization... As we look down we feel the presence of all the centuries of European history, a score of civilizations dead and lying in state one beside the other; and in the midst of their eternal monuments mankind still swarms and labors, after all its strange and varied experience, still intent to live, still busily weaving the remote future out of the immemorial past.*

Augustus Hare, the acceptable face of the nineteenth-century *inglese italianato* (since he was very far from being the traditional *diavolo incarnato* or devil incarnate that Italianate Englishmen were meant to be) tried to "show" the city thoroughly but with a less rhetorical flourish in his annual program of walking tours. Though wholeheartedly adopted as the only way to see the city by the impressionable females of polite expatriate society, another perhaps equally valid approach was employed by the eighteenth-century English "Mi Lord" who hired an open carriage to drive him No Stop (as the Italians would have it) around the town, accomplishing a complete viewing within the day.

I once accompanied a friend on her visit to two of the four great basilicas of Rome, S. Maria Maggiore and S. Giovanni in Laterano. Perturbed as we set off only at 11:00 AM, and with the prospect of a late lunch at a *trattoria* in a part of Rome I did not know, I was overjoyed to be back home for drinks before lunch at 12:45 PM. My friend's refreshing concept of visiting a church was to take a fairly brisk stroll through it following the shortest possible direct route. A day or so later, she also successfully cast a new light on the Vatican galleries for me, concentrating on the lavishness of their interior decoration, the most obvious feature, in fact, if you view your visit as mainly an opportunity for a reasonably long walk.

Seeing something of everything has to be set in the balance against seeing everything of hardly anything. Rome gives plenty of scope for both approaches. It is possibly because of this twin fact that visitors to Rome have generally planned a return. From this comes the superstitious tradition of visiting the Trevi Fountain on the last day in the city to throw in a coin to ensure another "turn." Clearly this might simply be the cheapest possible form of life assurance as it not only cabalistically underwrites future travel plans, but also guarantees longevity. Provided you are not resident, return to Rome implies the continuity of life itself.

Pen, Fork, and Film Portraits

Dr. Arnold, of Rugby fame, catches something of the seriousness with which the returning visitor can be visited, as he wrote to his wife in 1840: "Again this date of Rome; the most solemn and interesting that my hand can ever write, and even now more interesting than when I saw it last." Fleeing from the awesome responsibility of seeing and telling it whole, many have tried to suggest a "taste" of Rome, acknowledging just how hard it is to communicate the experience *in toto*. In his eccentric travelogue *To Noto— or London to Sicily in a Ford*, Duncan Fallowell almost wastes some wise words on a tiny pen portrait as he ostentatiously omits the city from his itinerary:

*And we are not going to Rome. I do love Rome and it's a wonderful
town for love—sweeter than Paris, freer than London, safer than
New York, funkier than Madrid, happier than Berlin, cleaner than
Istanbul, more human than Tokyo.*

But what sort of "taste" is best? Literary, musical, pictorial? Perhaps we
should first stick close to our metaphor and opt for gastronomic. I like
the food in Rome, but not all visitors agree with me; Fallowell again:
"But it's bland. All the bars and restaurants are identical because Italians
only ever want Italian food." He is perhaps half right, but errs on the
side of understatement. All Italians only ever want to eat their *mother's*
food. And that's why the best Roman restaurants are those that are really
extensions of a family table.

Successive films about Rome have tried to catch the *tinta*, the
defining "color" of the place. *Satiricon*, Fellini's *Roma*, *La Dolce Vita*,
even Hollywood's *Cleopatra* and a wonderful series of biblical epics tell
us of the Rome of excess. *The Bicycle Thief* is more honest, more painful,
as is Rossellini's *Roma, Città Aperta*. We see a town that portrays the
parti-colored nature of human experience, subject to love and war.

Rome, set in the center of two nations, inevitably suffers
condescension from both North and South. Giuseppe Tornatore's films,
from his definitively modern Sicilian perspective, show Rome as a place
where the open spirit of the *meridionale* or southerner is broken or
perverted. Visconti, already romanticizing the South, chooses virtually
to ignore Rome, remaining an outsider, a cosmopolitan visitor from the
North, a typical *Milanese*.

Christopher Kininmonth's rather fey and over-written early 1950s
account of Rome has its moments of precision; this is one of them:

*Rome is a hybrid sort of place where the real Southerner feels
undernourished. The Mediterranean southerner's diet consists of
sunshine and those foods most directly produced by sunshine,
whereas Romans eschew all but the gentle sun of Spring... But if
Neapolitans, Sicilians, and Calabrese feel themselves to be, when
in Rome, in the chill north, Italians from the north, even Tuscans,
feel they are already in the primitive, animal, dilatory and
dissolute south. One could say that Rome is a synthesis of all Italy*

but it would probably be nearer the mark to say that it is not particularly Italian.

Luigi Barzini adds a biographical edge to this realization when he comments that "only a foreigner, perhaps, can manage to be (so) crudely Italian." He was writing of Curzio Malaparte, a German with an Italian name and taste for reactionary Italian politics, but it might as well be said of those who find in Italy, and in Rome, the home that they somehow have missed in the places of their birth.

In trying to encapsulate Rome's spirit one is repeatedly brought face to face with what appear to be irreconcilable extremes, thus further distancing the searched for the "whole." Let me list some of the contraries that make up the place: the enduring class distinction of plebeian and patrician, filtered through twenty centuries; the constant juxtaposition of the old with the new in every age; the dialectic of pagan with Christian, and clericalism with a rooted anti-clericalism. And last but by no means least, is the partisanship of *calcio*, soccer, with a choice between Roma and Lazio (although really there was no choice when the local derby on April 10, 1999 saw Lazio romp home to a sixth successive win). Commiseration was still the dominant mood at my favorite restaurant on the following Tuesday, with Antonio dell'Omo, the junior proprietor and Roma fan, handing out *digestivi* so that we might all learn to forget... The new season has brought happier days.

So it really is a question of choice; make a decision about which Rome it is that you want to see and stick to it. "Let's ignore everything ruinous," a literary friend once decreed on a very short trip to the city. His taste was then, and from his publications still appears to be, for the *barocco*. But it was a manageable dish from Rome's menu, and so I joined him in the meal with relish. For centuries, though, visits have been controlled for the visitors by the wisdom or the tastes of others. The Roman Church dictated which shrines, saints or even doorways imparted the most grace, and this denial of choice is reconstructed for a post post-modern age as the Holy Doors of the principal basilicas are unbricked by the pope for *il Gran Giubileo*, the sacred "take" on the millennium. Guidebooks as such did not become common until the middle of the eighteenth century, but influential accounts of visits to Rome abound long before there were recognizable tourists. Latin writers from Horace to Juvenal satirized their capital. The priggish Pliny in his letters polished for publication makes clear what he, the very model of a second-century bureaucrat, thought appropriate behavior while "in Town." Dialect poetry like that of Belli and the short stories of natives such as Moravia point to the "real" Rome that provides yet another *gusto*, or taste, to be sampled.

Roman Holidays

But for most of us *stranieri,* foreigners, the more accessible Rome is created by the literary visitors themselves; romanticized by Shelley, Goethe, and Byron; apostrophized by Henry James and Oscar Wilde; defamed and ridiculed by Mark Twain, Wilkie Collins and even Dickens. Keats died here, we know only too well; it is terribly sad that his Roman life was spent entirely in a rented small room, with the pathetic exception of two exhaustingly agonized donkey trips up the Pincio hill. Comments in the visitors' book of the Keats Shelley Memorial Library in Piazza di Spagna often quote imperfectly from the Cockney poet's more plangent verses, while a rather refreshing voice once announced in a bold hand: "What a lot of silly young men they were!"

Silly young women there seem fewer of in Rome, whether they be local or from out of town. But if silly they be, it is usually in a rather heroic and grand fashion. When in Henry James' *Portrait of a Lady*, Isabel Archer falls into the trap of a miserable marriage she takes some warm cold comfort in Rome's environment:

> She had long before this taken Rome into her confidence, for in a
> world of ruins the ruin of her happiness seemed a less unnatural
> catastrophe... She had become deeply, tenderly acquainted with
> Rome; it interfused and moderated her passion. But she had
> grown to think of it chiefly as the place where people had suffered.

Rome's own thick detail is splashed with blood and tears, perhaps disproportionately female, as well as washed in the water of its myriad fountains. English literature likes its Roman heroines sad, and unhappily married; George Eliot permits her Dorothea Casaubon only one painstaking outing from the confines of Middlemarch, and that symbolically is to the Eternal City.

A particularly perceptive visitor, Elizabeth Bowen, the Anglo-Irish novelist, wrote of the dullness of the perpetual quest for the whole Rome. How boring to have to identify the Seven Hills upon which the city is always said to have been built:

Capitoline and Palatine are unmistakably hills—the Aventine too. But the Caelian, Esquiline, Viminal and Quirinal are ambiguously webbed together by ridges. On the whole I have come to suppose that these are the Seven—but if so, what of the Pincian, "Hill of Gardens," and Janiculum, bastion across the river? I asked a number of friends, but no two gave me the same answer; some did not care to be pinned down, others put forward their own candidates. That I should be set on compiling a definitive list of the Seven Hills, eager to check on all, to locate each, was, I can see, disillusioning to people who had hoped I might show more advanced tastes.

No, she's right, the only whole Rome worth having is the one which you find and keep for yourself; to try to acquire anything else is fruitless. Most of the text—observation, trivia, and anecdote—that follows is my attempt to share a little of what I've stored up in my own inexhaustible quest.

On the Eve of All Hallows, 1989 I had an impacted wisdom tooth extracted by a Roman dentist of Belgian nationality, the good Dr. Decaesstecker. His premises were in a Renaissance Palazzo on the Corso Vittorio Emanuele, and proved to be the epitome of Italian gadget-chic. On the ceilings eighteenth-century *putti* floated, illuminated by delicate and cleverly concealed up-lighters. The fashionable patients (I was clearly an exception) waited in a tastefully furnished gallery with doors that gave straight into a suite of small cubicle-like surgeries. Softly piped harpsichord music played continually, giving the experience a slightly incongruous but not unwelcome celebratory, if not decadent, air. Against this background of luxury, the framed photos of the dentist being presented to John Paul II, exhibiting a fair amount of perfectly regular dazzling white teeth in the process, added the spiritually reassuring note to balance the worldly elegance. Out of the window, even when prone in the hi-tech operating chair, I could just see the cross on the gable of the Chiesa Nuova across the road. There followed the most painful fifty minutes of my life. However dentistry is dressed, even when dressed so attractively in Rome, it is largely about brute force and instruments that can easily be turned to the torturer's trade. As I staggered home through the darkening, autumnal streets, I felt as if I had been struck in the face by a sledgehammer. Religion, music, the glamour of both the old and the new, art, architecture, and just a touch of the perpetually foreign and slightly gothic—oh, and some pain: here it all was, and I was missing a tooth.

CHAPTER ONE

The Early Republic: Cloaca Maxima

divina natura dedit agros, ars humana aedificavit urbes
"Divine Nature gave the country, human skill built the cities."
Varro, *Roman Republic* 3.1

The Tiber does not force itself upon one's consciousness in Rome, as do the Thames and the Seine in London and Paris; it literally insinuates itself, curving yellow and sluggish through parts of the city that you might not even come across without the time or the inclination. Even if forced or tempted to take the wheel of a car or hop on a vespa, it is quite possible that the flow of urban traffic would never insist upon your encounter with the river bank, the *Lungotevere,* nor with one of the Tiber bridges, ancient or modern. There is one spot, however, which is inevitably exceptional, there just to prove the rule. A stretch of road from the Testaccio district forms a near expressway alongside the river until it joins two more busy streets pouring out traffic from what appear random directions into the maelstrom of a piazza. It is to this unlikely spot that I first want to guide the visitor to Rome.

Here, in the Piazza della Bocca della Verità, we are not so much at the heart of Republican Rome as loitering around its back passage. Even the crude monumental face with gaping mouth that attracts countless

visitors to the portico of the nearby Church of S. Maria in Cosmedin points to the reason for our visit. Tourist tradition insists that Romans believe the *bocca* or mouth to bite off the hands of liars foolhardy enough to pop them in. The truth that the mouth speaks of is far less exotic. As an ornamental grid cover, the grotesque face tells us that the earliest Rome to deserve the title "city" was built upon a large drain.

The *cloaca maxima* (literally "the biggest drain") is amazingly ancient, and it still works. It started life as a natural watercourse running through a marshy area near the river, and it is here, at a natural fording place of the river, that tradition speaks of the finding of the twin founding brothers, Romulus and Remus. Later it became part of an extensive drainage system serving the valleys between the Esquiline, Viminal, and Quirinal hills as well as the nearby Roman Forum.

Its canalization was attributed in ancient sources to the semi-mythical reigns of two of Rome's seven kings, Tarquinius the Elder and Servius Tullius (616–535 BC). The *cloaca* was later arched over at the beginning of the second century BC and so vanished except in its absolutely necessary effects. The marsh, known as the *velabrum*, recalled in the names of a nearby street and church (Via del Velabro, S. Giorgio in Velabro), together with the Tiber Island just a little further upstream were, in parallel with the fabled brothers reared by the she-wolf, the obvious twin causes for the beginning of settlement here.

In Book 8 of the *Aeneid*, Virgil imagines the pre-Republican village clinging to the bend of the Tiber and climbing the slopes of the Capitoline and Palatine hills. There definitely were Paleolithic burials on the Palatine, but little evidence of the Greek colonization envisaged by Virgil's politically motivated fancy. His invention of a settlement called Pallanteum, ruled by a Greek king, Evander, is a sure way of showing that the site of Rome is the true successor to Greek culture, though his account of Evander sacrificing to Hercules as Aeneas disembarks is rooted in local fact. For the oldest of the Republican temples (c.200 BC) in the Piazza della Bocca della Verità, with its distinctive circular marble sanctuary and conical roof, long thought to be the Temple of Vesta, was in fact dedicated to Hercules. An archaeological find has proved that there was once a statue to this powerful god on the site.

Next to the temple, a side conduit of the *cloaca maxima* is visible, covered by a large slab of travertine stone. The connection between this mighty drain and sacred space is not, however, isolated to this juxtaposition. In the Roman Forum itself, only a quarter of a mile away, the graceful, curved sanctuary of Venus just down the Sacred Way from the Senate House is named after the public utility upon which it stands. The temple to the erotic goddess and founder of Rome's fortunes is nicknamed *Cloacina*, for it is here that the sewer is diverted into the valley of the Forum. As if a county councilor's wet dream, here civic efficiency meets carnal pleasure, and "Love" makes her home in the office of public works.

Public utility and sex were to have a certain contiguity in the Roman state. The first emperor Augustus' ardent attempts to encourage procreation with the reward of titles and pensions for those who fathered five children spring to mind, as do Mussolini's award of medals to mothers of ten and more. Roman religion, in its official form, also seems to have been an expression of civic virtue rather than one of life's rewarding mysteries, even where it approached the exotic. Modern fantasies centering upon the activities of the Vestal Virgins might fall a little flat when we note that their principal daily functions were to keep a fire alight and to fetch water from a pure spring outside the city walls. In so doing they were perpetuating the myth of Egeria, one of the *Camenae* or local water sprites, who managed to marry another one of Rome's kings, Numa Pompilius. Drainage and water provision, even when mythologized, maintained their practical political importance.

Despite the Tiber, water is as much a visitor to Rome as the tourist or pilgrim. It is true that there are a few naturally occurring springs in the vicinity. In antiquity the *camenae* guarded one; the one most likely to be first heard and then seen nowadays is that in the *scavi* of the church of S. Clemente. But such natural local provision of water was never going to be enough for a city that always had aspirations. The first aqueduct was built for the city by the censor, Appius Claudius Caecus in 312 BC; he was a member of the family that was later to unite with the Julian house to provide Rome with its first emperors. The Republican censorship was an extraordinary office, supplementing the executive consulship for the purpose of demographic survey and the commissioning of public works. By extending his tenure of the post, Appius was able not only to lend his name to his aqueduct but also to the Via Appia, the main route to points south. Ten more aqueducts were to be built in the years to AD 226, drawing most of their water from the Alban hills to the south, or the spurs of the Apennines around Tivoli to the east. A couple of them were supplied from the north, around Lake Bracciano. The water they provided was distributed at public fountains or could be piped direct to large homes and commercial bath complexes. The aqueduct system was modeled directly on that of the drains and sewers, and although aqueducts still provide some of the most spectacular evidence of Roman public works when lifted upon arches (look at the double-decker near Porta Maggiore, or those which cross the *campagna*), they were for the most part underground, silent, invisible.

The invading Goths, led by Vitiges, cut the aqueducts in AD 537 and in one stroke humbled the city that had been Mistress of the World, *caput mundi*. Subsequently the medieval inhabitants of Rome settled on the *Campus Martius* in the curve of the river, from which they took their water, and it was only in the mid-fifteenth century that the process of restoration began. It fell to the pope, as temporal successor to the emperor, as well as spiritual monarch, to provide for the city. Paul V Borghese (1605–21) so marked his early seventeenth-century pontificate with the provision of fountains that he earned the nickname "Fontifice Maxime," punning with his title Pontifex. But it was Nicholas V (1447–55) who in 1453 had commissioned the engineer-artist Leon Battista Alberti to restore the ancient Virgin aqueduct, given its name either by the sweet purity of its waters or a legend concerning the discovery of its source, and so started the papal conservation and provision of water. Sixtus V (1585–90) provided the Acqua Felice in 1586; Paul V (the Fontifice) the Acqua Paola in 1611. Pius IX (1846–78), never wishing to be left out, restored one of the ancient channels and added his own name to it, forming the Pia Antica Marcia. When he presided over its completion early in September 1870, watching as the water splashed into its fountains, he was performing the last public duty a pope would perform as temporal ruler of the city and the Papal States. Ten days later, the troops of the Kingdom of Italy broke through the wall at the Porta Pia and Rome fell to secularism.

Water works continued into the twentieth century, under monarchy and republic, with the Vergine Nuova of 1937, and the Peschiera of 1949. With a couple of minor additions the grand total of aqueducts supplying modern Rome had reached eight by 1972, the same number there had been during the reign of the Emperor Claudius in the middle of the first century AD.

Display and Convenience

Talk of aqueducts inevitably leads us to consider one of the most striking features of Rome's street furniture: the fountain. Choosing Roman fountains, together with pine trees and holidays as the defining subject of the city's personality, Ottorino Respighi, Rome's most celebrated twentieth-century composer, described four of them in music, and such public celebration does not seem out of place. If the ancient Romans built their reputation as suitable rulers of the world on engineering excellence and the provision of drains, the later inhabitants gloried in the extravagant display that even civic amenities might entertain. Each of the aqueducts possesses a *mostra*, a display fountain, for display has always gilded utility in Rome.

The Trevi Fountain, for example, is the *mostra* of the Acqua Vergine, as is the Pauline Fountain half way up the Janiculum for the Acqua Paola. In this respect, baroque practice followed antique hydraulic systems; the two best known ancient fountains were themselves *mostre*: the Meta Sudans set between the Colosseum and the Arch of Constantine, and the Julia fountain, the remains of which can be seen close to Stazione Termini, in the Piazza Vittorio Emanuele. Formally the plinth for the ancient sculptural piece known as the Trophies of Marius (removed to the balustrade of the Piazza del Campidoglio in the sixteenth century), the Julia Fountain was the *castellum*, or holding tank and terminal, for either the Aqua Claudia or Aniene Nuova. It was built in the period of Alexander Severus (222–235 AD), and no doubt served the needs of a busy market like the one that is still held in the neighboring piazza.

Much is known about the way in which the fountains, aqueducts, and drains of the ancient city were maintained because of the writing of one Sextus Julius Frontinus, the chief commissioner for water in the reigns of the Emperors Nerva and Trajan (end of the first, beginning of the second centuries AD). His treatise, *De aquis urbis Romae,* was rediscovered at about the same time the papal rulers of the city became interested in supplying water by aqueducts and celebrating the fact with fountains. The department over which Frontinus presided, the *statio aquarium*, had been founded by Marcus Agrippa, the loyal lieutenant of Augustus, nearly a century before. Agrippa himself had provided a new aqueduct, the Aqua Virgo, in 33 BC, the spring of which was indicated to his engineers, according to legend, by the mysterious appearance of a mute girl (once again the flat dough of civic works receive their leaven of sex), a story recorded in Nicola Salvi's eighteenth-century bas relief above the current Trevi Fountain.

If the Republic instituted the drain and sewer, the aqueduct and fountain, and the early principate regulated them, it was an emperor of a slightly later date who gave Rome its other specific "public conveniences." Modern Romans to this day rejoice in the names of the great rulers: Cesare, Massimo, Claudio, Tito, and even Tiberio. But no one is christened for the Emperor Vespasian simply because he gave his name to the urinals that he provided for the city's men. On an early trip to Rome with student friends, we punished a particularly surly waiter at our favorite *trattoria* by referring to him privately as Vespasiano; he is still waiting, but has mellowed with age.

If you are looking for relief in Rome, bars are probably your best bet, although there are a few "independent" public lavatories, in metro stations and near parks and the Roman Forum. The big stores have them (Standa, Upim and Rinascente), and shop keepers and patrons of restaurants are usually understanding. Best ask for *il bagno* (pronounced banyo), since long ago I inadvertently caused considerable trouble for a clerical friend who wanted the name of the most famous ecclesiastical tailor in Rome (Gammarelli) by telling him the word for toilet (*gabinetti*). I know better Italian now, but I would hate to think of a desperate reader seeking a bathroom finding themselves confronted with a display of cassocks and birettas.

Water, Water

The water supplied to Rome is uniformly hard and the enduring problem for those holding Frontinus' brief in antiquity or more recently has been to ensure that lime deposits do not entirely block the channels. Other problems for the ancients were the myriad leaks that were more than likely over the considerable distances run by the aqueducts (the Aqua Virgo was over twelve miles long), and the unauthorized tapping of the public supply by individuals for home or business. The work is carried on today by the Azienda Comunale Elettricità ed Acque, and some of the problems remain the same, especially with the explosion of domestic building in the suburbs since the end of World War II, and the resulting increased demand.

Roman mythology about the city's water does not stop with picturesque tales to titillate the lubricious. More practical wisdom exerts itself in determined prejudice concerning the various merits of the

differing supplies. Stories abound in which elderly gentlemen trudge with buckets of water from their nearest supply of *acqua felice* because it is perfect for cooking vegetables and they have only *peschiera* on tap at home. It is, however, easily provable that *acqua paola* is scarcely drinkable, with its source in the brackish Lake Bracciano, and for many years homes were often supplied with a separate supply of it for washing up dishes (and some purists did not even trust it for that). So complex is the current supply from the various aqueducts that many fountains are fed by two simultaneously; one source providing the ornamental jets, the other the drinking water.

Other notable *mostra* fountains are the Fontana dell' Acqua Felice and the Fontana delle Naiadi, the former in the Piazza San Bernardo and the latter more prominent in nearby Piazza della Repubblica. Neither boasts much artistic finesse (the ungainly Moses of the Felice dates from the 1580s, and its attribution is contested), but the effect of the Naiad Fountain (1870, sculptures by Mario Rutelli, 1901–1911) is attractive, especially at night. Pius IX (or *Pio Nono* as Gladstone insisted on calling him in the House of Commons), the restorer of the aqueduct feeding this fountain, would have approved neither of the dedication of the piazza to republican ideals nor of the seedy cinemas that used to surround it.

The prize for the *mostra* must then be awarded to the Trevi Fountain, which is enduringly popular with visitors to Rome. The tradition that throwing a coin into the fountain guarantees a return to the city remains habitual for even the most skeptical, and after extensive recent renovation it is as spectacular as was intended. When Nicholas V restored the aqueduct feeding it, the fountain was no more than an elegant bowl by Alberti, but this was removed when Urban VIII (1623–44) had more works done on it, financed reputedly by taxing wine. Plans for the replacement fountain were drawn up by notable artists including Bernini, but it was only in 1732, when Clement XII (1730–40) held a competition, that the commission was won by Salvi. As an example of kitsch it can have few rivals in Rome, the Vittorio Emanuele Monument perhaps being a notable exception. But then again, Marcello Mastroianni and Anita Ekberg did not disport themselves all over that mighty pile in *La Dolce Vita*, while the shot of the waters being turned off in the Trevi as they splash about in it is one of cinema's most enduring images of erotic bathos. The Acqua Vergine feeds other notable fountains, including those of the Piazza di Spagna, Piazza Navona, and Piazza Farnese. Their underground link lends its name to one of the most fashionable of Rome's shopping streets, Via Condotti. The playful pretentiousness of nineteenth-century English ex-pats extended to renaming this thoroughfare Conduit Street.

Walking Rome and finding the many street fountains to quench real thirst is one of the wonders of the city. The trick of placing the finger under the direct downward flow and so forcing the jet through an upward aperture convenient to drink from is so elegantly simple that it escapes the notice of many visitors. And yet it is also sufficiently tourist in its appeal that it hovers close to *brutta figura* (or looking "uncool"); only the most self-confident of the city's beautiful youth can carry it off convincingly. Even the grander *mostre* often have smaller cascades or basins equipped with such a makeshift drinking fountain. Only the most fastidious need to buy bottled water in Rome. If anyone suffers an upset stomach the local experts are more ready to attribute it to a change in the grade of flour used to make pasta than to find fault with what has been drunk.

Rivers of Blood

The frequency of fever, which is reported as a hazard of living within the city during the Middle Ages, probably stemmed from the close connections between water provision and the disposal of sewage and household waste. The river was used for both purposes, and the location on the Tiber Island of what may well be the oldest hospital in the world in continuous use was either a happy coincidence or a poignant irony. Founded in Republican times, it was the site of a temple of Aesculapius, the Greek god of healing, and, according to the historian Livy, the recipient of a sacred serpent from Epidaurus, the center of his cult. Today it provides a base for the river police, as well as boasting a helipad for emergency admissions alongside its Church of St. Bartholomew. These facilities proved just a little too far away and came a little too late for one of the most notorious murder victims to find his way into the river at one of the sewer mouths. Juan Borgia, Duke of Gandia and eldest surviving son of the second Borgia pope, Alexander VI (1492–1503), died in mysterious circumstances one night in the early summer of 1497. The papal master of ceremonies, Johann Burchard, gives an unforgettable account of the finding of the body and the testimony of witnesses in his diary of life at Alexander's court:

> *Of those who were questioned, one man, Giorgio Schiavi, was a wood dealer who used to have timber unloaded from a ship near the sewer, and in order to keep a watch on his wood to prevent it being stolen, Schiavi would sail up and down the river in a boat. When asked if he had seen anything thrown into the river on the preceding Wednesday night, he replied that, as he was watching over his logs, two men came on foot down the alley to the left of the Ospedale of Schiavoni at about midnight... Thereupon a rider had*

appeared on a white horse with the body of a dead man slung across its back, the head and arms hanging over one side, the feet over the other... The party had moved further away from Schiavi, crossing past the end of the sewer, and then they had halted. The horse had been turned with its tail toward the river, and the two men on foot had taken the body, one by its hands and arms, the other by its feet and legs, and had dragged it from the horse. They had then lifted it up by its arms and flung it with all their strength and might into the river. The man sitting on horseback had asked if the body had sunk, and the others replied, "Yes, sir," but then looking back at the river he had caught sight of the dead man's cloak still afloat. On inquiring what the black object was that he could see, he had been told that it was the cloak, whereupon he had thrown stones on to it until it had disappeared under the water... When the pope's servants asked [Schiavi] why he had not revealed such a crime to the city governor, his reply was that he had seen a hundred bodies thrown into the river at that point on different nights and he had never thought anything of it.

For five days the pope, Rodrigo Borgia, did not eat or drink and could only be persuaded out of his private room by the cardinals of the most gentle reputation. It is a story of harsh political realities (the man on the white horse was probably Juan's brother, Cardinal Cesare Borgia, murderous for power), and one that fits the popular picture of the notorious family involved. But the story also describes the persistence of human responses to those realities that have their more recent echoes. The discovery of Aldo Moro's body in the boot of a car in the Via delle Botteghe Oscure, close to the political offices of the Communist Party, and of Roberto Calvi hanging from London's Blackfriars Bridge are perhaps ranked equal among them. In a chilling parallel the former is said to have broken the spiritual health of his aging friend, Pope Paul VI (1963–78). We will return to the Borgias later, to give them at least a chance of making a slightly different impression.

Between the island with its ancient and modern facilities and the mouth of the *cloaca maxima*, a noble ruin can be seen. This is the so-called Ponte Rotto, or broken bridge, though its proper name is the Latin *Pons Aemilius*. Its fame rests on the fact that it was the first stone bridge over the Tiber, and its piers date from 179 BC, the arches connecting them from 142 BC. The Ponte Rotto survived into the Middle Ages but after frequent repair it collapsed in 1598. The other ancient bridges that survive with varying degrees of restoration are those with shorter spans, linking the island to the left and right banks. The Ponte Fabricio, springing from the left bank, dates from 62 BC and an inscription over the well-preserved arches records the builder as Lucius Fabricius. It is truly delightful and is well worth walking across to get a feel of real Roman pavement beneath your feet, though beware the vespas, for although the bridge is pedestrianized, they still manage to make themselves felt. The bridge is sometimes also known as *dei quattro capi* ("of four heads") because of the carvings of four-headed Janus on the parapet. The Ponte Cestio, probably built by Lucius Cestius in 46 BC, leads over to Trastevere and was restored at least twice, with a virtual rebuilding in 1892. It does, however, appear to preserve the dimensions of the three original arches.

Although the body of Juan Borgia never made it downstream this far (the sewer by which it was dumped being close to the Ponte Sant'Angelo, and the sewerage in two senses coming from the Vatican), plenty of other bodies must have passed beneath these venerable arches. The Republican practice of executing traitors by flinging them from the Tarpeian rock of the Capitoline Hill was completed by dragging the corpses with hooks to the Tiber and throwing them in. Such deaths reached their peak in the proscriptions of individuals and whole families during the Civil Wars that led to the end of the Republic. It was this image that Virgil contrasts with the idealized peace brought by his patron Augustus, when he has the Sibyl of Cumae foresee the river running red with blood. This image was itself used by Enoch Powell, the darling of the 1960s British political right wing, to commit parliamentary suicide as he predicted similar civil strife resulting from mass immigration. The cruelty of the Roman mind often showed itself in the spectacle of death; to merit mere strangulation in the privacy of the Mamertine Prison at the foot of the Capitol one had to be a defeated general of an enemy army. And even then, you were first subjected to the ritual humiliation of being exposed as principal captive in the victorious general's triumphal procession.

Politics in Rome was pretty squalid from the start, however high-minded Cato and later Cicero can sound and the French classical revival painter David could make the early patricians look. The evidence of a founding myth that rejoices in the wholesale "rape" of the female population of a neighboring district, as Romulus and Remus carried off the Sabine women, speaks of values considerably misplaced. How educated Romans of a sensitive disposition could tolerate the gladiatorial shows remains something of a puzzle to scholars even to this day, for there is remarkably little outcry. Cicero finds it vulgar and boring rather than horrific, but then it is worth remembering that his *cognomen*, Tullius, itself derives from the Latin for a drain or sewer.

To say that post-war Italian politics sometimes resembled a sewer is perhaps something of a caricature. But the revolution following the discrediting of the Christian Democratic and Socialist leaders and the emergence of new political forces during the 1990s had something of the explosive purification of flushing the lavatory. The political traditions of the Italian unified state are difficult to appreciate. They are comparatively new, receiving a definitive form first in 1870 with the fall of papal Rome, and then again with that of the Republic of 1946. The overriding concept that has marked every government, with the possible exception of the Fascists', is *trasformismo*.

"Transformism" could simply be the inevitable political outcome when a state generates as large a variety of political parties, each commanding some clout, as Italy did. In order to keep a government afloat, with a small majority and an official coalition, it is necessary always to be working to transform your opposition into your supporters. The cynic may recognize in this the manifestation of the maxim that political wisdom consists in knowing everybody's price. The Fascists, the exception, knew only their own. *Trasformismo*, pioneered by Agostino Depretis (Prime Minister between 1876 and 1887), was re-minted for the politicians who arose from the resistance movements of World War II. It gave the country the largest conceivable number of governments of any European state, with the smallest number of veteran politicians. These matched the center-right Christian Democrats first with the Socialists in the 1960s, and then, ten years later, even more improbably with the Communists. It seems naive to have thought that such a system was not open to abuse. Italians, and particularly Romans, show a distinct lack of naiveté. There must have been a price worth paying; it just got too high.

Leaning over the balustrade of the modern bridge (Ponte Palatino) that takes the traffic from Piazza della Bocca della Verità where we started this chapter over to the Trastevere district, one can see, when the river is low, the opening of the *cloaca maxima*, that immense Republican public convenience. Be careful not to step into the road precipitately, overwhelmed by the excitement of seeing such a civil engineering turn-on, as almost uniquely the traffic on this bridge, through a vagary of one-way planning (*senso unico*), has the cars driving on the left. It pleases me that an interest in drains might lead one to notice that here in Rome, motorists can be forced into Anglo-Saxon habits.

CHAPTER TWO

The Early Empire:

Ara Pacis

avanti a lui tremava tutta Roma
"before him, all Rome trembled"
Illica after Sardou, *Tosca*

Rome is a woman, but with a man's face. Ask anyone what they think of when the city is named, and after a moment they will probably start using words like graceful, glamorous, sexy, even feline. The models strut their way down the Spanish Steps each summer; women window-shop for jewels and furs along the Via Condotti; the majority of male heads follow a girl with a short skirt on the back of a vespa. Yet for all this attention given to women and the high profile that the city affords them, this is a male town.

The dominating personalities in the city's history have been almost exclusively male, be they consuls, emperors, or popes. At a time when Byzantium brought itself to allow Theodora and Irene to rule, Rome was already under the sway of a male hierarchy. Those with a taste for fantasy would have us believe that a woman was elected in AD 855 as John Anglicus (Pope Joan) after Leo IV's (847–55) death, having successfully passed herself off as a man throughout her youth and the many steps of the Church's preferment. But even such travesty only serves to prove the point. In an earlier period, Livia, the wife of the first emperor, Augustus, did exert real influence, and other empresses followed her lead with the poison bottle, but they never thoroughly emerge from the shadows, even if their husbands terminally deified them. A little later, the Senatrices, the two Theodoras and Marozia, scandalously brokered the power of the papacy through a delicate game of sexual entrapment and dynastic marriage, but their reign was brief and considered so outrageous that it remained a blip. *Il Duce*, Mussolini, dated a woman who had little to recommend her other than her coiffure and a conveniently distant husband. Marginalization, thy name is Roman woman.

The city is, of course, feminine in both Italian and Latin grammar, not only because all cities are, but because its name might be a woman's name. The depiction of a goddess "Roma," with specific attributes and an officially recognized cult, comes relatively late in the imperial period. At the beginning of the second century AD, she seems to have been chosen as a symbol for the exaltation and indeed worship of the idea of the Roman Empire itself, shifting the focus from individual, fallible emperors. Roma was given a huge temple in the Forum by the Emperor Hadrian, but even he, married and with a taste for Bithynian boys, had to add the goddess Venus to the dedication in order to evoke something specifically feminine.

To a British observer the goddess Rome looks strangely like the reassuring image of Britannia from the old penny piece. In front of the Palazzo Senatorio on the Campidoglio, a fine statue represents her, but the figure started off as the goddess Minerva, and was only converted into Roma late in antiquity. In 1824 Giovanni Ceccarini produced a Roma still to be seen in the hemicycle niche of a fountain in the Piazza del Popolo, directly underneath the belvedere of the Pincio Gardens. Hardly anyone recognizes it as such since a cursory glance, even in its startlingly bright restoration, would leave you thinking it represented a rather muscle-bound youth in his late teens. The best example of the true Roma is probably the relief sculpture from the Column of Antoninus Pius in the Vatican Museum. A seated woman warrior, with shield and helmet, her right breast bared Amazon-fashion, looks up to see the deified Emperor Antoninus and his wife Faustina carried up into heaven. Roma is there to see others exalted, to wear their expressions, to carry their names. It is lucky that she has next to no feminine personality as she is called upon to front a male mask.

Rogue Males

Augustus, Charlemagne, Rienzo, Mussolini, myriad popes: all men who have in their extremely different ways imposed their features upon the city. Their faces have in one way or another promoted their political programs, and the traditional ancient Roman practice of keeping the death masks of male family members for use in official ritual accords with the masculine vanity that so often accompanies *realpolitik*. This chapter looks at a personality whose manipulation of traditional form and appearance to mask political revolution may have been equaled but has never been surpassed. The man is Gaius Octavianus, the heir of Julius Caesar, who reigned as the Emperor Augustus for almost fifty years.

Octavian, as his name is usually anglicized, was born in 63 BC, the son of Julius Caesar's niece. Caesar adopted him in 45 BC, when he was just seventeen, and only six months before the fateful Ides of March. After the murder it was Octavian's precocious political ability as much as his legal position as Caesar's heir that delivered him a share of power. Over the next thirteen years he converted that share into a sole interest, by removing all rivals, finishing with Mark Antony at the Battle of Actium. As First Citizen (*princeps*), he established a system that steered a course between overt dictatorship and the old Republican government of senatorial institutions. In 27 BC the grateful Senate gave him the title *augustus*, which was to become the form of address for all later emperors.

The monument that captures something of his genius and just a little of his physical presence is unique in the story of Roman propaganda and art history. It vanished almost completely for well over a millennium, only to be restored through archaeological and political will power in the 1930s. The *Ara Pacis Augustae,* the Altar of Augustan Peace, was buried over thirty feet below street level, and was first discovered by accident in 1588 when the foundations of the Palazzo Fiano-Almagia were being dug. Ten large fragments were recovered and split between a number of aristocratic collections, principally that of the

Medici in the Uffizi. Later in the mid-nineteenth century, when the palace betrayed its precarious foundation with the appearance of huge cracks in the walls, a further seventeen pieces were brought to light. Again in 1903, after a major archaeological campaign, yet more of the altar was dredged up, but the project had to be abandoned because of the fear of flooding.

Finally, in 1937, to crown a monumental plan of yet another of Rome's dominant male faces, Mussolini, the site was totally explored at huge cost and with considerable resourcefulness. The palace was underpinned and the surrounding water-soaked earth frozen, thus walling a space that could then be adequately drained to permit complete excavation. The various fragments were then brought home (with the exception of the panel in the Louvre, Paris) and reunited in a scholarly reconstruction.

Visiting the *Ara Pacis* today is an odd experience. It forms part of the archaeological interest for a piazza created at Mussolini's request along the modernist lines beloved of the Fascist regime. The other ancient monument framed by the towering walls of concrete is the Mausoleum of Augustus, as ugly now as the buildings surrounding it. H.V. Morton is blunt in his assessment of it in his *A Traveller in Rome* (1957): "The Mausoleum of Augustus stands near the Tiber and is one of those miserable ruins which refuses to disintegrate...[a place] where lame cats seek refuge from small boys."

It is difficult to imagine how different it must have appeared in antiquity: a massive circular tumulus (300 feet in diameter) planted with cypresses and crowned with a statue of the emperor. It remained the burial place for Augustus' successors until Nerva in AD 98 and was revered throughout the imperial period. By the time Mussolini decided to give it a facelift, it had been successively a medieval fortress, a beast-bating pit, a concert hall, and most surprisingly of all, a cinema. Its appearance has not improved since the 1950s. But we cannot afford to let the depressing aspect of the Piazza Augusto Imperatore deflect us from our goal, Augustus' Altar of Peace, even though we still have to surmount one last hurdle.

The altar is housed in a glass and concrete pavilion, closing Mussolini's piazza on the riverside. Its shabbiness is exemplary. In *Rome*

Alive (1950), Christopher Kininmonth passes some characteristically sharp comments upon its design and maintenance:

> *One would never guess at what this blank box contains while the disintegrating pillared canopy, so jerry built and washed a tell-tale* fascisti *pink, looks like some dishonoured shrine to Mussolini's optimism. It is commonly used as a public lavatory and a roosting place for down-and-outs, nameless bundles of dormant misery whose personalities seemed to be merged into their subhuman condition.*

The canopy finally managed to disintegrate completely some years ago, but to little effect, as the place refuses to improve. Remarkably the 2,000-year-old monument that the pavilion houses not only manages to appear infinitely more attractive but also considerably more modern. Surrounded by a high enclosure built from the same high-quality Luni marble, the altar itself is approached by a flight of steps broad enough to have allowed access to a crowd of people together with the sacrificial animals. As with all classical monuments the whiteness of the clear chiseled stone belies the fact that in antiquity it would have been painted in bright colors. As a "working" altar, all the surfaces, plain or decorated, would also have been subject to regular splattering with sacrificial blood.

The size, design and position of the altar seem never to have been impressive in traditional terms. It is not especially big (the platform 40 x 35 feet, the altar 10 feet high); inspired by Hellenistic models from the Eastern provinces of the empire, its plan of near cube within near cube is austere and conventional; its original position, some 500 yards from the present site, backing on to the *via flaminia,* now the Via del Corso, was eminent, though not spectacular. This restraint is emphasized when you briefly consider the different "effect" of a direct, if distant, descendant—the Vittorio Emanuele Monument, officially designated the Altar of the Fatherland (*Altare della Patria*). Love it or loathe it, no one can deny that *la macchina di scrivere* (the typewriter) as it is locally known, is immense, exuberant and artificially prominent. The equestrian statue of Vittorio Emanuele, Italy's first King, which perches atop the pile of unrelentingly crystalline marble is still claimed to be the biggest in the world (his mustache alone is six feet long). Augustus, it would seem, was less interested in size.

The sculpted decorations which compliment the architectural environment of the enclosure of the *Ara Pacis* are of great beauty. Over almost the whole lower zone, exquisitely modeled acanthus plants, which have been called the "indispensable ingredients of Augustan imagery," are entwined with ivy, vines, and swans. Above this, relief sculpture of consummate artistry celebrates Augustus' victorious peace. On the long sides, flanking the two doors, are mythological scenes: Romulus and Aeneas to the left and right of the steps; *Pax* (Peace) and Roma on the two panels that would have been seen from the road. Sadly, the altar's Roma is extremely fragmentary, but Peace goes a long way to make up for it, though even she was subject to heavy eighteenth-century restoration. The masterpieces of the monument are, however, the processional friezes on the short sides of the enclosure, representing either a real or idealized occasion of public worship, presided over by Augustus and attended by members of his family. It could even represent the occasion of the altar's inauguration on January 30, 9 BC, which by accident or design was also his wife Livia's birthday.

Many late Republican and early imperial sculpted portraits survive. There is a wearisome number of such busts on display in the Vatican Museum. They are naturalistic, often unprepossessing in their warts-and-all approach, but at the same time they are representative of the traditional Roman virtues of frugality and decorum. The sculptures on the *Ara Pacis* are different. They still look real (the figures are three-quarters life size) and some of the faces are undoubtedly portraits, but they promote the ideology of a new regime. At last, they seem to say, after the bitterness of Civil War, the *pax romana* allows elegance and promotes style. There is an ease in the way that these people chat as they walk to the sacrifice; they are clothed in the "high fashion" uniform of Augustus' revolution, official togas and high-laced patrician boots for the males, and stole and mantle for the women. Office holders such as Augustus and his son-in-law and lieutenant Agrippa have heads covered as tradition dictates, but the children of the imperial family peep out from behind the legs and skirts of the dignified adults, undercutting the formality. The chief priests (*flamines*) of the four principal state cults are present; they are the men with leather caps topped with spikes, but the

adult members of Augustus' circle are crowned casually with laurels. This is beautiful dignity with a human face; and, as always, such naturalism is the product of deliberate artifice. Here we see a public image as constructed as the Camelot ideology of John and Jackie Kennedy, and it bears the same hallmark: glamour.

Public Images

Augustus was obviously proud of the monument as he picks it out for precise comment in the autobiographical inscription *res gestae* (literally, Things Done), the text of which is reproduced on the exterior of the pavilion, its one interesting and redeeming feature. The original inscription was discovered in Ankara and reads:

> *When I returned to Rome from Spain and Gaul after having successfully attended to affairs in the provinces, during the consulship of Tiberius Nero and Publius Quintilius (13 BC), the Senate, in honor of my return, decreed that an altar of the Augustan Peace be consecrated in the Campus Martius, and ordered that the magistrates, priests and Vestal Virgins should perform annual sacrifices on it.*

Within the frieze, Augustus himself is just slightly taller than the rest of the figures, an eminence that he shares only with Agrippa. But, by a twist of fate, Augustus, unlike his friend, is virtually faceless, his features little more than a blur upon the marble's surface. The whole monument could, however, be said to bear his likeness and it is certainly a manifestation of his most celebrated claim—that he found a Rome of brick, and left a Rome of marble (*urbem lateritiam invenit, marmoream reliquit.* Suetonius, *Lives of the Caesars*, Augustus 28).

It is rather hard to appreciate the reality of these proud words if you visit the site on the Palatine Hill that is generally thought to contain the remains of the house to which Augustus moved from the Caesar family mansion on the Roman Forum. Confusingly, the house the emperor bought from the distinguished orator Hortensius is now reckoned to be that which has been traditionally termed "The House of Livia" rather than its neighbor known as—you guessed it—"The House of Augustus." Neither gives to the casual visitor any real sense of the elegance that an aristocratic dwelling of the early principate possessed. However, the internal frescoes (still *in situ* but not open to visitors without special permission) are of the highest quality and typify the advanced stage of the so-called Second Style of Roman wall-painting. Crammed onto a site that includes three sizable temples (two old, those of the Great Mother and of Victory; one new, to Apollo, Augustus' special patron), the houses gained prominence from their proximity to the carefully preserved iron-age hut in which tradition said Romulus and Remus had been raised by the shepherd Faustulus (after, that is, the she-wolf had done her bit). This bit of ideological designer-living gives us the word "palace," as the succeeding emperors, for as long as they lived in Rome, kept the Palatine as the seat of their private government.

Like others before and since, Augustus did not hesitate in promoting an official image of himself. The most enduring of his portraits is that which we know as the Prima Porta type, a name that derives from the small town eight miles to the north of Rome, where a fine example was found in the ruins of Livia's summer villa. Elizabeth Bowen, herself noting the difficulty of coming into contact with Rome's feminine side, made a visit to the archaeological excavations: "I visited Prima Porta: a friend and I and her cocoa-colored, aristocratic dogs climbed the slope to where Livia's villa was—two women paying a morning call on a third, gone (though not quite) as were the surroundings."

Augustus' portrait persists. The statue found at the villa is now in the so-called New Wing of the Vatican Museum (it was built in 1817!). The emperor is depicted in middle age, though the face still bears something of the youthfulness that distinguished his meteoric rise to power. Greek models, primarily that of Polykleitos, the greatest sculptor of the classical age, are evident in the pose, and its idealization, heightened for political purposes, recalls the portraiture of Alexander the Great and his successors. But the statue is not merely political in tone; like the *Ara Pacis* it is deliberate in its celebration of an administration and its achievements.

The scene on Augustus' breastplate depicts an event of pivotal consequence for his regime; the return in 20 BC of Roman standards captured by the Parthian Empire 33 years earlier. The battle of Carrhae, where the eagles were lost and Julius Caesar's colleague in the First Triumvirate, Crassus, was killed, was one of the most humiliating defeats ever suffered by a Roman army. Augustus' campaigning and diplomacy in the east of the empire bore fruit with the propaganda coup of regaining the symbols of military might. It was an achievement that he could literally wear somewhere rather more prominent than his sleeve. The Prima Porta Augustus is not only an example of artistic manipulation of a historic event for political ends; it is the point of departure for all those who have succeeded in imposing their own features upon those of Rome herself.

Faces and Facelifts

The Roman nose is famous and common, and it is a refreshingly leveling observation that it was also an especially striking feature of a good few emperors, Augustus included. It remains a striking feature of a good few Romans traveling on the buses and metro today. Visitors, like me, captivated by the look of them, have a job not to stare at times. But staring is not in the nature of the Romans themselves. Here I diverge from the opinion of a reflective and intelligent colleague who recently remarked on the first and lasting impression made upon him by the faces and especially the eyes of those traveling into the city from the airport on the train. Everywhere he looked he seemed to catch the eye of people staring back. What my friend's intelligence and reflection failed to reveal to him is that the Romans' attention was probably stirred by his habit of speaking so loudly that all heads turn toward him. Normally speaking, the Romans show little interest in what other people look like, so busy are they with their own appearance, its care, and its contemplation. This is not to say that they are unaware of what is

attractive (or not) around them, but their standards are self-imposed.

Cheek by jowl with the *Ara Pacis* and the mausoleum are the two restaurants Alfredo, once the haunts of Rome's most recognized and recognizable visitors and natives. One is in the colonnade of the Fascist building that closes the square on the Corso side, the other around the corner in the Via della Scrofa. The latter is the original (dating from

1914), and yet it is the transplant of the1950s that continues to capture the imagination. The place owes its celebrity to the dish named for the owner, pasta Alfredo, *fettuccine al burro*. In the anteroom you enter before passing through to the gourmand's inner sanctum, the walls are covered in signed photographs. They are masks that you know better than your own face, features that you have seen in the sensuous dark of the cinema or the flat, dull brightness of a room with a TV. Celebrities, especially movie stars, rule supreme here. But it is the silver fork the *padrone* is said to have reserved for the final twirl of the spaghetti before serving that acts as the principal object of reverence. "Alfredo" is not the only eponymous pasta; Sophia Loren had her name added to that distinctive taste experience, *spaghetti agli'olio*. Try it, even if La Loren leaves you cold; gazing upon the faces of the powerful can be a surprisingly famishing task.

Following the example of screen divas, Rome decided to have a facelift to celebrate 2000. And considering the city has been officially celebrating the opening of each century with a religious Jubilee (*Il Giubileo*) since AD 1300 it might be thought high time. It was a brain-wave of the then pope, Boniface VIII (1294–1303), to designate a special holiday every fifty years both in accordance with the tradition of the jubilee year outlined in the Hebrew Scriptures and also celebrating the supposed anniversaries of the birth of Christ. And lest it be thought that such an attractive and life-affirming decision was the result of a happy personality, it is well to remember that Boniface was probably the most abrasive and haughty of the medieval popes. Accused of murdering his predecessor, Celestine V, after encouraging his abdication, Boniface himself was thus summed up by J. N. D. Kelly in his *Oxford Dictionary of Popes* (1986):

> *a man who... was singularly unsympathetic, combining exceptional ability with arrogance and cruelty, insatiable acquisitiveness for his family, and insensitive contempt for his fellow-men; feared and hated, he could not keep a friend.*

Dante confined him to a particularly sticky part of the *Inferno*, and he actually died as a result of injuries and the shock of an attempted kidnapping by his French enemies. Such a man did not grant holidays for the good of the health of others: *Il Giubileo* was conceived of and remained a moneymaking scheme. The offer of plenary indulgences to any pilgrim in Rome during the year 1300 is said to have increased the tourist trade ten-fold. Those who planned the Millennium celebrations and Rome's accompanying facelift lived in the same hope and expectation. Interestingly for the subject of this chapter, Boniface was also accused of encouraging idolatry because he erected so many statues of himself. He also assumed some of the imperial insignia, claiming to be both pope and emperor, thus recalling Augustus' assumption of the High Priesthood (*Pontifex Maximus*) to compliment the principate.

Before the concerted clean up of recent years, visitors new to Rome could easily think the place neglected, the buildings and monuments uncared-for. The dominating but muted colors of burnt umber and old gold quickly fade, and the best efforts of private owners or the Istituto delle Belle Arti e Culturali cannot hide the town's natural tendency to look just a little seedy. Until recently you could come back time and time again to Rome, only to find a particular monument still swathed in scaffolding and plastic sheeting, living or partly living in the nether world termed *restauro*. This suited the temperament of a society that often places a premium upon the internal life of a building rather than being preoccupied with its external appearance. It is worth noting that many a Roman building granted the designation "palace" still looks to all extents and purposes like a slum from the pavement.

Fresher Faces

But things are changing. Laura Biagiotti can suddenly without any sense of irony name perfumes, for both women and men, "Roma," and actually sell them, albeit to foreigners. Gone are the drain smells, in comes the fragrant chic. Very much in keeping with this trend was the appointment of Giovanna Melandri as minister of culture in 1998. Brought in by the ex-Communist Prime Minister Massimo D'Alema, and chosen successor of the groundbreaking Walter Veltroni, who single-handedly revolutionized the moribund museum system, she was a striking 36-year-old, who scandalized Italian parliamentarians by attending the Palazzo Montecitorio while heavily pregnant. Born of wealthy Italo-American parents and mixing in an exclusive circle of fashionable actors and media stars, Melandri had to struggle to deny charges of being a champagne (former) Communist, appealing to the tough working-class district of Rome which she represents. She could not successfully deny, however, that she was a figure of considerable allure. In conversation with the Rome correspondent of *The Times* on her appointment she rejected the suggestion that she owed her success to her good looks. "I am not a model," she remonstrated, "I am a representative of the people." Maybe Rome had finally found a woman who did not need the superimposed image of a man to explain her sufficiently, or to steal her thunder—or maybe not.

In today's Rome, all politicians and public figures, including Signora Melandri, are faced with unbeatable competition from the charismatic Green Party mayor, Francesco Rutelli. The so-called *Sindaco Verde* was re-elected for a second term in 1998 and has continued his highly successful policy of improving the city's environment; introducing pedestrianization wherever possible and improving the flow of traffic in a city that is a byword for congestion (a former *sindaco,* following a heart attack, notoriously died in an ambulance held up in traffic). Immensely popular, not least among women voters, for his film-star looks, Signor Rutelli's main opposition has come from the archaeologists and cultural gurus with whom he has had much publicized run-ins. Plans for parking lots, underpasses and the Metro Line C have all been questioned by those who would have the city's heritage of the "dead" given priority over facilities for the "living." Depending on your priorities, it might be a good thing that the dead have no votes.

Consonant with all this glamour in national and local Roman government, an element of elegant whimsy was introduced in the works to clean and restore the principal facade of the Palazzo Farnese. The metal and plastic skin that veiled the nobly austere face was itself the product of radical architectural design. Post-modern fittings, fancy un-Roman colors and zany lettering made the virtual "absence" of the building a source of entertainment. Admittedly, as the French embassy, the Farnese Palace makes rather more than a local point, but it set the standard for merely native projects to emulate. The hiding of the Campidoglio's statues of the Heavenly Twins, Castor and Pollux, beneath the necessary restorative but drab hoardings was relieved by cartoon-like depictions of the pair. It was the urban equivalent of childish doodling upon a plaster cast: an unsatisfactory, but amusing, attempt at distraction from a painful if necessary evil.

Nor is the cosmetic surgery always an improvement. Quite close to the central offices of the Istituto delle Belle Arti e Culturali, hard by the flight of steps leading from the Via Cavour to the church of S. Pietro in Vincoli, a tiny, undistinguished and (in my researches) nameless baroque church bears the mark of the thorough make-over. Perhaps it was a test piece, or just that those working in the city's facelift department could not bear to see something so close left so unrestored. Whatever the explanation, today its marble gleams with a deathly, bone-bright whiteness, reminiscent of those phases of the city's taste when women, and not only those of loose morals, used lead-paste to cover their faces. Borgia's courtesans and the most respectable of Republican matrons alike, perhaps even Caesar's wife herself, are not above suspicion of participating in this suicidal practice.

Rather more successful to my mind, and far more in keeping with the general lovable shabbiness of the town was the comparatively early (1980s) restoration of the only rococo church in Rome. S. Maria Maddalena is due north from the Pantheon and rejoices in an intimate square filled with attractive restaurants. Dismissed as "faulty in style" by the Jesuit author P. J. Chandlery, who throughout his *Pilgrim-Walks in Rome* of 1903 seeks to diminish anything of merely secular attractiveness, this beautiful church has a yielding, feminine grace that perfectly matches the mythical qualities of its patron. Its stucco front was painted in the subtle traditional shades of the Roman street, and recently, ten years on, had merged happily into the surroundings. One fallen woman at least, it seems, is totally at home with her surroundings.

Few portraits in Rome have assumed as great a significance as the bronze of the Emperor Marcus Aurelius to be seen on the Campidoglio. If the sculptures of Augustus' *Ara Pacis* had not vanished from view for centuries they would have given it a run for its money, but so long unknown, fragmentary and of the less prized marble they remain the favorites of only the *cognoscenti*. Bronze statues dating from antiquity are rare because of their value as bullion in the Middle Ages, and so this unique example of an equestrian subject from late in the emperor's reign (c. AD 180) is doubly prized. It seems to have survived because of mistaken identity. Standing outside the Lateran Basilica from the mid-eighth century, it was believed to be a representation of Constantine, the emperor who recognized Christianity as an official religion. It became the single most reproduced symbol for Rome in the medieval period and kept its currency when it was moved to the Capitol from the Lateran in 1538 to become the centerpiece of Michelangelo's newly designed square. Writing of it in 1873 Henry James says: "I doubt if any statue of king or captain in the public places of the world has more to commend it to the general heart."

You can now see the real thing inside the Museo Capitolino, freshly and wonderfully re-gilded since its restoration in the 1980s, and an impressive copy on the plinth outside in the square. The Capitol's porphyry statue of Roma herself, mentioned at the start of this chapter, is presented with an unrivaled view of the horse's backside. The town has had to put up with a great deal from its rulers, notwithstanding what the general heart might feel. Luckily, Rome is like her women, beautiful in spite of everything that the male sex, or indeed horses, can throw at her.

CHAPTER THREE

The Later Empire: The Pantheon

> *"On each side an imperial city stood,*
> *With towers and temples proudly elevate*
> *On seven small hills...*
> *By what strange parallax or optic skill*
> *Of vision multiplied through air, or glass*
> *Of telescope..."*
> John Milton, *Paradise Regained*

Roman light often plays a particular trick. At odd times throughout the day the architectural and natural environment presents itself as if it were a piece of theatrical scenery. A church facade, the pine-crowned prospect of an urban hill, the vanishing point of a receding street; given a fleetingly appropriate lighting effect, each can seem the backdrop for the eternal drama that is Roman life. Sitting on a bench in the autumn dusk atop the Janiculum hill I once saw the whole city transform itself into a two-dimensional curtain, with palaces lifted upon church domes, and towers overlapping themselves to the cloud line. Perhaps it was not quite the view of Rome given to Jesus by Satan in Milton's epic, but it was something special. Depth and distance were transfigured into the darkling essence of the town.

This is not to imply only the sort of artificiality, the constructed image outlined in the preceding chapter, but to claim for the city a real universality, a monumentality that rejoices even in the trivial. And yet the "show" offered by Rome evokes the most varied of responses from those who purchase the ticket, from the disappointment voiced by Daisy Miller's mother in Henry James' novel of that name:

> *We had heard so much about it; I suppose we had heard too much. But we couldn't help that. We had been led to expect something different...*

to the author's own contrary expression of sheer wonder and infatuation:

> *At last—for the first time—I live! It beats everything: it leaves the Rome of your fancy—your education—nowhere. It makes Venice— Florence—Oxford—London—seem like little cities of pasteboard.*

Certainly many of us find ourselves among the city's groupies. We bore our friends describing it, seek out like-minded fanatics and even presume to write books on the place. Listen to Thomas Gray, the poet, and companion of Horace Walpole on their mid-eighteenth-century Grand Tour. Gray was a rather pallid man, but no lukewarm observer of Rome's theatrical initial presentation:

> *The first entrance to Rome is prodigiously striking. It is by a noble gate,* (The Flaminian, my italics) *designed by Michel Angelo, and adorned with statues; this brings you into a large square* (Piazza del Popolo), *in the midst of which is a vast obelisk of granite, and in front you have at one view two churches of a handsome architecture, and so much alike that they are called the twins* (SS Maria dei Miracoli and di Montesanto); *with three streets, the middlemost of which is one of the longest in Rome* (Via del Corso). *As high as my expectation was raised, I confess, the magnificence of this city infinitely surpasses it.*

Robert Adam, the Edinburgh architect, spent a whole two years in Rome, studying with such natives as Piranesi, while maintaining his place as a gentleman among the British noble tourists. He was struck by Rome's pre-eminence among Italian cities:

> *Rome is the most glorious place in the universal world. A grandeur and tranquillity reigns in it, everywhere noble and striking remains*

> *of antiquity appear in it, which are so many that one who has spent*
> *a dozen years in seeing is still surprised with something new.*

But there are those who fail to get the point. Famously E.M. Forster characterizes the type in *Room with a View* (1908):

> *"You know the American girl in Punch who says: 'Say, Poppa, what did*
> *we see at Rome?' And the father replies: 'Why, guess Rome was the place*
> *where we saw the yaller dog.'"*

When I was traveling through Europe by train with a school friend in 1984, we met up with a Canadian by name of Ian whose principal delight in any town visited was its provision of a beer-stein for his collection. Rome failed on this score, but in his words was still a great place "because everything is on one street." It has puzzled me ever since which single street he could have walked down, unless by a miracle he was transported directly from Stazione Termini to Piazza del Popolo and was introduced, like Gray, to the Via del Corso ("one of the longest in Rome") straightway.

Rome has the vulgarity to make itself a smash hit. But it is an irony not wasted on people like Henry James that its very theatricality can hide a profundity that makes other cities seem like rehearsals. You cannot have a "crush" on Rome: the relationship appears to be for life. But how well this demonstrative love fits the public display of human emotion we expect upon the stage, and especially the melodrama of the Roman stage.

An Architectural Saga

Visible from my vantage on the Janiculum and part of that scenic, evening curtain described above was a dome considerably shallower and wider than its neighbors. The building that it roofs has been a feature of the cityscape for nearly 1,900 years, and it stands on the site of another, which was built over 2,000 years ago. It is the Pantheon, or more accurately La Chiesa della Santa Maria Rotonda, and I cite it as the most impressive structure that the city has preserved from antiquity, and so the fitting monument to record the later periods of the Roman Empire. Part of the impression that it makes, however, is the result of those Roman theatrical effects that are the subtext of this chapter.

Looking at the building from its own auditorium, the delightful

Piazza della Rotonda, the first thing to strike you is an instance of the illusions that abound in its design. The bold inscription trumpets the building's maker and dedicant: "*M. AGRIPPA L.F. COS TERTIUM FECIT* (Marcus Agrippa, Son of Lucius, Consul for a third time, built it)." This, taken at face value, dates the Pantheon exactly to 27–25 BC, but it is not so. An examination of the brick-stamps has conclusively proved the building we see now to have been built between AD 118–125, during the reign of the Emperor Hadrian. But even that does not end the saga, because Agrippa's original had already been rebuilt after the great fire of AD 80 by the Emperor Domitian. It seems that when struck by lightning in AD 110 this first reconstruction also burned, leaving the way open for Hadrian's temple. Some people have even suggested that he designed it himself. He certainly showed considerable interest in this area of town, the heart of the *Campus Martius* (Mars' Field), with the site of the temple to his deified self (and to Matidia, his mother-in-law, and Marciana, her mother) just around the corner. Someone who had the imagination to engage in a major building project in honor of the divinity of distant female in-laws (even if they were also close relatives of his predecessor Trajan) may well have been up to designing the miracle of the Pantheon.

The potential of the *Campus Martius* as an extension to the monumental center of the Roman state was first really exploited during the late Republic. The Theater and Portico of Pompey, scene of Caesar's assassination, was a prominent early example of its architectural development. Formerly just a low-lying open space in the curve of the Tiber to the north of the Forum and outside the city walls, Mars' Field, as its name implies, was the place for military reviews and maneuvers. It was also the scene of elections, where Roman citizens would vote according to their traditional "tribal" designation, a family-based local form of registration. As Augustus secured control of the state he also began the process of reserving the right to build public monuments for himself, his family and close associates. Munificence, through the endowment of public spectacles such as gladiatorial games and the erection of temples, theaters and circuses, was an established tool in the armory of the popular politician. Augustus' monopoly, first on building and later on such other Roman traditions as the award of triumphal processions following notable victories, was a sure way of keeping potential rivals "voiceless."

The *Campus Martius*, together with the residential area immediately to the east of the forum, became the sites of successive major imperial building campaigns. In the last chapter we saw how Augustus' tomb and the *Ara Pacis*, both constructed on the *Campus,* were principal elements of this architectural politics. Closely related to it was the completion of the Basilica Julia and the Forum of Caesar, started by his grand uncle, and the building of the Forum of Augustus. The latter's temple of *Mars Ultor* (Mars the Avenger), is in token of Augustus' defeat of Brutus, Cassius and the rest of Caesar's assassins. It became the custom for most of his successors to add their own forum to this procession of imperial squares.

Easier than the complicated real estate deals that the construction of the fora entailed, since they encroached on already built-up residential areas, were the green-field projects of the *Campus*. As Augustus' son-in-law (he was married to the emperor's daughter Julia) and potential successor, Agrippa seems to have been given the honor of complementing his leader's building projects with a number of his own. He completed a plan of Julius Caesar's to monumentalize the old temporary voting enclosure (*saepta*), built a *porticus* dedicated to the god Neptune and some sort of sports complex with an associated ornamental park and artificial lake (*stagnum Agrippae*) fed by the new aqueduct, the Aqua Virgo. Not least in this prestigious project was the original version of the Pantheon.

The concept of a temple dedicated to all the gods (the literal meaning of the name Pantheon) is not one that was known before in Rome, or indeed elsewhere, and there is some scholarly debate as to whether it ever really served this function. The building's very name, then, could itself be something of an illusion, according to Amanda Claridge's *Oxford Archaeological Guide to Rome* (1998):

> *The city of Rome (unlike the empire at large) never took kindly to the idea of worshipping emperors as gods during their lifetime but it is possible that the Pantheon provided a setting—not a temple in the conventional sense—in which the living emperor would appear in the company of the gods.*

Certainly the Pantheon became particularly associated with the person of the emperor, being one of only three places (the Forum and the Palatine Palace being the others) where he would sit on a public tribunal and, as the highest magistrate, receive petitions and pronounce judgment. So it is quite possible that the Pantheon's religious significance was, at the very most, skin deep. There were statues of the gods housed within it (Mars and Venus, for instance), and the seven alcoves within the rotunda itself surely must have housed significant others, but perhaps the statues of Augustus and Agrippa themselves, which were lodged in the portico, were the presiding spirits.

In the face of this political reality, the commentaries concerning the Pantheon that derive from later ages rather misplace their judgments. It remained an architectural wonder, but was always somewhat suspect as the supposed center for the worship of the pagan gods. Medieval visitors to the city, intent on a spiritual rather than artistic tour, showed relatively little interest in the antiquities, but the Pantheon was simply too impressive to ignore. An English pilgrim of the eleventh century, one Master Gregory, gives an appreciative description of the building, although only "briefly because it was once the image of all the gods, that is, the demons." P. J. Chandlery, the Jesuit apologist of papal Rome at the turn of the twentieth century, was similarly ambivalent in his estimate, judging it:

...one of the most remarkable and interesting architectural structures in the world... unique in design, solidity and grandeur; but, alas! in its pagan days it was defiled by a sensuous worship, that was a scandal to the very heathens.

It is puzzling why Catholic commentators needed to be so guarded, if not downright bigoted, about the Pantheon when we consider its "cleansing" of AD 610 by Pope Boniface IV (608–15) in order that it might become the church of S. Maria ad Martyres, or more commonly now, S. Maria Rotonda. There is even a suggestion that the first keeping of the festival of All Saints is connected with this "deliverance," hardly an event that true children of the Church would have wanted to question. Perhaps it was the continued association that the Pantheon had with the civil power that perpetuated the doubts. Pope Boniface could, it seems, only convert the church with the agreement of the Emperor Phocas, one of the last Byzantine rulers to have a direct monumental influence on the city. He is only really remembered for having dedicated the last commemorative structure in the Roman Forum, the column that bears his name, even though his direct rule of Rome was temporary and fleeting. It is possible that the Byzantine governor of the city, the Exarch Smaragdus, actually raised the column in honor of the transfer of ownership of the Pantheon, from imperial to papal hands.

Declining Days

When we think of the survival of any imperial Roman remains it is worth pausing to consider the medieval city and its physical state. When Constantine the Great (emperor AD 306–337) moved his capital from Rome to Byzantium (renamed Constantinople), the city went into a slow decline. Though remaining the Mother City of both the Eastern and Western Empires, Rome's political priority was stolen. The Senate remained, but gradually degenerated into a glorified town council, and the papacy was still in its political infancy. Emperors not only stopped residing in Rome; many of them never even visited the city. The decline in economic stability that accompanied political change was exacerbated by the wave of barbarian invasions of Italy and successive sacks of Rome (first by Alaric and the Goths in AD 410). The city, which had once boasted a population of more than a million, dwindled in size, and there simply was not enough money to maintain the civic fabric. Added to this was the dilemma facing the one potentially powerful force left to Rome, the Church.

What made the city important was its imperial past, but this was intrinsically linked to paganism, as represented by the hundreds of temples and monuments to the gods. Churches and Christian monuments were being built, often using material recycled from former pagan buildings (just look at the huge number of ancient columns used in the naves of Christian churches). But for papal claims to a special authority higher than that of the other original patriarchs of the Christian churches, an appeal to Roman primacy *per se* was needed. The seat of the Bishop of Rome was in the former imperial residence of the Lateran given by Constantine to Pope St. Silvester I (314–35), and his cathedral was the associated church of St. John the Baptist. Throughout the long centuries of the medieval period (from the fifth to the fourteenth centuries) the power of the papacy was counterbalanced by successive, and even at times competing, civil authorities which claimed "imperial" dignity.

Crucial to an understanding of this rivalry is the appreciation of the symbolic role of yet another important church in the city. The Basilica of St. Peter remains one of the principal reasons for many people to visit Rome at all. We will return to it again and again during this book. But now we are visiting it for the first time, as an idea. As noted above, Constantine gave the pope and his successors a cathedral, S. Giovanni in Laterano, but he built an imperial church, S. Pietro, for himself. Throughout the Middle Ages this distinction was maintained, with St. Peter's preserving its close connection with royalty and fostering the concept of Christian kingship. Thus it was on the steps of St. Peter's, not at the Lateran, that Charlemagne was proclaimed Holy Roman Emperor. Equally, it was in the Borgo, the neighborhood of St. Peter's, that we find the royal Anglo-Saxon pilgrims settling and developing a location of patronage. It would be mistaken to say that St. Peter's was not a papal church, but it was primarily an imperial shrine under papal protection.

As the papacy's direct political significance increased, its own imperial claims grew accordingly. Thus, by the end of the Middle Ages, with the Papal States an established and clearly defined political entity and with an independent pope back from Avignon, where for seventy years he had been subject to French "imperial" manipulation, the distinction between papal and imperial became blurred. Finally in the mid-fifteenth century, the Vatican adjoining St. Peter's became the principal papal residence, completing the ideological journey that had begun when Constantine had vacated the Palatine twelve hundred years before.

We seem to have made quite a journey from the Pantheon where this digression began, but distance, like perspective, can play tricks in Rome. The Pantheon was the place chosen by the royal House of Savoy for the interment of the modern kings of Italy, the next "imperial" power successfully to displace the papacy in Rome. (Napoleon Bonaparte had tried, but with limited, temporary success.) Following the series of political accidents and skillful diplomatic maneuvers presided over by the Savoyard Chief Minister Count Camillo Cavour that led to the proclamation of the Kingdom of Italy in 1860, Rome and a small area of surrounding land was virtually the only territory on the peninsula to remain sovereign; and this was only due to the presence of French troops guaranteeing the position of Pope Pius IX.

When French power was shaken with the defeat of Napoleon III by the Prussians, the Italian state seized its opportunity, invading Rome by breaching the walls near the Porta Pia on September 20, 1870. The aged pontiff left his summer palace on the Quirinal hill to the "usurping" Savoy dynasty, choosing to immure himself as the self-styled Prisoner of the Vatican in invisible, but morally palpable, opposition to the secular power of Vittorio Emanuele. It was a tradition to be followed by his successors until the Italian government under Mussolini came to an agreement with the papal diplomats, granting sovereign status to the

Vatican and various other churches and associated buildings throughout the city, and recognizing the Catholic faith as the official religion of the Kingdom of Italy. Ironically, the Vatican, which had once conferred the idea of kingship to the rest of Christendom, had become the last remaining territory of the papacy.

In the Pantheon you can see the tombs of the first two kings and the first queen of Italy (Vittorio Emanuele's second wife did not qualify for the title "queen" as he had married her, a former mistress, morganatically.) Umberto I's wife, Margherita, a haughty and domineering woman, and first among the aristocratic supporters of Mussolini, accordingly became Italy's first queen. Today, the Pantheon also provides the principal platform for the minute monarchist faction left in Italy. Here you can sign a petition to seek burial for the remaining members of the Savoyard dynasty in this "family" church; and here, on All Souls' day each year, you can attend a requiem for the dead monarchs. The Republican Constitution of 1947 does not permit members of the former royal house even to visit Italy. And so Vittorio Emanuele III (king 1900–1945), and Umberto II (1945), remained in exile for life and death. From time to time, their successors test the Republican temperature with a quick visit to Alto Adige for the skiing, but to no effect, since hardly anyone is interested enough even to enforce the law.

A Tale of Two Domes

The connection between the Pantheon and the Basilica of St. Peter does not stop with the concept of monarchy. Both are substantial buildings crowned with domes, and although this point might seem obvious, it is worth remembering that for centuries the Pantheon was the city's only model for a dome. It is also worth remembering that for centuries St. Peter's did not look as it does now; the current basilica is "modern" in Roman terms.

Constantine's original church, built on the site where a small grave shrine to St. Peter had been established within a few years of his death, was a great hall-like basilica after the fashion of the Roman civil law courts. Most early churches dating from the beginning of the period when Christianity was tolerated and then gradually achieved religious dominance follow this pattern. The Basilica of St. Paul's-Without-the-Walls is of this type, although it is a nineteenth-century reconstruction of the original that was destroyed by fire. But St. Peter's is of another type altogether. It is a Renaissance church, on the site of a demolished original basilica, and it took over a century to build.

Planned first by Pope Nicholas V in the middle of the fifteenth century, the work was put into the hands of the architects Rossellino, Alberti, and Sangallo the Elder. Work stopped, after some initial restoration, for almost fifty years until Julius II brought Donato Bramante on to the job. He demolished what was left of the old church and really got started on the ambitious new project. When he died in 1514, having acquired the nickname "Ruinate" for his pains, only the four central piers and the arches of a dome had been completed. Other architects visited the project: Raphael, Fra Giocondo and Peruzzi. The years went by and the basilica remained not only unfinished, but virtually unfinishable. In 1539, under the patronage of Paul III (1534–49), Sangallo the Younger took on the work, further adapting the designs of his predecessors. When he too died in 1546, the pope commissioned the 72-year-old Michelangelo to get the job done. He radically altered the plan and demolished what had been built of the dome. Part of his revised scheme was a facade based on that of the Pantheon. Clearly there was a connection in his mind between these two buildings. Michelangelo continued his supervisory role until his death in 1564. The dome was finally completed by della Porta, assisted by Fontana, in 1590. Maderno completed the facade under Paul V, and the church was at last consecrated under Urban VIII on November 18, 1626, the 1,300th anniversary of the original building.

Rome became used to St. Peter's being unfinished and domeless (or at best partly domed). Indeed, it became so used to this state of affairs that Raphael included the building works and, significantly, the dome space without its dome in one of his most famous paintings, the so-called *School of Athens*. This Vatican fresco, painted for the private apartments of Julius II (1503–13), is one of a series depicting Wisdom, human and divine. It shows a group of ancient philosophers, modeled upon contemporary lights of the artistic and cultural Renaissance, standing in an elaborate architectural setting drawn directly from the unfinished St. Peter's. This clearly links the project with the philosophical aspirations of the humanist papal court and its artistic entourage. But it also seems to be passing an ironic comment upon the apparent inability to complete the building, for the work of the pagan philosophers itself is envisaged as being incomplete without the addition of Divine Wisdom provided in Christian revelation.

Providing the missing ingredient in the theologically designed program of the fresco cycle and facing the *School of Athens* is its major companion, the *Disputation on the Nature of the Sacrament*. It bears a classically perfect design, closed in the formal sense. Rows of Christian worthies face each other as if in choir stalls, with an altar blocking off the middle space. Above the earthly scene, the presence of Christ and attendant apostles and other major saints is depicted as if on a traditional apse, curving through a semi-circle. An apse had closed the eastern end of the original basilica, as in all churches of that type, examples of which were everywhere to be seen in Rome. Perhaps Raphael wished the old church had never been dismantled, that he had never got the thankless job of rebuilding it, and this was the only way he could say it. In any case, he chose as his final resting place a building with its dome complete, the Pantheon itself, and it is there that his tomb with its elegant epitaph by the great humanist scholar, father of modern Italian, Cardinal Pietro Bembo can be seen:

ille hic est Raphael timuit quo sospite vinci rerum magna parens et
moriente mori

Living, great Nature feared he might outvie
Her works, and dying fears herself to die.

(Alexander Pope's translation, adapted for Godfrey Kneller's tomb)
Dame Antonia Byatt in her literary love story, *Possession*, chooses the same inscription for her fictional poet-hero's grave, going to the extent of personally supplying a supposed translation of the Latin by her subject, R.H. Ash, himself:

Here lies the man, who, whilst he was in breath
Made our great Mother tremble that her skill
Was overmastered, who now, by his death
Fears her own powers may grow forever still.

What Art Conceals

The domelessness of the Christian basilica chimes with one of the most striking architectural features of the imperial monument, temple or not, which is the subject of this chapter, for the Pantheon's dome is not closed. Its oculus (the circular ceiling opening) is thirty feet in diameter and is the building's only source of light. It also lets in rain and birds. The effect of shafts of sunlight penetrating the gloom of the interior is one of the building's magical features, and this is heightened whenever a section of the floor bears a shallow reflecting pool of rainwater. The dome itself is a perfect hemisphere with a diameter of some 150 feet, meaning that the diameter of the internal rotunda is exactly the same height from the floor to the oculus. The dome seems much steeper inside than out as the true dome only begins at the third row of coffered decorations, the first two being architectural components of the twenty-foot thick wall. In this way, the architect of the Pantheon (Hadrian or another) played the reverse optical trick to that employed by Sir Christopher Wren at St. Paul's Cathedral in London, where the decorated interior ceiling is far shallower than the acutely pitched and separated outer dome. Rome, however, has an even better trick to play than that. Sant'Ignazio Loyola, the Gregorian University's home church, is incomplete, its cupola never having been finished. In its place in the crossing is a perspective canvas that gives the impression of a dome soaring above the worshippers. Only the clergy in the choir and at the altar could see how things really were: painfully skewed and made nonsensical when viewed in reverse. Clearly the suggestion of a dome was more important than its reality in the ideology of baroque Rome.

In spite of its high reputation, the Pantheon itself is far from being architecturally perfect. The transition between the rotunda and the pillared portico is uneasy and calls for the imposition of a rectangular member, which provides a second pediment higher than that fronting the porch. It may be that the original plan called for fifty-foot shafts for the columns that would have carried it to this height, but their unavailability led to forty-foot shafts being used instead. Similarly, the porch itself has been criticized for the sheer number of its columns, giving the effect of entering a marble thicket to pass through to the rotunda.

Some of these lapses in elegance would be relieved were we able to see the building as it was designed. It stood upon a platform and was approached up a flight of four wide marble steps. It formed the close to a large porticoed square much larger than the piazza before it now. The majority of the exterior would have been veneered in white Pentelic marble. The bronze decorations are missing from the pediment, and even more tragically and notoriously, the bronze girders supporting the porch roof were removed by Pope Urban (Barberini) VIII in 1626. This act of vandalism, perpetrated to provide cannon for the papal fortress, was the foundation for the Latin witticism—*quod non fecerunt barbari, fecerunt Barberini*: where the barbarians failed, there Barberini succeeded. Pope Urban also insulted the Pantheon further by commissioning Bernini to erect two towers topped with cupolas on either side of the porch. Always known as the "Asses' Ears," they did not make it into this century. The royal house of Savoy wanted to be buried in an *echt* Roman monument, not one spoiled by seventeenth-century "modernization."

An oft quoted urban (Urban?) myth is that the Barberini pontiff wanted the Pantheon's bronze to build the great *baldacchino* over the high altar in St. Peter's, linking the two buildings again in the popular imagination. John Milton was a visitor to Rome in the late 1630s, and he received generous hospitality from the English Catholic colony there, in spite of their sharp religious differences. When he came to write his most famous work, *Paradise Lost*, what he had seen of the completed St. Peter's seems to have inspired the description of the palace of Pandemonium, to which Lucifer and his cohorts withdraw after their expulsion from heaven at the close of Book I. The simile of the bees, which Milton uses to capture the arrival of the demons at their new home, alludes directly to the Barberini family crest, which swarmed with bees, as the *baldacchino* designed by Bernini did with bronze ones. Michael Dibdin's crime novel *Cabal* provides us with a more recent excursus on the dome's sinister potential. The opening murder is staged as a suicide as the victim plunges from the dome's gallery to a sticky end on the marble beneath. Dibdin goes on to make a further intellectual leap by paralleling St. Peter's dome with that of the nineteenth-century Galleria Vittorio Emanuele in Milan. But that's another book...

So, repeatedly, we find specific links between the Pantheon, once viewed as "the seat of all the gods, which are the demons" and its rival dome, St. Peter's. The two buildings made their points about imperial power and both were disguised more or less as places of worship. Down the centuries Rome has enjoyed employing the sleight of hand that claims that the spiritual is pure and then lends that purity to the dirty work of politics. We may not be deceived, but we enjoy the entertainment produced by the attempt. If you doubt it, try to be displeased by the Pantheon.

CHAPTER FOUR

The Early Church: Constantia's Mausoleum

"The transition from pagan to Christian is the point at which the ancient world still touches ours directly. We are heirs to its conclusion..."
Robin Fox Lane, *Pagans and Christians*

A news item to hit Italian TV screens and some front pages early in 1999 seemed a salacious editor's dream come true, combining as it did physical violence, religion (Catholic, of course), and sex. Reports had reached Rome that persecuted Chinese priests were being subjected to sexual torture. Prostitutes were being admitted to their prison cells and the outcome filmed through close-circuit cameras. The news items illustrated the story with juxtaposed images of topless, high-heeled oriental girls dancing and an aged pope, John Paul II (1978–), making his laborious way across picture—this, I suppose, in lieu of footage direct from the cells of the clerical "unfortunates."

On the same broadcasts, another story further down the interest/importance scale told of an old priest from Viterbo, a town a little to the north of Rome, who had been taken ill while on a solitary walk in the countryside. An unearthly figure clothed in white, it was said, had indicated to the helicopter search party where to find him. The old man, recovering in his modern hospital bed, surrounded by the technological panoply of both hospital and mass media, murmured, "*un miracolo, vero.*" Switch to a close up of his gnarled fingers telling the beads of his rosary.

The practice of a Catholic Christianity still runs through the heart of Italian, and particularly southern Italian, culture. To this extent, Rome, though the capital of the United Italy properly belongs to the South, the *mezzogiorno*. But Rome belongs to the Church in a far more profound way than simply falling on one side of a national divide. For centuries this city was the capital of another state, the so-called Patrimony of Peter and its adjoining territories, ruled over by the pope, administered by his cardinals, protected and policed by his armies. At times the Papal States stretched as far as Bologna and embraced the Romagna. The medieval popes claimed suzerainty over the Kingdoms of Naples and Sicily; they gave the German Holy Roman Emperors a considerable proportion of their support and generated most of their trouble; they dealt in numerous other duchies and principalities, largely to the benefit of their own family members.

This legacy of direct, and often intransigent, priestly rule makes Rome one of the most anti-clerical of cities. At the same time it is still acutely aware of its dependence upon a hieratic tradition. The news stories I cite above are not unusual; they are just a couple chosen at random to illustrate a continuing fascination, almost an infatuation, which is linked to a hearty, disregarding irreverence. This obsession is spiced by the regulations that have forbidden priests to marry since the eleventh century, when the monk Hildebrand, elected pope as Gregory VII (1073–84), realized that by enforcing clerical celibacy he might successfully control his subordinates, making them easier to move around and less costly to maintain. Thus, mention of priests and sex in the same Roman sentence has always been enough to cause literally a "cheap" thrill, coining as it does nothing more than a local cliché.

Gioacchino Belli, the great nineteenth-century dialect poet, caught something of the disgust a Roman might feel both for the unmanly males who ruled him and for the commonplace breaking of their vows in his alliterative and pithy description of the city—*Papa, preti, principi, puttane, pulci, e poveri* (Pope, priests, princes, prostitutes, poop, and paupers). Numbers of recorded and licensed whores have always appeared disproportionately high in Roman censuses—at the time of the Borgias, almost incredibly so—as inevitably have nuns and monks! (The 1676 records show the following: 150,000 inhabitants in total, set against 12,000 monks and nuns and 1,000 licensed prostitutes). Roman slang and aphorisms have long centered upon the dealings between the laity and their religious rulers: one of my favorite phrases, should one lose something or need a replacement for something worn out, is "*Il Papa è morto; si scelt'un altro*—The pope's dead? Choose another!"

According to Romans, the venality of the clergy does not stop at sins of the flesh; they have been typically imagined as uniformly corrupt. This belief gave birth to the oft-cited remark that accompanied the traditionally pious funeral of a notoriously anti-clerical and irreligious prime minister: "When the priests are paid, they sing." Wordplay with the city's proudly enduring acronym SPQR, (*senatus popolusque romanus*—The Senate and the People of Rome), which adorned ancient statues and is still stamped on twenty-first-century drain covers, reflects

the same scorn. For some the initials stand for "*solo i preti qui regnano -* it's only the priests who rule." The wits, as we shall see later on, had further interpretations of the acronym for the Fascist regime in Rome, but not even the creation of the Vatican City State and its car registrations marked SCV give the priests a break, for this has come to mean, for the cynic, "*Se Cristo Vedesse...* If only Christ could see...!"

The root of this kind of antagonism is buried deep in the strata of the city's past. Christianity, and particularly its Roman brand, has long traded on the fact that for the first three centuries of its existence it was a persecuted sect. Theologically, this was converted into the rather dubious theory that God preserved and strengthened the early Church through its many bloody trials and tribulations in order ultimately to crown it with the power to engage in the same persecution of dissenters. At the other extreme of theorizing, this time historical rather than theological, there are those like Gibbon, and more recently, Robin Lane Fox, who have blamed the Christian culture, which from the beginning of the fourth century gradually became dominant in the Roman world, for the decline and ultimate fall of the glorious imperial past. The period which this chapter looks at is the workshop for both of these fabrications, the age that articulates pagan and Christian culture. The monument that we will consider in this light is one of the least frequented and most interesting of a number of remarkably well preserved buildings of the early fourth century.

A Suburban Sanctity

Via Nomentana leads northeast out of Rome, the ancient road to Nomentum, now Mentana, about fifteen miles from the city. Once outside the walls it passes through a district developed in the last years of the nineteenth century, the Umbertine period. There are large villas and gracious apartment blocks, just the hint of gardens behind high walls, and an architecturally eclectic antiquarianism that enabled Henry James to contrast this and other new parts of the city with recent developments in New York. One day, he said, the new parts of Rome would look old. He was right. Finding yourself about a mile along the road beyond the Porta Pia, the complex of ancient buildings clustered around the Catacombs of St. Agnes hardly look out of place at all.

A truly suburban atmosphere has managed to survive, one that finds a resonance with what would have been there in late antiquity.

In the classical period, burials were forbidden within the walls of the city, and so the roads leading out of Rome inevitably became the last resting-places of its inhabitants. The Via Appia Antica tells us the story most clearly because of the failure to transform it into a major modern thoroughfare. The excavations that have been possible along it and in the land through which it passes, have yielded the richest evidence of the burial practices of the Romans of antiquity. From rich to poor, from Republic to Empire, from pagan to Christian, they are all found here. Some were buried after cremation in little niches (*columbaria*, literally dovecotes), others interred in impressive mausoleums, or sealed in the wall spaces of the excavated passages we call catacombs. Roman death was the leveler that it is ever destined to be. The other roads out of town also provided access to cemeteries; there was one on the Vatican hill, where St. Peter was to be buried after his martyrdom. St. Paul was buried just off the Via Ostiense, and the tombs of other Christian martyrs are found encircling the city following the pattern of the roads. St. Agnes' church, catacombs and adjoining buildings are reputedly where they are because her family owned a villa there on the site to which her body was brought for burial after martyrdom.

Virgins proliferate in the lists of the Roman sanctified. But Agnes provides the further exquisite refinement of having been a young child. As Henry James wrote, not on this occasion intending a Roman allusion, the suffering of children provides the turn of the emotional screw. The classic account of her martyrdom comes to us from St. Ambrose, the fifth-century bishop of Milan, through the medieval writer on the lives of the saints, Jacobus de Voragine. If Jacobus had been alive in the present century he would have been a scriptwriter for soap operas, so eventful, detailed, and melodramatic are his lives of the saints. His book, *The Golden Legend* (*Legenda Aurea*), is the necessary guide for anyone seriously interested in Renaissance art, providing as it does the source material for all Giorgio Vasari's "greats." Agnes' story is typical in the violence it records and the contrasting atmosphere of calm that pervades the spiritual disaster-movie script. It starts almost like a fairy tale:

One day Agnes was on her way back from school [note the Lolita-like setting] when the prefect's son saw her and fell in love. He promised her jewels and great wealth if she consented to be his wife. Agnes answered: "Go away you spark that lights the fire of sin, you fuel of wickedness, you food of death."

As Agnes' rejection of the young man's advances grows ever more vehement through her allegiance to her spiritual bridegroom, Christ, she is subjected to attempted gang rape and burning alive. She survives these horrors, protected by miraculous aid, only to die from the rather pedestrian stroke of a dagger. The climax of the martyrdom is traditionally held to have taken place in the Stadium of Domitian, the shape and foundations of which are preserved in the Piazza Navona. Borromini's church of Sant'Agnese in Agone is this tradition's most eloquent reminder. Beneath it, in one of the arches (*fornices*) of the stadium is said to have been the brothel (*fornix* in Latin) to which Agnes was consigned. Fortunately, a timely and general growth of hair over the girl provided both a veil and a successful rapist-repellent. The prospect of fornicating with such a spectacularly hirsute woman was obviously beyond the potency of even the most hardened pagan.

The martyrdom is dated c. AD 305, only seven years before Constantine's triumph over the Emperor Maxentius at the Milvian bridge, and the start of official toleration, and ultimately promotion, of Christianity. Thus the cult of Agnes would have been very fresh at exactly the time when it was most possible to popularize it. The growth of Christianity and the increasing level of charitable and social work organized from its structures threatened the authority of successive "divine" emperors, for whom a monopoly on poverty relief had secured popularity. Harsh persecution was not only, perhaps not even, a religious issue for Diocletian and Galerian; it was a political strategy. For all its fantastic *grotesquerie*, the product of a more romantically inclined Middle Ages, Agnes' story has obvious power, as the symbol of vulnerable courage in the face of domineering and demanding authority. To acquire a better perspective on the issue of martyrdom, and virgin martyrs in particular, the extant correspondence and contemporary accounts of the noble woman Vibia Perpetua, her slave Felicitas and their companions, who were executed at Carthage in North Africa about a century before Agnes, is more illuminating than the hagiography of later male propagandists (and fantasists?).

Robin Lane Fox comments on the power of these stories to impress a society that was still able to enjoy the cruelty of the arena:

> In the early church, martyrdoms were exceptionally public events, because Christians coincided with a particular phase in the history of public entertainment: they were pitched into the cities' arenas for unarmed combat with gladiators or bulls, leopards and the dreaded bears... Violence made excellent viewing, and the crowds could be utterly callous... When the well-born Perpetua and Felicitas entered Carthage's arena, "The crowd were horrified when they saw how one was a delicate girl, the other fresh from child-birth..." First they called for them to be clothed more modestly. Then like a crowd at a bullfight they roared their applause while the girls were brought back to die before the wild beasts. This same high-pitched mixture of torture and female martyrdom was later to inspire the works of art which Christians patronized in their own counter-Reformation.

Arriving at the church of Sant'Agnese Fuori le Mura, either by bus or by walking up from the Piazza Bologna Metro station, seems just about as far removed from martyrdom as it is possible to conceive. But it is worth remembering that it is because of the facts of what was probably in truth a particularly gruesome and poignant death some 1,700 years ago that we are actually visiting this place.

You enter the monumental complex either directly from Via Nomentana or by walking around the corner and down the hill on Via Sant'Agnese itself. The basilica we now see is the second in the area and was built by Pope Honorius I (625–38). It is a beautiful building best appreciated in the afternoon; its position is well below current street level, and with windows mainly facing west, the declining sun supplies its best light. It is unique in the location of a *matroneum*, a gallery for women, built over the central nave, whereas it returns to type in being one of those churches mentioned in the last chapter, the columns of which were taken from the ruins of older classical buildings. The decorative mosaic and the marble paneling in the apse are original, with a representation of Agnes standing between two popes, Symmachus and Honorious, the latter holding a model of the church, set against a background of dull gold. A modified antique torso was worked up around 1600 to represent the saint, and it stands beneath the high altar's *baldacchino*. At the same time Pope Paul V gave the silver casket that now houses Agnes' relics. As if one virgin martyr were not enough, pious tradition holds that Emerentiana, her foster sister (smacking of over-coincidence), was also martyred and buried in the same place. The position of the current church is determined by the traditional site of the saints' joint tomb within the catacomb, immediately below the high altar.

This catacomb was part of what appears to have been a major suburban cemetery from the middle of the first century AD. Evidence for this is found in the large collection of inscriptions, mostly of a memorial nature, which now decorate the walls of the staircase leading down to the basilica from the Via Nomentana entrance. Near the bottom is the famous epitaph composed by the poet and sainted pope, Damasus (366–384), in honor of Agnes. The significance of the whole site received a real boost, however, when Constantina, the elder of Emperor Constantine's daughters, built a large basilica and her own mausoleum in the vicinity during her residence in Rome from AD 337–357. The remains of the church form the walled garden set upon the slight hill to the right of the mausoleum.

By doing this Constantina was following family tradition. Her father had endowed the establishment of the popes at the Lateran with the building of a basilica, a baptistery and a residence. He also assisted with the foundation of the gigantic funerary basilicas of Saints Peter, Sebastian, and Lawrence, all sited at the martyrs' tombs in established cemeteries along the roads out of Rome. Although it is often argued that Constantine's relations with Christianity were more a question of accommodation than adoption (he was only baptized on his deathbed), his political sense accorded with the developing spirituality of his family. His mother, the fabled Helena, sainted for her reputed discovery of the relics of the True Cross in Jerusalem, also built a basilica for these trophies in the equivalent of her back garden, the grounds of her favorite palace, the Sessorian (the present-day S. Croce in Gerusalemme). She later added a mausoleum and an accompanying church on the Via Labicana to her architectural legacy.

Constantina's Mausoleum, a jewel of fourth-century architecture and decoration, was long known as the Church of St. Constance, as it was clearly *de rigueur* for the family, which had recognized Christianity to be conventional recipients of that religion's highest honor. Although unlikely to have been a virgin (she married at least twice), Constantina may in widowhood have ranked as a "nun," the early Church designating its orders of religious women either as widows or virgins. However, even this flies in the face of the historical accounts of her life, which record her and her husband Hannibalianus as particularly nasty examples of ruthless political opportunism. What is perhaps perplexing about the mausoleum, in the light of this mix of considerations, is the absence of specifically Christian motifs in decoration or design. As Christopher Kininmonth points out in his *Rome Alive!* of 1950:

It is a church, which, one cannot but feel, is consecrated in name only, and that mistakenly. It is possible that Constantine thought of it as a temple for his daughters when they should have joined the other imperial gods. But they died Christian ladies.

The building is annular in plan with an external diameter of 120 feet and internal diameter of 70 feet. An inner colonnade of granite columns supports arcades that in turn further support a clerestory of twelve windows leading to the concrete dome. It is true that the mausoleum resembles contemporary and later Christian buildings such as the Lateran baptistery and S. Stefano Rotondo (it shared the design of an apsidal porch with the former, now demolished). But it is its similarities with pagan buildings of the period that are most striking.

Just before his defeat by Constantine in AD 312, the Emperor Maxentius was engaged in a major building project about two and a half miles outside of the city on the Via Appia. It was at least in part a funerary complex (as might be expected from its location) in honor of his infant son, Romulus, who had not only recently died of a childhood disease aged four, but had also been deified with a temple in the Forum. Enough for any toddler, you might think, but Maxentius disagreed. A large annular mausoleum was constructed in the vicinity of a whole series of imperial buildings (known as the Villa of Maxentius), which in turn were connected to what was planned as one of the largest circuses known in the Roman world (only slightly smaller than the *circus maximus*). Among all the unfinished public works undertaken by Maxentius, this was the only substantial one not to be adopted by his conquering successor. And for obvious reasons. This was a family memorial, undertaken with the succeeding generations of Maxentius' dynasty in mind. That it provided both a source of public entertainment as well as imperial resort is incidental to its purpose of political aggrandizement and propaganda. We do not know whether the circus was ever used either for chariot racing or for the execution of the criminals known as Christians.

This Mausoleum of Romulus gives the architectural type not only for future imperial mausoleums like that of Constantina at the Sant'Agnese site, and of Galla Placidia at Ravenna, but also for the Lateran baptistery and the round church of S. Stefano in the Parco del

Celio. The baptistery follows the plan of the mausoleum, not the other way round. The association of imperial "death" and its attendant *cultus* was made directly with the theological implications of Christian initiation, in a baptism that mimics mortality in its symbolism of drowning. But there is a further refinement in this nexus of imperial and religious metaphor.

The basilicas built by Constantine's successors and family members take the form of circuses. At Sant'Agnese this is easy to see, because the later church is not built upon the site of the original, and so its ruins have been converted into the garden described above. Its aisles were covered, but its nave may always have been unroofed. This perhaps reinforced the idea, conveyed by its plan of a long rectangle closed by an apse, that these martyr churches were signs pointing to the places where so many martyrs had met their deaths: the arenas and circuses of the city. They are more than a simple demonstration of the current ascendancy of Christianity; they are a picture of its triumph over the culture which had formerly triumphed over it.

For all this subtle theological point-scoring, Constantina's Mausoleum remains profoundly a product of its transitional cultural climate. The mosaics that adorn the outer vaults of the ambulatory are broadly secular. Starting as mere geometric designs near the porch, they move both ways around the inner colonnade toward the burial niche opposite the door. As they approach the sarcophagus of imperial purple porphyry, (the original is now in the Vatican Museum), they become more figurative. They remain, however, secular in tone; cupids engaging in the vintage, still-lives of flowers, fruits, wine jars and birds, and portrait medallions of the Princess and her first husband, Hannibalianus. This is the resting-place for a member of the imperial family, and designed to be appropriate to pagan or Christian.

The Christian faith has for centuries over-emphasized the completeness and rapidity of the defeat of paganism. Nearly a century after Constantine's victory, it still took a Christian martyr, the monk Telemachus, to die as a suicide, throwing himself to the wild beasts, to put a stop to the shows in the arenas. At the time of Alaric's siege of Rome (AD 410) the pope, St. Innocent I (401–17), suffered pagan priests to return to the Capitol to make sacrifices, believing at worst that they were nothing more than an irrelevance, but allowing his and others' hopes to be placed in the most desperate of theological measures. The power of the stories of girls like Agnes, however, has a quality that transcends rhetoric and special pleading. Something of its bittersweet nature is still preserved in the annual tradition of the blessing of lambs which takes place at S. Agnese Fuori le Mura on her feast day (January 21). After the service, the animals are taken to a convent in Trastevere where in due time the nuns use their wool to weave the *pallium*, the symbol of an Archbishop's office, which is sent as a gift to each newly appointed prelate by the pope. It is this kind of tradition that can sometimes make the connection between our world and that of martyrs, virgins, princesses and a dying culture, the Rome of late antiquity.

CHAPTER FIVE

The Middle Ages (1: The Papacy): Castel Sant'Angelo

> *"Beatrice Cenci: ...Tortures! Turn*
> *The rack henceforth into a spinning wheel!*
> *Torture your dog, that he may tell when last*
> *He lapped the blood his master shed... not me!*
> *My pangs are of the mind, and of the heart,*
> *And of the soul..."*
> Percy Bysshe Shelley, *The Cenci* (1820)

Afternoons can seem dull, even endlessly so, in Rome, especially if you reject the haven of a long lunch, a half-liter of wine and a short sleep. Churches close between noon and four PM, so if they are your addiction, there is a definite dry period each day. Many museums operate on bizarre schedules seemingly designed to keep their treasures hidden. But the crown of dull afternoons is Monday, when everything seems to close. In fact, nothing ever opened, for the morning is the same. For visitors to the city in summer, the torture of abortive sightseeing is made exquisite by dust, heat and the inflated prices of soft drinks. This truly is tourist hell. Until very recently I could have calmed your fears with an easy remedy. What Monday afternoons had to offer was a trip to a place more often associated with torture than its relief. Almost unique among Roman monuments, the Castel Sant'Angelo opened its doors on washing day. Now its submission to Monday closing seems the *coup de grâce*.

The fortress of the popes is an extremely complex sight, and its influence on the Italian imagination has been fruitful in various ways. (The fruit of housing the national military museum here smacks of a rather specialized taste, however; I'd face the heat and dust rather than troop by its cabinets of arms and armor any day.) Its original purpose was to house the ashes of Hadrian, and the subsequent line of Antonine emperors. It was not quite finished in AD 138 when Hadrian died, even though its construction was started almost twenty years before. A bridge, the *Pons Aelius*, linked it to the *Campus Martius* on the other side of the river. Although the bridge has been restored often in the past two or three centuries and was adorned with the Bernini-designed angels, the Ponte Sant'Angelo is today substantially the same ancient structure.

As a tomb, the castle follows in much the same tradition as Augustus' Mausoleum: a tubular construction, after Etruscan models, but on a far

grander scale. A direct connection was made between the two imperial tombs by making the base of the new one equal in width to the outer diameter of the old. But where in the earlier tomb there was space bounded by terracing, in the other there was solid masonry. The result has properly been called an artificial mountain, which now, after the accumulation of nearly two millennia, rises over 150 feet above the Tiber.

Many commentators have described Castel Sant'Angelo as "grim." H.V. Morton's assessment has become the standard: "Anyone who knows Castel S. Angelo will, I think, agree with me that it is one of the most frightening buildings in the world... Compared with [it], the Tower of London is almost a happy place." Another author, Cecil Roberts, less good though almost contemporary with Morton, has the strange notion of opening his book, *And So To Rome* (1950), with an extensive visit to the castle and an obsessive description of its creepy atmosphere:

> The building has seen enacted within its walls a terrible story of assassination, hanging, beheading, strangulation, poisoning and torture, with grim variations in the mode of murder and execution, such as death by starvation in its dungeons, or swift exit from the living world by its dreadful oubliettes.

I cannot join Roberts in thinking this place a suitable starting place for any tour of the city, hence my now abortive decision to save it for a Monday afternoon, judging few would arrive in the city late on Monday morning.

It is true, though, that after Castel Sant'Angelo had lost its outer facing of marble and most of its original decorative features through being incorporated into the city's defenses, the charm which the structure must once have boasted was lost. It becomes for me, as for others, a symbol of the change that is articulated through the passage from Ancient to Dark Age Rome, from antiquity to the Middle Ages. Here is the Rome which, especially in the Northern imagination typified by Morton and Roberts' treatment, is a gothic destination. Scheming and bloodthirsty cardinals, the fallen women they further corrupt, wretched prisoners in the depths of the deepest dungeons: these are the stock characters of such fantasies.

Light on the Dark Ages

However, unlike the brutish life that is proverbially said to have been led during them, the Middle Ages were, in cultural terms, attractive, sophisticated, and long. They span almost a thousand years and deserve a more thorough investigation, than, sadly, I allow. Out of the ruins of antiquity, two distinct forces emerged to fashion medieval Rome: the papacy, and the small-scale political life of a city-state. A chapter is devoted to each. The first of these forces increasingly developed an international dimension but was often brought back to the level of the second, as powerful local families vied for the papal tiara. During the whole period, outside influences were many. Barbarian invasions marked the end of ancient Roman culture proper, but occasional Byzantine resurgence meant that the city never quite lost its link with the continuing *imperium romanum* exercised from Constantinople. In the ninth century, Rome was sacked by the Saracens, who, unlike Alaric's Goths, did not respect the Christian holy places. Their example was again to be emulated by Christian armies in the subsequent sacks of 1084 and 1527. Also in the ninth century, the papacy was to forge a fresh political alliance with the newest European superpower, the empire of the Franks, ruled by its dynamic creator Charlemagne (768–814). Looking increasingly to the West rather than the East, the popes set the pattern of Rome's future that has lasted long after the close of the Middle Ages. The Treaty of Rome, which defined the movement toward European Union in the 1950s, owes not a little to this Dark Age cast of the die.

The first and defining anecdote concerning Castel Sant'Angelo comes from the very beginning of this period. During the pontificate of St. Gregory the Great (590–604), plague struck Rome. It was during a religious procession, designed to show penitence and invoke God's mercy, that the sainted pope is said to have seen a vision of the archangel Michael sheathing his sword upon the peak of the *castello*. This pious legend is commemorated by the gigantic statue cast by Verschaffelt in 1752, and which has taken the place of what crowned the structure in Hadrian's time. This is variously thought to have been a representation of the emperor himself portrayed as the sun-god driving a four-horse chariot, or the enormous bronze pine cone now to be seen in the *cortile* of the Vatican's Belvedere. In either case, neither has the gothic piquancy of St. Michael, now threatening, now merciful.

The vast Roman structure had been incorporated into the city's defensive system by Aurelian in the late third century, and further additions date from periods as late as the sixteenth century. The castle was only decommissioned as a working fortress in 1911, and until 1870 it had been the base for the occupying French troops who propped up the papal government in its last, ailing years. Jauntily perched upon the artificial mole are whole suites of papal apartments that attest to the considerable periods of papal occupation when the Holy See was under threat. Pope St. Gregory VII took shelter there when besieged by the German Emperor Henry IV. And the second Borgia pope, Alexander VI, withdrew into the *castello* as King Charles IX of France passed by on his way to attempt to seize the throne of Naples.

Most famously, Pope Clement VII (1523–34) fled there along the elevated covered walkway from the Vatican, the *passetto*, as the imperial troops comprising a multinational force of Catholics and Protestants burst into the city early on the morning of May 6, 1527. (Occasional entrance to this concealed passage is one of the more welcome of the jubilee year's touristic innovations, even if it does not make up for closing on Mondays…). The Medici pope was in St. Peter's, determined to shame the invaders by confronting them in full regalia, but so terrible was the alarm when news reached him that the troops had massacred the inmates of a nearby hospital, that he gave up his noble but foolhardy plan. He was considerably hampered in his flight by the length of his court train, which had to be hoisted over the arm of an attendant cardinal. Luckily, Clement was not as incapacitated physically as had been his cousin and predecessor Leo X (1513–21), who could only make it up to the safety of the castle's apartments by means of a highly decorated lift. Dependent upon strong men, as well as an elaborate system of pulleys, this might truly be the lift defined by Proust as "dating from the period before lifts were invented." Clement VII did not need the lift in his panic, as the covered way delivered him directly to the outer bastions and the curtain wall.

He might well have needed the bathroom that bears his name, however, after the considerable fright and indeed danger, as he dodged arquebus shot aimed through the passage's narrow windows. The bathroom, sumptuously decorated, and apparently able to deliver hot and cold running water directly into the vast marble tub, was a luxury facility amid the more practical amenities of a fortress under siege. It would be possible to make a short, but I insist, fascinating tour of Renaissance clerical bathrooms were you minded to do so. Those designed for Cardinals Riario and Bibienna in the Palazzo Altemps and Vatican respectively might form the points of departure. But leaving the opportunity of initiating research into fifteenth-century bidet prototypes to others, we return to the more *macho* territory of Castel Sant'Angelo under attack.

The building had shown its mettle even before it was militarily equipped. During the gothic siege of Rome in AD 573, defenders had scrambled up the monument and hurled down fragments of the statues that lined the cornices. In the more infamous assault of 1527, the Sack of Rome, it was from the fully developed battlements that Benvenuto Cellini, the artist, biographer and teller of tall tales, had claimed to have fired the fatal shot to dispatch the Constable of Bourbon, commanding officer of the imperial troops.

It will come as a shock to those who have grown accustomed to the pacific image of the papacy established and developed during the twentieth century that the popes have ever actually needed a stronghold. Everyone is used to the idea of the Vatican's army, the Swiss Guard, but their status as real soldiers is diminished by their picturesque costume, often erroneously attributed to Michelangelo's design. Is there nothing that could not be ascribed to the artistic capabilities of that somber Florentine? In fact, the role of pope, as secular as well as spiritual prince, in as much need of an army as the next territorial power, was established as the civic importance of Rome declined. In the political vacuum, the papacy gradually assumed the reins of power and took on the role first of city prefect, held variously under a barbarian king or the Byzantine emperor. Later, the popes relied upon the fabrication of testimonial documents supposedly originating with Emperor Constantine. This so-called "Donation" granted the popes the temporalities of not only the city, but also a large stretch of land surrounding it. They were ideologically supported in this by the line of Holy Roman Emperors starting in AD 800, although, as we have already noted, it was sometimes as uneasy allies that such worldly and spiritual cooperation existed between emperor and pontiff.

Gothic Guided Tour

Visiting the castle today presents an experience considerably more interesting than the plain bulk viewed from outside might suggest. Although it has lost all of its external decoration, the quality and style of which are known from pre-Renaissance sketches and a fragment of cornice now in the castle's museum, a substantial part of the internal design survives. Entering from a park on the eastern side, you approach the main and original entrance along a circular street once covered by vaulting. Arriving on axis with the bridge, a short corridor leads into the heart of the structure, terminating in a vestibule with a niche that would once have contained a statue of Hadrian. The head of a likely candidate is in the Vatican's Sala Rotonda. From the vestibule, a helical ramp, the architectural wonder of the building, takes a full circuit of the cylinder's drum, climbing some forty feet in so doing. A further corridor then leads to what was the chamber in which the imperial funerary urns were deposited. This, however, was transformed into the point of departure for another ramp, constructed under Pope Alexander VI, which cuts right through the cylinder, bisecting the lofty, sepulchral *cella*. When the Borgia pope added this refinement to the structure, a drawbridge carried the ramp through the open space of the *cella*, emphasizing the change of use from classical tomb to medieval castle.

Where the urn of Hadrian once rested, a modern inscription quoting his most famous words has been installed. Hadrian's *Address to his Soul*, five short lines of Latin verse, has a melancholy that perfectly suits this crepuscular, cavernous space:

> *animula, vagula, blandula,*
> *hospes comesque corporis,*
> *quae nunc abibis in loca,*
> *pallidula, rigida, nudula,*
> *nec ut soles dabis jocos*

Confronted with literally hundreds of translations of these few words (a pamphlet containing 116 was published in 1876), I will conform with

H.V. Morton in quoting the youthful Byron's version, while joining with him in criticizing line three as having no foundation in the text:

Ah! gentle, fleeting wav'ring Sprite,
Friend and associate of this clay
To what unknown region borne
Wilt thou, now, wing thy distant flight?
No more, with wonted humour gay,
But pallid, cheerless and forlorn.

Marguerite Yourcenar chooses the wistful stanza as the epigraph of her fictional autobiography, *Hadrian*. For her, the emperor's soul is rather more forthright about its "gay" element than even Byron might have been able to be, though no less humorous.

Hadrian's resting-place was not the only antique Roman monument to undergo the change from tomb to castle. A number of substantial ruins were converted into the strongholds of various powerful families during the Middle Ages. At different times, the Frangipani and Annibaldi held the Colosseum, while the strong men of the Theater of Marcellus were the Pierleoni, Orsini, and Savelli. Once they had fortified it, the Mausoleum of Augustus was kept in the hands of the Colonna. The Caetani took the tomb of Cecilia Metella about two miles out of town on the Via Appia as their country base of operations, and the Cenci held the Theater of Balbus.

The last named family, though small beer in the internecine rivalries of the Middle Ages proper, assumes epic proportions when the gothic legacy of Rome is considered. A lurid story in which a cruelly tyrannical and ultimately incestuous father is murdered by his wife and children was internationalized by Shelley in a verse drama. Its departure from popular western culture is attested to by the fact that it was the subject of a recent modern opera (Goldsmidt's *Beatrice Cenci*), but commentators on Rome always assume that everyone has heard of the beautiful Beatrice. As one of the accomplices in the murder plot, but also as the principal victim of incestuous rape, she earned both a death-sentence and the extravagant pity of both contemporaries and subsequent devotees of gothic horror. She was executed on a scaffold set up on the bridge by order of Clement VIII (1598–1605) in 1600, after being held in the Castel Sant'Angelo.

As if one Roman literary (and operatic) beauty were not enough for the grim fortress, it is here that Floria, la Tosca, heroine of Sardou's play and Puccini's opera, takes her one small leap for womanhood and the race of overweight sopranos. Her lover Cavaradossi is held in the castle because of his revolutionary ideas. After killing Scarpia, the chief of police, with a knife filched from his supper table, Tosca arrives at Castel Sant'Angelo, only to witness the death by firing squad of her beloved. What else is there for a girl to do but to throw herself on God's mercy by leaping from the battlements? The rather cruelly termed "shabby little shocker" (Stafford Dean) is a wonderful opera; the real shabbiness comes in the open competition entered by all impersonators of the title role to tell the most outrageous story about the leap. The claim to have bounced back from the trampoline positioned to take the fall has been made by at least three divas (most recently by the nonagenarian Dame Eva Turner— clearly age did not prevent her telling fibs). Far more believable are the accounts of those who broke limbs through the absence of any soft landing. I have seen rather stately women simply step off into the high wings, with no suggestion of a jump being made at all, and I have seen *tours de force* as athletic youngsters took a run up. Most ludicrous was the recent production at London's English National Opera where the actress took a bow and the audience saw the slow-motion fall of a dummy.

Not So Brutish or Nasty

In previous chapters, I have already mentioned some of the changes in physical circumstances that befell the city during the Dark Ages. The water from the aqueducts stopped flowing. The vast complexes of public buildings became first deserted and then derelict, the most imposing adapted to more pressing uses. Recent excavations (1981 onward) of the area around the Theater of Balbus, where the Cenci made their medieval home, have revealed important findings for understanding Rome's economic life during this period. In the substantial *porticus* that ran down the Tiber side of the Via delle Botteghe Oscure, evidence of early medieval metalworking and glass manufacture has been found. As already noted, the focus of the city shifted to the *Campus Martius* because of its access to the river's water supply. The areas around the Jewish quarter, the Campo dei Fiori and the Piazza Navona, give us the strongest taste of the medieval domestic and economic adaptation of Roman ruins.

Further "out of town" (although not outside the walls), the monastery and church sites of late antiquity survived and became increasingly surrounded by gardens and vineyards as the domestic buildings which had existed in these quarters fell into total disrepair or were plundered for reusable materials and so demolished. The changes can be witnessed very readily in such churches as S. Clemente near the Colosseum and SS. Giovanni e Paolo on the Coelian. In the celebrated case of S. Clemente, three different layers of occupation can be visited. At the lowest level, an alleyway, part of a large house, and a temple of the Mithras cult dating from the first century AD have been uncovered in excavations by the resident Irish Dominicans. Above these is an early medieval basilica (fifth century) with some traces of early fresco work, and built upon this is a mature medieval church with important architectural and decorative schemes (AD 1108). At SS. John and Paul, not dedicated to the Apostles, but to early Roman martyrs of the same names, a villa complex and more humble residences form the foundation of the church, and can be visited beneath it. Even more accessible is a viewing of the *Clivus Scauri*, the Roman street that descends the Coelian hill to the side of SS. John and Paul, and the third-century shop fronts, which have been totally incorporated into the design of the medieval church above.

The history of church buildings, in spite of so much excellent first-hand evidence in Rome, remains a murky science. No thoroughly antique building intended as a church has come down to us unscathed. Constantine's basilicas have been so knocked about or completely destroyed that all they can really give us is a sense of scale and plan. The earliest proper examples come from the beginning of the medieval period. The common Italian word for any large church, not only one designated the seat of a bishop, is *duomo*, deriving from the Latin for home or house, which implies the truth of the oft-cited, but never proved, contention that Christians continued to worship in domestic circumstances right up to and possibly following the Constantinian period. Thus, the large houses below both S. Clemente and SS. Giovanni e Paolo may have been the original churches of these martyrs, later memorialized in the formal basilica-type structures above them.

The basilica had started its architectural history as a simple hall with aisles to house Roman law courts. Such were the Julian and Ulpian basilicas of the Roman Forum. Over the centuries, however, the form was enlarged and modified, so that in the massive ruins of the basilica of Maxentius/Constantine we have a multi-aisled hall with lofty vaulting and two apses (although the original plan only furnished one). It seems that it was such buildings, together with the funerary-circus tradition explained in the last chapter, which produced the regular form of churches from the early Middle Ages on. The height of the Maxentian basilica and the complexity of its vaulting, where main hall meets aisle, may have suggested the further refinement of adding transepts to religious basilicas, thus giving the traditional cruciform plan to which we have grown accustomed. Yet the most typical medieval basilicas in

Rome do not have transepts. The best examples of an attempt at total restoration to the medieval plan and decorative scheme are the churches of S. Maria in Cosmedin (the church with the Bocca della Verità in its porch) and S. Sabina on the Aventine. Although in both these examples the features are not always original, the intention of twentieth-century restorers was to return these early buildings to a state that really suggests the atmosphere of the early Middle Ages. Almost all churches in Rome underwent the process of baroque adaptation and so it comes as a great pleasure to find some that have been stripped of their seventeenth-century tinsel in order to create spaces of simple and solemn dignity.

Another link these churches have with the antique past is the durability of the taste for mosaic work. The principal decoration of the medieval churches in Rome are the mosaics that adorn their apses, and in the cases of larger ones such as S. Maria Maggiore and S. Maria in Trastevere, the triumphal arch as well. These works span a period from the fourth to the thirteenth centuries, although it is almost certain that by the later date the workmanship and design were consciously old-fashioned, and in some cases actual reworking of much older originals. It is very likely that at least the design for the apse mosaic of the upper church of S. Clemente came from the lower church. The delicacy and finesse of these glowing images, where deep blues and reds rise like jewels from a sea of dull gold, gives the lie to the popular image of the Dark Ages.

Another striking and original feature of medieval Roman craftsmanship is the ubiquitous *cosmatesque* decoration of everything from tombs to candlesticks. This appliqué technique, named after its principal practitioners, the extended Cosma family, employed fragments of colored marbles harvested from the shattered fields of inlay, which once decorated thousands of antique public buildings. Recycled in this way, pieces of a marble panel from a shady and salacious second-century bath house can find their way onto the inlaid floor of a particularly sacred shrine. Fragments of Roman decoration are a little like the air we breathe and the water we drink: in a constant human merry-go-round of re-use.

Although times could be troubled, economically and politically during this period, there still were standards of beauty and civilization to which the city of the popes aspired. Take the pontificate of Pope St. Paschal I (817–24). Politically, Paschal had to play a careful game of cat-and-mouse with Charlemagne's successors, particularly Louis the Pious and Lothair. The papacy and the empire were still recent allies, but complacent enough to start finding that the arrangement could chafe. Paschal was implicated in the murder of pro-imperial clerics, and by the end of his short but active pontificate was the object of local and international detestation. However, as a patron of the arts he has few medieval equals. The mosaics that decorate his mother's memorial chapel in the church of S. Prassede (Browning's St. Praxed's) are as fine as the best contemporary work at Ravenna or Constantinople, and may have been completed by Byzantine craftsmen fleeing renewed iconoclasm in the east. Another church that owes its glories to this pope is S. Maria in Domnica; there is Paschal, up in the apse, sporting the square blue halo of the living among the gold nimbuses of the sanctified dead. Although he is awarded the title Saint in some of the early calendars, it appears he did little to deserve it except to display a fine artistic judgment.

A Bit Brutish after All

So that we can appreciate the depths to which the medieval papacy really could sink, it is necessary to take a small detour at this stage into the careers of two Roman women of the tenth century (high- or low-achieving, depending upon your point of view). The Senatrix Theodora, wife of the noble Roman Theophalyct, began the female domination of the papacy, which later was to be termed the Pornocracy of the Holy See, around the year AD 904. The opportunity had arisen through a vacancy in the imperial office and theological chaos resulting from one half of the clergy refusing to recognize the ordinations of the other. (Relating to this, Pope Formosus (891–896) had been tried and sentenced in the bizarrely macabre Cadaver Synod, which he was forced to attend in person six months after his death.) Pope Sergius III (904–11) became a puppet of the unscrupulous Theodora after he was seduced by her fifteen-year-old daughter, Marozia. Their child was later to become Pope John XI. Marozia herself succeeded to her mother's influence and was to be the principal mover in the deposition and murder in Castel Sant'Angelo of John X (914–28), shortly followed by the rigged election of her 22-year-old son, already cardinal deacon of S. Maria in Trastevere. She rounded off her unassailable dominance by marrying the Lombard King of Italy, Hugh of Provence. Stirred up by another of her sons and disturbed by this increasing foreign influence in Roman affairs, the mob stormed Castel'Sant Angelo, and imprisoned Marozia, her royal husband, and pontiff son. A tradition tells that she lived in the appalling conditions of a castle cell for over fifty years, only to be brutally put to death when a later city governor learned she was still alive.

Roman politics has more recently shown itself to be susceptible to rather obvious feminine charm. La Cicciolina ("Bunnykins"), a superstar porn-queen, and partner of Jeff Koons, the creator of Trash Art, was elected as a Radical Party deputy in the late 1980s as the disillusionment with the traditional parties and career politicians began to mount. Her successful election address delivered on televised hustings was crowned by the unbuttoning of her blouse and bra to show the electorate what she was made of. Inspired by her guiding spirit, another pornographic actress, Moana Pozzi, founded the Partito del Amore (Love Party) in 1992. Considered an intellectual because of the weighty tomes lining her bookshelves, she proposed a free market in sex and the provision of love stations to be visited by workers in their lunch hours. She confided in the BBC's Matt Frei at her party's launch at a large discotheque in Rome that Italy was "going through a profound transition... The breaching of the Berlin Wall and the fall of Communism has deprived the Christian Democrats and their allies of the reason for perpetual re-election." The danger, she said, was that "this so-called revolution" of theirs would "fizzle out ... in a *coitus interruptus*." Sadly, things did come to a sudden end for Moana herself, who was diagnosed with cancer in 1994 and dead a few months later. She has since avoided the universal condemnation of the Pornocrats, Theodora and Marozia, being elevated to a kind of pseudo-sanctity on the Eva Perón model. Even the Archbishop of Naples, Michele Giordano, spoke of her at Sunday mass, saying how she had shown the spark of faith dwelling under the ash heap of humanity. As Frei goes on to comment: "Italy may be the home of the Vatican and boast more saints per square mile than any other Catholic country, but it is also one of the least prudish societies in the world."

It is in that same Italian spirit that I move us from Santa Moana slowly back to our consideration of medieval Roman church buildings. The abiding Roman basilica style of architecture froze out styles that predominated elsewhere. The Romanesque and gothic get little exposure in Rome. The exception in stylistic terms is the proliferation of Romanesque bell towers, or campaniles, conjoined to older basilicas. Richard and Barbara Mertz, in their customarily warm style, describe the type well in their *Two Thousand Years in Rome:*

> *The form is typical and unmistakable—tall square towers made of the lovely rosy Roman bricks. The airy look implied by the tall slim shape is augmented by the design, which is a series of arches supported on slender little columns. Sometimes as at SS Giovanni e Paolo, the towers were decorated by majolica work, circles of colored pottery set into the masonry.*

The much-cited unique example of a truly gothic church in the city is S. Maria Sopra Minerva. Even though it is true that its windows and arches rise to the lancet point characteristic of the gothic style, the church's similarities with its neighbors far outweigh these differences. To look for real examples, we have to wait for the nineteenth-century neo-gothic of either my own church, All Saints, the Church of England shrine in Rome, built by George Street in 1882, or on just the other side of the river, back near the Castel Sant'Angelo, the church of SacroCuore del Succorso. This brings us back to our starting-place.

Any visit to the massive fortress is aimed at reaching the top for the view, one of the best in the city. But don't miss the café out on the bastions on the way up, patronized in both senses by the American journalist Robert Hutchinson, who describes it, in his book *When in Rome*, as serving "surprisingly good tortellini." Looking down from it, you get a good view of the popes' escape route, the bit spruced up and the more distant parts still overgrown by weeds. Also, after the glories of Clement VII's bathroom, pause to look at the brass-bound chest in which Leo X kept the entire treasury of the Papal States. Somehow it seems smaller than you might have expected. There are also some pretty frescoed rooms where you can easily imagine grossly corpulent clerics sipping wine and tossing bones over their shoulders while their prisoners were racked, seared, and pierced in nearby dungeons. If this is too fanciful, then stop to consider the tiny chapel of the Crucifixion out on the bastion. It was here that those condemned to death were forced to attend mass before execution. Although we might agree with the concern given to the spiritual condition of those about to die, the element of emotional torture in this obligation was insidiously cruel. Gothic scenarios are often more ordinary than we think. By the same token, the small tragedy of a frustrating and wasted Monday afternoon could once have been transformed by Castel Sant'Angelo's gloomy delights. Not any more.

CHAPTER SIX

The Middle Ages (2: The City): Statue of Rienzo, The Capitol

> *"It is not impossible to rule the Italians, it's pointless... I wear no rings, it will not happen to me."*
> Mussolini in private conversation.

He cuts a ludicrous figure. Alone in a sea of trouble, perched at a precarious height, and robed in a costume mocking the clownishness of all officialdom: the white gloves and white-domed hat of a traffic policeman. He used to be a regular and welcome source of diversion for travelers on buses crossing his particular stormy passage, the junction of the Corso and Piazza Venezia. We don't see him so often now, since under Sindaco Rutelli and his regime of *Roma per Roma*, Rome for Rome, an attempt to rationalize traffic flow has re-routed some buses and increased the number of one-way streets. There may be fewer *bloccati*, traffic jams, but life seems poorer for the silencing of his whistle and the disappearance of his exemplary gesticulation.

Telling Romans how and where to go is a sport in which the state engages without any real expectation of success. Traveling by taxi from Ciampino airport, having been quoted a ridiculous price (it had been 30,000 lire cheaper only six weeks before), I lived both to prize and to regret my exhortation that we should go fast, as otherwise I would be late for lunch. The driver obliged. So fast were we that he outmaneuvered a line of waiting cars at some traffic lights by pretending to be turning right, only to pull out across the intersection when the signal was against us. When I commented that it was like being on a fairground ride ("*Come si chiama... rollercoaster?*"), he replied that he was faster. I could vouch for more exciting. Road signs and signals, the ubiquitous but useless pedestrian crossings, even the loitering of police cars and the observation of *vigili urbani* do not rein in the enthusiasm of Roman drivers. The chariot race from *Ben-Hur* is daily re-enacted along the roads flanking the *circus maximus*, the location of the scene from the film, as Charlton Heston in a white convertible Fiat Punto, outdoes his surly and cruel rival, the red Alfa Romeo with chrome trim. Ten years ago, when faced as students with a pedestrian journey to lectures, a friend devised a sure way of getting across the busiest streets. He would bring the most demonic lane of oncoming traffic to a screeching halt simply by walking into the middle of the road, holding out his hand and proclaiming, "Let me through, I'm a diabetic." The combination of foolhardiness and the element of surprise provided dividends, but I don't recommend it as a technique to be emulated.

The Piazza Venezia is one of the most confusing of the road junctions in town. The mile-long, centrally placed Corso empties into it. This is an ancient street that follows the line of the *via flaminia* across the *Campus Martius* to the gate at Piazza del Popolo, and was used during Carnival as a racecourse until the nineteenth century. The boulevards, Via Nazionale and Quattro Novembre cascade into Piazza Venezia to the left of the Corso, and the similar Via Plebiscito and Via Vittorio Emanuele II fail to cope with the egress on the right. Just to add further problems, the major Fascist-era road, Via dei Fori Imperiali enters the far side of the piazza with what, at a conservative estimate, appears to be about nine lanes of traffic. In the midst of this maelstrom is a patch of rather unprepossessing lawn overshadowed by cliffs of masonry. On one side, the bleak early Renaissance bulk of the Palazzo di Venezia rises, with its disproportionately small window and balcony from which another ludicrously dressed Italian gesticulated. Behind, is the Sala della Mappi Mundi, the office occupied during the tenure of the premiership by Benito Mussolini. Make just a half turn, and there to your left towers the *Altare della Patria*, the monument dedicated to the memory and patriotism of Italy's first king, Vittorio Emanuele II. People say that this artificial mountain of white Brescia marble, 250 feet high, provided a safe seat for the deputy from that city for the quarter century it took to build (1885–1911).

Call it what you like (wedding cake or typewriter are currently most popular; Augustus Hare in the nineteenth century said it resembled a money box), but the monument certainly blocks one of the most significant views you can get from here. Neither the posturing policemen nor Mussolini from his balcony could have caught even a glimpse of the Capitoline hill, which has symbolized the civil power in Rome for two and a half millennia. It was the location for the most important religious shrines of Republic and Empire, the temples of Jupiter and Juno, the heavenly king and queen. It has been the site of Rome's town hall, the Palazzo Senatorio, since the end of the eleventh century. It was here that Petrarch was crowned as imperial poet laureate, here that Pope Clement VII received Emperor Charles V once they had patched things up following the Sack of Rome. It was here only a few years ago that John Paul II made the first official visit of any pope in modern times to the city. In a strong sense, this area has always been an alternative power base to the Lateran, Vatican or Quirinal, and the popes who held sway from these various strongholds. It is to this place that we come now to consider Rome in the Middle Ages from a secular perspective.

Approaching the Capitol from Piazza Venezia's automobile circus and the gloomy bus station to the side of the wedding cake, we are faced with three choices. A precipitous flight of 124 steps climbs to the western end of the medieval church of S. Maria in Aracoeli, which now occupies the site of the ancient shrines of Hera. As you can get into this

church far more easily from the back, it is best to leave the steps to the mountaineers. To the right, a winding, shady road allows access for cars, as it did for carriages when it was laid in 1873. Although the least challenging as a climb, it is of little interest, meandering past some temple fragments and a short stretch of archaic wall—perhaps a must for those who wish to see every last bit of ancient Rome, but otherwise not fascinating. Straight ahead stretches the *cordonata*, a stepped ramp, designed by Michelangelo to be the ceremonial approach to the heart of Rome's civic life. This is the way for us. Passing the Egyptian lions, brought here from the ruined temple of Isis and which guard the foot of the ramp, you make your progress toward the Campidoglio and the Capitol's piazza. But if you pause for just a moment, letting your eyes drift from the statue of Marcus Aurelius, which is gradually revealed as you mount, you will see to the left a smaller, lonely statue perched on a rather inadequate plinth and set in a tiny garden. This unobtrusive nineteenth-century monument is the focal point of this chapter, not for its intrinsic artistic merit, but for the significance of the man it commemorates, a figure of considerable ambiguity, great talent and vision shaped by the vices of his time and place.

A Political Personality

Nicholas, son of Lawrence, known to the world as Cola di Rienzo, was born either in 1313 or 1314. His family members kept an inn, around the corner from here in the Regola quarter, next to the ghetto. The young Cola grew up at a significant time for Rome, during the long pontificate (almost twenty years) of Jacques Cahon, John XXII (1316–34), the French pope who firmly established that the papacy need not be resident in the city. His predecessor, another French prelate, Clement V (1305–14), had actually done the deed, moving after his election at Perugia over the Alps to France. For seventy years, the papacy was to be established at Avignon, the so-called "Babylonic captivity" under the direct influence of the French throne. The reason for this move was, of course, political. The pretext was the scandal that arose from the increasing violence and crime perpetrated by powerful families in Rome itself. The feud between Boniface VIII and the Colonna family, which culminated in the pope's notorious kidnapping, mistreatment and death a few days after his rescue, left its mark. But the true macro-political cause was the increasing antagonism between the two European superpowers, France and the Empire, and the increasingly uncomfortable role played between the two by the papacy.

In previous periods, the popes had lived in other towns, when things got too hot for them in Rome. Viterbo and Perugia, both within their political orbit, provided cool summer palaces and alternative bases of government should mob violence and rioting make Rome uncomfortable. Yet no pope had actually traveled with the intention of taking the Apostolic See away with him. This was the effect of the time at Avignon. It slowly dawned on members of Rome's patrician elite that they had killed the goose that laid the golden eggs, for by now whatever prestige Rome possessed was derived from the papal office. However much they prided themselves on being descended from noble *gentes* of the Roman empire and being members of the Senate, now the oligarchic town council, the Colonnas, Orsini, Gaetani, and so on were just a group of strong-armed barons in a peninsula overcrowded with such types. The thing that had made Rome different and special was the papal, and by extension, the imperial links the city still possessed.

It was into this chaotic vacuum that Cola appeared, a self-taught lawyer with a very persuasive tongue. Stories told with hindsight point to his early pretensions of grandeur, even while resident at his parents' inn, where he would claim to be the illegitimate child of a leading noble foisted upon a cuckolded husband. It is little wonder that he had a poor relationship with his father. Cola was chosen as a junior member of an embassy that was sent to Avignon in 1342 to try to persuade Clement VI (1342–52) to return to Rome.

International pressure to the same end had been steadily building, especially within the community of artists. Dante, in *The Divine Comedy*, laments the departure of the popes to France, and Petrarch was disconsolate to find the city of Rome a shadow of its former glory in the Holy Year 1350 ("Nowhere is Rome less known than in Rome," he wrote to a friend). Dante's complaint is justifiably famous:

> Vieni a veder la tua Roma che piange,
> Vedova, sola, e dì e notte chiama:
> "cesare mio, perché non m'accompagne?"

> *Come see thy Rome that weeps,*
> *Widowed, alone, and calling day and night:*
> *"Caesar my son, why art thou not by my side?"*

Soon, St. Catherine of Siena, the visionary ascetic, was to add her slight physical weight and immense spiritual muster to the pleas for return in her near-hysterical epistolary style, and even more alarming ecstatic presence at the court of Avignon. Cola's embassy failed, but Cola did not. By hanging around long enough, he brought himself to the notice of those with political influence at Avignon, and he was sent back to Rome with an official title, position, and salary, as Apostolic Notary. Luigi Barzini, the percipient Rome correspondent of the London *Times* during the 1950s and 1960s, and a veteran native journalist, comments wryly in his *From Caesar to the Mafia* upon Cola's failure in these circumstances to act as would other Italians: "His job was one which most Italians fancy; he had a steady income, some authority, underlings to do the real work, and time to pursue his own studies."

Cola's difference was to attempt to realize the full potential of his personal power through further effort, rather than remain comfortably where he might stay undisturbed. Inspired and stirred by his appreciation of Rome's past and present, Cola staged a coup on May 9, 1347. Unlike its modern counterparts, it left the post office, TV station, and airport alone, focusing on an all-night vigil, similar to that practiced by those receiving knighthood, in his parish church of Sant'Angelo in Peschiera. In the morning, he emerged from church wearing a suit of shining armor, and unfurled his banner (an uncanny portent, a red flag with no emblems) as he and his companions advanced upon the Capitol to take control of the Palazzo Senatorio.

The populace of Rome rallied to the cause of one of their own number, and rapidly the bad government of the aristocracy was replaced by the personal dictatorship of Rienzo. By dispensing justice equitably, he quickly consolidated his grassroots support, but further alienated the ousted political class. At the same time, Cola gained legitimacy by successful diplomacy with pope, emperor, and other powers. The nobles were unmanned. Yet they need not have been concerned; Cola would be the cause of his own downfall. The same taste for show and theatrical gesture that had made his May coup successful was to lead to his fall from grace. On the August 1, he staged a pageant which took him and his court to St. John Lateran, the papal cathedral. He rode there upon a white horse, an honor customarily reserved for the pope. And on arrival at the church, after a near sacrilegious bath in the font of the Baptistery, he was crowned with six crowns in a ceremony that explicitly employed symbolism evoking Christ himself.

This attack of *hubris* had its counterpart in the political field. After he had invited the majority of nobles to a banquet, he arrested them all and quickly passed the death-sentence upon them. This was too much, not only for the former rulers, but even for some of the ruled. Threatened with insurrection, Cola backed off and released the prisoners, but he was unable to reassert his authority following this climb-down. By December 1347, his perceptiveness told him that discretion was the better part of valor, and he left Rome for voluntary exile. But that was not the last history was to hear of him. He did the rounds of the royal courts of Europe, seeking support for a restoration. Finally, backed with imperial authority, he returned to the city of his birth on August 1, 1354.

Things had changed. Between a third and a half of Europe's population had been killed by bubonic plague, and, rather less dramatically, Cola had passed from vigorous youth to corpulent middle age. This time, he was to rule for just over two months. His regime cracked on October 8, and Cola, disguised as a coal-vendor with shabby clothes and a face blackened with soot, crept from the back entrance of the embattled Palazzo Senatorio. Alas, he had not removed all his jewelry. A ring or bracelet (accounts differ) caught the attention of someone in the crowd, and he was set upon, to be killed by the mob on the site of the present statue.

Late Medieval Change

This story of a brief Roman dictatorship seemed worth telling in full, as it highlights so much of what makes medieval Rome different from its neighbors. The northern and central cities of Italy developed strong communitarian governments in the mid-to-late Middle Ages. Guilds of merchants and lawyers were the driving force for the foundation of public and private institutions such as the oldest university in the world at Bologna, and Europe's oldest surviving bank, the Monti dei Paschi di Siena. In the south of Italy, development had been promoted by a strong and imaginative Norman government, which was followed by the lengthy direct rule of the Holy Roman Emperor Frederick II. Frederick's enlightened court had been the wonder of the world during the thirteenth century, memorialized in the enduring Latin tag *stupor mundi* and uniting Christendom with the scientific, cultural, and architectural innovations of Islam. Rome, caught between these two, was a backwater. Popes did not generally rule for long enough to see through a program of reform, and in any case, were weighed down by the twin problems of a violent city dominated by warlords and the pressures of maintaining an international standing. Rome, then as now, belongs neither to Italy's north or south, but is classified by both as belonging to the other insofar as it remains hostile and alien. Strikingly though, it is still the unobtainable prize of each.

There had occasionally been strong and influential medieval popes. There was Gregory VII, the monk Hildebrand, who centralized authority in the papacy and imposed clerical celibacy. Even this strength, however, especially where it concerned the theory that the pope was above any other human judgment, was not unproblematic. It led directly to his major clash with the Emperor Henry IV and to the Sack of Rome in 1084. Innocent III (1198–1216), who held the fourth Lateran Council of 1215, successfully renewed canon law. He also took the earlier medieval idea of crusade and directed it inward, creating the Inquisition to root out the Albigensian heresy and its adherents, the Cathars. Even Hadrian IV (1154–59), the only English pope, who had trodden the careful line of diplomacy with the German Emperor Frederick Barbarossa to strengthen the political position of the Papal States, might be held up as an exception. But these achievements were always subject to sudden and irremediable reversal, in part because of Rome's lack of any significant civil authority. The city was caught between a rock and a hard place; it could not better itself without the papacy, but the principal reason for its failure to do so was the presence and authority of the pope.

The architectural remains of the high Middle Ages in Rome are disappointing. The Torre delle Milizie and the Torre dei Conti, both fortress-like towers built as new, rather than within ancient structures, look broodingly down on the valley of the Forum from the Quirinal and Esquiline respectively. Richard and Barbara Mertz, whose excellent book *2000 Years in Rome* is among the most systematically thorough in the field, found enjoyment atop the Torre delle Milizie, which once could be visited as part of a package for entry to Trajan's Market:

> *From the top of the tower, one gets a magnificent view over the fori and the Colosseum area, but the stairs, which are inside the tower and not very well lit, are somewhat nerve-wracking to climb. There is a little stone table on top of the tower; it is one of the most unusual and most private spots we found for a picnic.*

Sadly, the tower is now closed. You will have to nibble your *panino* elsewhere.

Two palaces which variously reflect their origins are the Palazzo di Venezia and the Palazzo Senatorio itself. The first looks medieval and recalls the gothic architecture of its mother city. In fact, dating from the 1450s, it is really the first great Renaissance palace in Rome, built for the Venetian Cardinal Pietro Barbo, later Pope Paul II (1464–71). The Palazzo Senatorio on the Campidoglio, however, looks at least from the front like a creation of the High Renaissance, but is actually solidly medieval. Built upon the foundations of the *tabularium*, a large antique building of the Roman Forum, the town hall was designed as a fortress by the Corsi family early in the twelfth century. The Senate was established there around 1150, but it was not until the middle of the sixteenth century that it got the Michelangelo facelift it had been waiting for, part of his total makeover of the Capitol. It still houses the offices of the mayor and of the city council, and is therefore usually closed to visitors.

As mentioned in Chapter One, there is much to admire in Sindaco Rutelli's attempt to get Rome to work. But as I make the transition from visitor to resident in the city, I become increasingly aware of the gripes people have about him. The *Roma per Roma* project, which was supposed to make life easier for people and return the city to its inhabitants, was nearly right. The thinking behind it—to improve the quality of the air by removing traffic from the *centro storico*, to smarten up the look of things in conjunction with the Vatican's preparation for *Il Gran Giubileo*—all this made and makes sense. But Romans are both impatient and slow. It seems to have taken an inordinately long time, and Rutelli's majority in a second term looks considerably less secure. I heard a very well-established expatriate lady married to an Italian facetiously order *acqua Rutelli*, that is, tap water, in a restaurant. As the Sindaco slides from his position of admired idealist to be the butt of jokes, the old story seems to be playing itself out. It seems unlikely that Rutelli, even after the criticism he earned for the chaos surrounding the millennium celebrations, will need to escape from the Palazzo Senatorio, Rienzo-like. He lacks the required level of egoism and theatricality; but he may be removed in the twenty-first century's democratic equivalent of a lynching.

Modern Strongholds

In some ways not unlike the medieval fortresses built upon the glories of the antique past, the party headquarters of the post-war period long nestled within the walls of Renaissance *palazzi*, close to the nation's political heartbeat. Within spitting distance of the Capitol (or in Roman terms the aim of a piece of small change, for this is how disgraced politicians are greeted by a crowd) were two of these magicians' caves. The Christian Democrats, appropriately enough, were found in Piazza del Gesù, and their supposed enemies, the PCI (Communists) were just around the corner at the Piazza Venezia end of Via delle Botteghe Oscure. Both parties fell in the great political showdown of 1993, but the Christian Democrats had farther to fall. An anecdote often related about the diabolical machinations of the Jesuits has a new currency when applied to their party building. The story goes that the devil and the wind once took a walk around Rome, and when they came to Piazza del Gesù the devil said to the wind, "You wait here, while I pop into the church to light a candle and say a prayer." All Rome knows that even on the stillest of days the piazza in front of the great Jesuit church remains peculiarly draughty. The devil might well have kept the wind eternally waiting as he popped into party headquarters to strike a deal.

My most abiding memory of the Gesù doesn't involve the largest piece of lapis lazuli in the world, affixed to St. Ignatius Loyola's tomb, and fixes instead on a requiem mass for seven Jesuits and some local women who kept house for them, martyrs in 1989 of the repressive regime in El Salvador. Hundreds of priests who were moved by the religious courage and political outspokenness of these men and women concelebrated at this most moving of liturgies. Thousands of ordinary Romans of all ages, fresh from offices and shops, crowded into the huge basilica to align themselves not only with a faith that speaks clearly of the power of life over death, but also of the weak being morally superior to the strong.

Despite the attempt to relaunch themselves by adopting the name Popular Party (a revival of the Vatican-influenced, mildly left-wing movement of the early twentieth century), the majority Christian Democrats still kept their emblem, a shield with a crusader cross, above their palazzo's main entrance. This PR slip seems to underwrite the party's political slump. *Plus ça change* will simply not do as an acceptable slogan for elections in the Italy of the new millennium.

The PCI already seemed a little more attuned to contemporary events, as did their old dispensation, TV and radio station Rai 3, with fewer programs in which housewives did striptease and more documentaries. Their headquarters rejoiced in huge plate glass windows, moveable at the flick of a switch through which Eurocommunist cars (small but chic) could pull up even into the building's ultra modern foyer. No gloomy courtyards reminiscent of the political past for them. The PCI was the first to change its name, dropping the "C" word as early as 1990. Gradually, the renamed Popular Party of the Left, at first within the Olive Tree Alliance, and more recently under Prime Minister D'Alemo, has finally received a moment of political ascendancy. The

Communists' taste of power goes some way toward paying them back for all the years when they were cynically kept at bay by other parties doing unscrupulous deals.

The downside of this ideological change is that in the Italy of the late 1990s the single most popular politician was Gianfranco Fini, the head of the neo-Fascist party. Confused by the run-away disillusionment with the old order and captivated by the political phenomenon that is Alessandra Mussolini, the *Duce*'s granddaughter (who also just happens to be a leggy blonde and deputy from part of Naples), the Italian electorate fails to see the jackboot, which is still the accoutrement of Fini's hardcore skinhead support. The neo-Fascists took part in Berlusconi's government of 1994, and yet together with Umberto Bossi's Northern League brought the media tycoon's premiership tumbling down scarcely a year later. The time was not yet right to deliver the policies upon which neo-Fascism is based. My own encounter with a man in his mid-fifties riding a bike through the Piazza Santa Maria Sopra Minerva and unashamedly singing *Giovinezza!*, the old Fascist party hymn, at the top of his voice makes me think that it might be drawing closer.

Moved to action by just such eventualities, politicians like Emma Bonino and Carlo Ciampi, recent contestants in the presidential elections, seem to be looking for a common cause of sanity after ten years of madness. Bonino's electoral slogan *Finalmente, un giusto uomo* (At last, a just man) had a sly humor that suggested a change for the better among the mainstream politicians. Over the past ten years the pious protestations aimed, seemingly by rote, against those who had formerly enjoyed power and its privileges were noticeably wearing thin. Some new thinking was being called for from the survivors of the revolution.

In conversation with Aldo Parini, a veteran Roman journalist of the mid-twentieth century, Benito Mussolini is reported to have reflected on Cola di Rienzo's fate. He drew attention to his own superstitious self-assuredness, "See, I wear no rings. It will not happen to me." He was wrong; so might others be.

CHAPTER SEVEN

The Popes
(1: In the World):
The Filarete Bronzes

"I have seen nothing like the extraordinary grace of his gesture, as he rose...
to bless possibly the pilgrims, but certainly me."
Oscar Wilde of Pope Leo XIII

During the early evening of December 8, the Feast of the Immaculate Conception, the pope always makes a public appearance. Traveling by limousine, he makes his way up the ultra-fashionable Via Condotti (usually closed to cars) and arrives in Piazza di Spagna, famous the world over as the place where the Spanish Steps begin (if, that is, they begin at the bottom). The pope has not made the journey here either to buy chrysanthemums from the celebrated flower stalls, nor indeed to order a Big Mac McMenu at the city's original McDonald's outlet. His goal is at the Quirinal end of the square in front of the palazzo that houses the Spanish Embassy to the Holy See and which gives the piazza its name; it is the column commemorating the publication of the dogma of the Immaculate Conception. The theological idea, an old one, is not, as many otherwise well-informed Christians think, to do with Jesus' Virgin Birth, but concerns his mother's conception. Mary's parents, traditionally called Joachim and Anna, were fully human, and conventionally pious, Jews. Old and childless, as in so many other Hebrew myths, they are blessed with a child after a pilgrimage undertaken by Joachim. The dogma asserts that from the moment of ordinary human conception, Mary, unlike any other creature, was sinless, in order to prepare her as the suitable vehicle for the incarnation of the Divine Word, Christ himself.

Pope Pius IX, the longest reigning pope (1848–76), because of his particular devotion to Mary and her place in the dogmatic scheme of things, decreed that the often unofficially held belief in her immaculate conception was to be a necessary teaching of the Roman Catholic faith. The promulgation of the dogma was made in 1854 following a lengthy but largely stage-managed series of theological debates. The occasion was marked by the decoration of a room in the Vatican, which is a must for anyone who wants to see what the whole papal court looked like in the reactionary climate of nineteenth-century Rome. The commemorative column itself was erected in 1857.

For over a century now, the firefighters of Rome have assisted in the annual celebration of the feast by providing a tender complete with extendible ladder. This is not (sadly) to raise the pope himself to the level of the statue of Mary in order to garland her, but so that, following his blessing, a burly *pompiero* may do it for him. When I attended this event in 1989, it was not the most attractive of Rome's December days. It was chilly and had drizzled throughout the afternoon. Bad weather had not, however, prevented a crowd three deep forming on all the pavements around the square. Immediately in front of me was a large American woman; she chatted away to her friends in a particularly loud voice, commenting on everything, from the arrival of the fire tender and its crew, to the facade of McDonalds just feet away. From her conversation, it was clear that she was neither a Catholic, nor a particularly well-informed tourist. She was just there. After what seemed an age (maybe an hour), the procession of black limos pulled into the space in front of the crash barrier, and on to a strategically-placed length of red carpet stepped the man in white. My neighbor went wild, and I have not forgotten what she chanted, with all the excitement of a teen fan at a rock concert: "Look, it's a little pope! A little pope!" Had she expected a large one, or just a series of the small kind? I'll never know.

In his early 1950s *Rome Alive*, Christopher Kinninmonth describes a period of this kind of religio-touristic waiting:

> *We are tightly packed now near the barrier; the tall English couple who had stood a little aloof are now pressed together and warmed into good-fellowship by the contact with their neighbours. There is a commotion by us and a fat lady is making great eyes and sighing as though suffering deeply. As she pulls at her furs people instinctively draw back to give her air, and, quite restored, she steps into a prized place at the barrier while gratefully thanking those about her. Preparations are still going forward before the great door in the now level light. Shadows have crept across the piazza and it is chill in the light wind. A big crimson curtain is hoisted behind the altar and hangs aslant; in a moment it is hauled down again. There is an officious acolyte who chivvies the priests gathering at the head of the steps where they obstruct the workmen.*

Things have not changed substantially. The pope still has to show himself, has to perform various actions, say various prayers on a regular basis, so that all visitors, whether religiously inclined or not, have the opportunity to see him. There are still moments of bathos or comedy as billowing altar cloths or draperies caught by the wind, which blows where it wills, are nailed in place by workmen in overalls only seconds before the dazzling epiphany of gorgeously robed prelates. Since the visitors are very many, the spaces large, and the Vatican hesitates to follow rock stars and politicians by flanking the pontiff with giant TV screens, the pope remains a little pope to most people. All see him, but most see him small.

Linked with this role of limited visibility, which underwrites the papacy's continuity and the security of its doctrine (for all that the pope does is a reflection of the Catholic doctrinal deposit), are the artworks that over the centuries have been commissioned by the papacy. As we saw with Emperor Augustus's artistic program for his capital, we will find that little has been done in artistic terms that was not to some degree planned to promote the required image of the papacy. This might be considered a political or a theological end, but best expresses the indissoluble link between the two. In the next three chapters, dealing broadly with the early and middle Renaissance, and the baroque age that grew from it, I will look at three very different works by three very different artists. Each will highlight an aspect of the papacy and the level of its visibility. We start with the papacy in public.

Full in the Panting Heart of Rome

Where is the most public place in Rome? At various times, the exact spot has been contested. The *rostrum* in the Forum was, Shakespeare would have us believe, where Romans lent their ears. In the last chapter, I mentioned the secular focus of both the Capitol and the balcony of the Palazzo di Venezia. As predicted earlier, however, our Roman wanderings bring us back time and again to St. Peter's Basilica. And it is this church's main entrance that we are now to visit.

The gigantic facade of the church is recognizable the world over, in part because of its central balcony from which the fateful words *habemus papam* (we have a pope) are spoken. Here, too, the reigning pope is wont to give his Christmas and Easter blessing to the city and to the world. The gold lettering telling both us and eternity that it was Pope Paul V who finished the Basilica's rebuilding has a perhaps surprisingly aggressive quality. But it isn't to the facade that I want to draw your attention. Go into the porch (making sure that you are not wearing shorts and that your shoulders are covered) and let the crowds surge past you on either side as they enter the Basilica. Go to the center of the space and look at the bronze doors, which from their position clearly mark the main entrance. There are five doorways in all—the one on the extreme right is opened only in Holy Years like AD 2000. Sometimes these central doors are open and in use as either "in" or "out" in a one-way system. They were "out" last time I visited St. Peter's, and so I had to position myself strategically at the corners of the threshold to get a good view and to avoid being swept away in the ebbing tide of bodies. Needless to say, scarcely a single visitor gave them a second glance.

The doors are of bronze, dark with age and without the extra polish of superstitious hands. There are three large and two small figurative

panels on each door, and the whole is bordered by a design of imperial busts entwined with ivy and vine leaves. If you look closely, it becomes obvious that the very top of the doors is an addition—the scrolls and legends look stylistically very different and you can clearly see the join. In fact, one and a half centuries divide these panels from the main body of the doors, which were made for the old basilica during the papacy of Eugenius IV (1431–47). When his successor, Nicholas V, realized that the basilica was in danger of collapse, and planned to rebuild it, the original facade and its main entrance were to have been incorporated into the design. This remained the case until Michelangelo got on the job, with his plans for a new front based on that of the Pantheon. Finally, 150 years after starting the project, it was Carlo Maderno for Paul V who demolished the facade and its entrance. Even so, the doors were considered significant enough to be incorporated into the new design, and the upper panels and some extra pieces at the side were added to make them fit the new threshold.

The doors themselves are the work of the Florentine Antonio Avelino, otherwise known as Filarete, a Greek pseudonym expressing his own belief in his love of virtue. He worked on the design and casting of the doors between 1439 and 1445, and although technically they are often compared unfavorably with Lorenzo

Ghiberti's bronzes for the Baptistry in Florence, they are textbook examples of how to incorporate a politico-theological argument into the design of a public monument.

Third-Rate City

Eugenius IV was the pope who consolidated a new age for Rome and for the papacy. He reigned for the comparatively long stretch of sixteen years, and followed a pope, Martin V (1417–31), who had reigned for fourteen years. Stability was what was needed most during this period. In the previous chapter, we saw how the popes were absent from Rome for most of the fourteenth century, and even as the fifteenth century dawned, problems continued in what is known as The Great Schism. During the period 1378–1417 there were at least two rival popes, one at Avignon and another in Rome, and at the worst times there were even three. The material condition of Rome declined still further, its palaces and churches neglected amidst the political wrangling of popes and anti-popes. These modern misfortunes magnified the wreck of empire represented by the antique ruins, which were being given new attention in the early Renaissance revival of scholarship and with the development of humanist sympathies. In 1430 Poggio Bracciolini reflected how things used to be in Rome when he and his fellow humanist scholar, Antonio Lusco, had visited the city during the Schism:

> (We) used to contemplate the desert places of the city with wonder in our hearts as we reflected on the former greatness of the broken buildings and the vast ruins of the ancient city, and again on the truly prodigious and astounding fall of its great empire and the deplorable inconstancy of Fortune. Here, after he had looked about for some time, sighing and as if struck dumb, Antonio declared, "Oh, Poggio, how remote are these ruins from the Capitol that our Virgil celebrated: 'Golden now, once bristling with thorn bushes.' How justly one can transpose this verse and say: 'Golden once, now rough with thorns and overgrown by briars.' But truly I cannot compare the tremendous ruin of Rome to that of any other city; this one disaster so exceeds the calamities of all other cities..."

Things were finally regularized, both for the good of the Catholic world and the physical condition of the city of Rome, at a general council of the Church held in Constance. Here the fifty-year-old Odone Colonna, a member of one of the aristocratic Roman families, was elected as Martin V. Rome was reestablished as the place for the papacy, and for the time being, with the extra security of a Roman as pope. It was also the time of the overwhelmingly optimistic middle period of the Renaissance, reflected in Poggio's remembering of the "bad old days." But less than thirty years after this lament, Platina, the papal librarian, could apostrophize his patron, Nicholas V, as the one "who restored the golden age to you, O Rome."

As we have seen, Rome had missed out on the start of the Renaissance, racked with its many internal problems, and the artistic heart of Italy had been undoubtedly established in Florence. Perhaps the first really great work of Renaissance art in Rome is the Chapel of St. Catherine in the upper church of S. Clemente. Decorated before 1430 by Masolino da Panicale, the chapel also reveals the hand of his greater pupil, Masaccio, or so scholars believe. It is well worth spending some time in this chapel when you visit this church, for the reasons dealt with elsewhere in this book; it was excellently restored in the late 1980s. Back to St. Peter's.

As Martin V had been the solution to The Great Western Schism, Eugenius IV, his successor, sought to be the solution to another, older division in the Church. Since the end of the eleventh century, the Eastern Orthodox churches, led by the example and doctrinal purity of the Patriarch at Constantinople, had refused to take seriously the growing pretensions of popes. Neutral, if not actually hostile, to the crusades, they contested papal claims to universal primacy, and had strong theological objections to some Western Christian doctrinal developments. Especially contentious was the belief that within the Holy Trinity, the Holy Spirit proceeds not only from the Father, but also from the Son (the "Filioque" controversy). Western and Eastern churches were actively hostile to one another during the late Middle Ages, particularly where they directly clashed such as in the crusader territories, in the lands between Poland and Lithuania, and in the Balkans. Conditions were not improved by the political and trade rivalry between Catholic Venice and orthodox Byzantium in the eastern Mediterranean and beyond. The low-point in these relations came with the sack of Constantinople in 1214 by the Catholic soldiers of the Fourth Crusade. The Byzantine Empire made another comeback in its long and checkered history of struggle against Persians, Turks, Bulgars, and Normans, to be relatively stable and on the offensive from 1300 under a new ruling house, the Palaeologues. And it is at this moment that the history lesson reaches our point of contact: the Filarete doors of St. Peter's Basilica.

Visible History

As mentioned earlier, each door bears five fields of figurative decoration: three large panels and two smaller ones forming the connections between the larger. The subjects of the large panels are fairly easy to read. In the upper field of the left-hand door, Christ sits in majesty, balanced on the right hand door by an enthroned Madonna. The central and largest panel on each door depicts one of the two founding saints of Christian Rome: Paul on the left, Peter on the right. Below each saint is a large square panel depicting his martyrdom. The twin panels dividing the larger ones form a narrative frieze, teeming with tiny people, horses, buildings and even ships. It is to these which we now turn our attention, returning (I apologize) to the history lesson.

Throughout the fourteenth and early fifteenth centuries, the Palaeologan emperors persisted in their defense of the Byzantine Empire against increasingly high odds. The Turks gradually took the territories surrounding the capital Constantinople until little of the empire, with the exception of southern Greece (the Morea), was left. Desperate measures were called for to guarantee even the survival of the capital. The Eastern Emperor himself made an extensive tour of Western Christendom, including Henry IV's London, appealing for support against the inevitability of attack. In Rome and countries that shared the papacy's pre-occupations, the question of the schism between Eastern and Western Christians arose. Placed over a barrel, so to speak, the Palaeologan Emperor John VIII sacrificed doctrinal purity for the glimmer of hope offered by a papal-led western alliance. Greek delegates were dispatched to the Church Council, then in session at Basel, and the preliminaries for this meeting, and its debates are depicted on the upper right-hand panel of the doors. We know that we are in Byzantium because the man sitting on the throne wears a hat a little like the one Errol Flynn sports in *The Adventures of Robin Hood.* Don't be surprised. This hat is a hugely important stylistic point in the history of western art. Only worn by the Palaeologan emperor and unknown until the 1430s tour and appeal for aid, the hat occurs relatively frequently from then on in Renaissance art to designate someone as either specifically the Byzantine emperor (as here), or a Roman emperor of the past presented in modern dress. The Tuscan artist, Piero della Francesca, chooses to represent Constantine the Great wearing this hat in the panel of the Milvian Bridge in his fresco cycle at Arezzo, *The Discovery of the True Cross.* The imperial headgear also makes an appearance in the same artist's celebrated panel painting in Urbino, once thought to be the Flagellation of Christ, and now properly identified as *The Dream of St. Jerome,* principally because of this important point of reference.

So here on the main entrance to St. Peter's Basilica, the imperial church *par excellence,* a scene showing the Eastern emperor's blessing being given to theological negotiations in Basel (later transferred to Florence) is exhibited as one of Pope Eugenius' trophies of achievement. On the left-hand door, Eugenius himself is depicted re-ordaining the Patriarch of Byzantium in a scene recalling the ordinations in Fra Angelico's frescoes inside the Vatican's chapel of Nicholas V. Lower down, and most significant in the narrative panel's artistic design, Eugenius, with the Patriarch riding alongside, is shown meeting Sigismund, the then candidate for the dignity of Holy Roman Emperor. He is the character depicted wearing ancient Roman armor. Together, the bronzes show the Western emperor on the basilica's left-hand door (west) and the Eastern on the right hand (east), the pope bringing them symbolically together. The entire work is in fact a manifesto for the reunification of the two halves of the antique empire under the patronage of the papacy.

As it happened, these panels commemorate a series of events that bore little fruit. The rank and file of the Orthodox clergy rejected the doctrinal compromises reached in Florence, and the Patriarch who had submitted to re-ordination died, only to be replaced by a theological opponent. In a parallel refusal to deliver the goods, the Catholic West failed singularly to provide the military and financial assistance promised, and the last Palaeologan Emperor died defending his capital the day before it fell to the Turks in 1453. Orthodox Christianity was guaranteed its doctrinal autonomy under the succeeding Sultanate, although for centuries the Patriarch remained the appointee of the Islamic government.

So much, then, for the technical ending of the great east-west schism. Even in the 1990s, the new Russian government was objecting to the appointment of Roman Catholic bishops for Moscow and St. Petersburg, since these prelates were seen as threats to the established Orthodox hierarchy. And clashes between Catholic Croats and Orthodox Serbs constituted an important factor in the shattered confessional mosaic axiomatic of the violence witnessed in the modern Balkans. The Filarete doors would perhaps be a rather pathetic historical document if we were able to leave them there. But they still hold considerably more interest as we turn our attention to the panels depicting the martyrdom of Peter and Paul.

The Saints Go Marching On

Today, St. Peter's Basilica and the Vatican palace immediately adjoining it are the places where people would most expect to see the pope. It is his most public of settings, but as we have seen, this is an expectation of recent origin in terms of the papacy's long history. For centuries, the Lateran was the seat of the popes, and during the eighteenth and nineteenth centuries, the Quirinal palace, originally a summer resort, became the principal papal residence. The growth of the Vatican as a series of linked grand palaces dates from the return from Avignon, and is connected to the project for the rebuilding of St. Peter's itself. Together, palace and church symbolized the new papacy of the Renaissance, in which the learned and urbane holders of Peter's Chair would achieve wonders for Christendom and for the world. Or so they would have had it. The Filarete doors, as well as depicting what Eugenius IV believed, however wrongly, to be a defining and positive moment in contemporary affairs, also reflect a timeless religio-mythical agenda. Tradition taught that both Saints Peter and Paul were martyred in the Neronian persecution of Christians during the 60s AD. Protestants, in the polemics of the Reformation, were to point out that there was no early documentary evidence (and most importantly, no biblical testimony) that Peter had ever even been to Rome, let alone become its first bishop. Pre-empting this kind of criticism, the doors' decorative scheme points to a specific material claim made of St. Peter's Basilica—that it is built on top of the Apostle's tomb.

The heads of both Peter and Paul were (are) relics kept at the pope's cathedral, S. Giovanni in Laterano, and the sites credited as the places of their martyrdom were venerated during the Middle Ages. Paul was said to have been beheaded at a place marked by three fountains on the Ostia road, near where the great basilica in his honor was built by Constantine. A small monastery still preserves the actual site. Peter, so the written sources stated, had been crucified upside down on the Vatican hill, and then *inter duas metas* ("between two turning-posts"). The interpretation of this Latin phrase had produced quite a complicated geographical solution in the medieval mind. A turning-post (*meta*) had the form in ancient Rome of a pyramid, and they stood at either end of the *spina* or "backbone" of circuses such as the *circus maximus*, forming the inside turns for chariot races. By association, *meta* came to be a word in Latin for "pyramid". Since there were two pyramids of some celebrity in ancient Rome that survived into the late Middle Ages—one by the Porta Ostiense, and the other just next to the Castel Sant'Angelo—the solution suggested was that Peter had been martyred at exactly the half-way point between the two. With the added complication that the site had to be on the Vatican hill, the chosen spot was identified and the church of S. Pietro in Montorio constructed, high above Trastevere. This plays just a little fast and loose with the geography, as the church is really on the Janiculum hill, which can only be called "the Vatican" by extension. Here then, at S. Pietro, a site had long been venerated as the post-hole into which Peter's inverted cross had been inserted. It is now commemorated by being covered by Bramante's exquisite miniature, *Tempietto*, a master work of small-scale Renaissance architecture.

Bronze reliefs depicting these instances of martyrdom (and, in Peter's case, the complicated topography) form the lowest panels of each of the Filarete doors. In St. Paul's martyrdom (the left-hand door), we see the saint three times as the story progresses. He is judged by Nero, seated on a throne under an elaborate canopy, to the bottom left, and kneels, about to be beheaded at the bottom right. He appears centrally, and toward the top as if from heaven, to his faithful female devotee Thecla. He gives her a handkerchief as a relic, in accordance with an important early Latin hagiographic work, *The Acts of Paul and Thecla.*

The martyrdom of Peter is depicted less as narrative than as topographical demonstration. In the lowest section, you can see the two pyramids: that of Gaius Cestius to the far left, and that in the Borgo to the far right, with a representation of Hadrian's Mausoleum nearby. The river Tiber is seen in the middle of the relief with a procession of horsemen forming a strong opposing line, moving your eye up to the work's central event, Peter's crucifixion. Another static depiction of Nero closes the processional movement. The upside-down crucifixion of the saint is strongly triangular in form, and together with the two lower pyramids, insists on an overall triangular design. Looking back to the relief of Paul's martyrdom, the three appearances of the saint also give a triangular design to that relief. The masterstroke of Filarete's aesthetic schema is thus to recreate in these panels the two pyramids between which Peter was crucified as testimony to the claim that St. Peter's Basilica covered his tomb. We can see, too, that the two representations of Nero balance each other, and perhaps comment ironically on the appearance of Eastern and Western emperors in the contemporary friezes.

Official Catholic thought now supports an opposing theory that *inter duas metas* refers to the turning posts in Caligula's circus, which was positioned here on the Vatican. This theory would place Peter's martyrdom in the traditional context of Roman public games. Archaeological work, begun accidentally during the 1940s, when Pius XI's (1922–39) tomb was being excavated in the *Grotte Vaticane,* have shown that the altar of St. Peter's Basilica is undoubtedly built upon what was thought to have been the site of Peter's tomb in Constantine's time. Constantine had to excavate half the Vatican hill and cover up a pagan cemetery in so doing to achieve this aim. Scholarly opinion varies concerning the tomb's further claims to authenticity. Various bones have been recovered from the area. You can make up your own mind about the likelihood of their being St. Peter's by making a visit to the Vatican *scavi.* The full story of the different findings and the various levels of development on the pagan cemetery site is extremely complicated. It is worth saying, however, that the Vatican guides are not entirely disinterested judges.

The Filarete doors were conceived to open, close, and frame the space in which the pope most formally appeared as successor to St. Peter. Through these doors for centuries, pontiffs were carried shoulder-high in the *sedes gestatoria* on their way to coronation. They were carried in their coffins through these doors to receive obsequies and internment. The doors' symbolic significance is underlined by their transposition from the old to the new basilica. They deserve a far higher profile than they receive in most guidebooks, which rarely even describe them, classifying them too readily alongside the bizarre modern bronzes that John XXIII (1958–63) and Paul VI commissioned for the doors flanking them. Before you leave them, just take another quick look at the large panel showing St. Peter. There, at his right hand, depicted on a far smaller scale, is a portrait of Eugenius IV receiving the keys of the kingdom from his heavenly predecessor's hand. Look, it's a little pope!

CHAPTER EIGHT

The Popes
(2: In Audience):
The Borgia Stanze

Sextus Tarquinius, Sextus Nero—Sextus et iste
Semper sub sextis perdita Roma fuit
Tarquinius and Nero were both named Sextus,
Now this man is also styled "the Sixth" (Sextus);
Rome was always lost under these Sextuses.
Pasquinade against Alexander VI

Political analysts and contemporary historians claim that once again, during the 1990s, Italy performed to type. It was as long ago as the early 1920s that E. P. Thompson described the Italian state as the laboratory of European politics. He was referring to the rise of Mussolini following the 1922 coup, and the way in which the Italian experiment foretold the course of events elsewhere, to be proved accurate more than a decade later in Germany and Spain. To get a feel for what has happened in Italy, and particularly in the capital during the last ten years of the last millennium, we have to go back to November 1989 and the events surrounding the fall of a wall and of an accompanying ideology.

I was on retreat above Lake Albano on the fateful day when our contemplative silence was shaken a little by a notice on the information board. The Berlin Wall was down, and Eastern bloc governments were falling like dominoes. The day of our return to Rome and to study saw a full-length broadcast on RAI Uno, the Christian Democrat-controlled TV station, of a High Mass of Thanksgiving for the Czech "Velvet Revolution." It was celebrated with considerable musical and liturgical pomp by the nonagenarian Cardinal Tomasek. There, enthroned in the front row, were Mr. and Mrs. Vaclav Havel, looking as much like a Catholic king and queen as the newly-elected president and first lady they were. The world had changed. Before Christmas every Italian newspaper, just like every daily around the world, would carry ghoulishly colored photos of the Ceaucescu corpses on their front pages. Communism was dead, and the controlling feature of Italian politics since the end of World War II was gone.

Fearful of the strength of Italian Communism, Washington and the Vatican had strenuously put their backs to the counter-revolutionary wheel. The US supplied billions of dollars in aid, and the Vatican its still considerable moral authority, ensuring that the Christian Democrats remained the dominant party of government throughout the entire post-war period. Political sleight of hand had led to the inclusion of the Socialist Party in coalition during the 1960s and 1970s. Further decline in grassroots support for the Christian Democrats had even led to a previously unthinkable *rapprochement* with the Italian Communist Party during the 1980s. The traditional Italian policy of *trasformismo*, which even conceded this crumb of influence to the PCI, led to what has since been termed *partitocrazia*, the rule of the parties. Each party, proportionate to its national support and standing within government, "colonized" the state and its foreign business interests over a fifty-year period. Part of this colonization consisted of the establishment of political fiefdoms, which not only distributed contracts and garnered profits through state subsidy, but also operated a well-developed structure of patronage designed to insure votes and the return of candidates. Always on the edge of the mechanism were the sources of oil that kept the machine running smoothly: money accruing from badly audited state accounts; billions of lire from the black economy operated semi-openly by the Mafia and associated groups; the wealth of individuals who really did contribute to the creation of a kind of economic miracle. Italy, as the world's fifth richest nation, outstripping the UK, took its place at the G7 summits with considerable pride.

With the revolutionary climate of a new decade, things were to change for the party bosses. These men, unlike any other European politicians, including the Communist leaders so recently removed from office, had held power in some cases since the mid-1940s. Chief among these was Giulio Andreotti. Prime Minister seven times, he had held cabinet posts in 30 out of 53 post-war governments and in 1946 had taken part in the congress that had created the Republican Constitution. His credentials extended even further back, to his role as a founding member of the Christian Democrat Party in 1942, at a time when no-one could have foretold the total collapse of Fascism between 1943 and 1945. A pious youth, who during his high school days had considered ordination, Andreotti maintained his character as a practicing Catholic by attending mass daily, acting as the editor of a Catholic journal, and by writing a book entitled *Popes I Have Known*.

Andreotti was the last Christian Democrat to serve as President of the Council of Ministers (the premiership) as the revolutionary scandal of *tangentopoli* (bribe city) exploded. It came in the early 1990s and was ultimately to sweep away the old political alliances and *modi vivendi*. It did this through the serving of *avvisi di garanzia*, the official notification of criminal investigations on the party leaders, as from minor cases of proven corruption, the trail inexorably led onward and upward.

In power, Andreotti had led a remarkably low-key existence. As with other party leaders and beneficiaries of the heady days of *partitocrazia*, he never paraded the ill-gotten gains that he was supposed to have stashed away. Most of those convicted of major corruption lived modest lives while amassing billions of lire in unnumbered Swiss accounts, or in one bizarre case, within the stuffing of a pouffe, a rich adornment for an unpretentious suburban sitting-room. What Andreotti—or Don Giulio, a name suited to his clerical leanings and base of political support in Sicily—actually wanted and got, was power. His now-famous aphorism, that "power only tires those who do not have it" is a conscious avowal of the phenomenal stamina that underwrote his political longevity. He has repeatedly denied links with *Cosa Nostra* and the allegations that he was Rome's Godfather, which were pinned on him by the Mafia supergrass Baldassare di Maggio. Further, he strenuously denied any corruption charges, differing in this respect from those who admitted them as mere participation in a system simply accepted as "the way of doing things." The end of his trial in October 1999 vindicated him judicially; his reputation, however, is changed forever.

During his ascendancy and dominance, Giulio Andreotti established a domestic ritual redolent of the lives of those kings and popes who most reflected his historically conservative temperament. Matt Frei, in his fluent account of what he terms Italy's "unfinished revolution," captures something of its archetypal grandeur:

> At the crack of dawn, he gathered a group of his closest advisors and friends in his bathroom to discuss world affairs, party politics, or just gossip. While the others sat on stools or the edge of the bath, Andreotti himself would lean back in a reclining chair and be shaved by his favourite Roman barber. Once the conclave was over, he would go to mass in his local church in Rome's via Giulia. Andreotti was a peculiarly Roman mixture of Machiavelli and incense. Half of his schoolmates have become bishops or cardinals. He became the high priest of the partitocrazia.

I do not think it fanciful to connect such *levées* with the arrangements of the papal household, in which the pope's position as absolute monarch of the tiny Vatican state still requires that a meeting with him be termed an audience. Andreotti granted a daily audience to his most trusted advisers while being shaved. The first daily papal audience is granted as a chosen few make their way, usually before dawn, to the pope's private chapel to attend his private mass. In the last chapter relating to the re-establishment of the popes in Renaissance Rome, we considered the public appearances that pontiffs have made and continue to make. Still within the context of artistic development, the present chapter introduces us to the idea of the popes in audience.

The small-scale representations of Eugenius IV on the Filarete doors cannot really be counted as portraiture. The award for the first major papal portrait goes to the seated statue of Innocent VIII (1484–92)

upon his tomb in St. Peter's, which has the singular honor of being the
only monument reconstructed in the new basilica after its rebuilding.
The bronze statue by Antonio Pollaiuolo shows the strenuous Genoese
prelate clutching a spearhead, an allusion to his recovery of one of the
sacred relics of Christendom lost at the fall of Constantinople. This was
the spear believed to have pierced the side of Christ on the Cross, and it
was a gift from the sultan Bajazet II. Along with this sign of goodwill
from the infidel enemy came a duty: the custody of one of the sultan's
ambitious brothers, Djem. We will see his portrait later. In the
meantime, Innocent gestures from his throne with an imperious
benediction, and his chiseled features, with hooked nose and beetled
brow, show, warts and all, that his was a personality not to be trifled
with. He had successfully outbid the nearest contender for the papal
throne, Cardinal Rodrigo Borgia, and kept his rival out for eight years.
When election time came around again upon Innocent's death, Borgia
spared nothing from his vast fortune, drawn from rich church livings
and his Spanish family estates, to ensure the papal tiara. With the Borgia
pontificate begun, the most lurid of the papacy's difficult passages was
also inaugurated. Or was it?

Borgia Orgies—Overrated?

Much has been written about the notorious Borgias: of Alexander VI's
insatiable appetite for sex, food, and gold; of the beauty and murderous
cunning of his daughter Lucrezia; of the wanton cruelty and ruthless
single-mindedness of his soldier son Cesare, model for Machiavelli's
Prince. While in no way intending to act as their apologist, at the same
time I want to avoid the trap of blindly following the easy wisdom of
hindsight by laying the political and religious failures of the papacy in
the sixteenth century solely at the Borgias' door. The Borgia court was a
worldly one, but was not one so significantly different from that of his
predecessors or successors as to warrant all of history's blame. The spice
of the matter lies principally in the accounts of the pope's incestuous
relations with Lucrezia, but these are far from being proven, relying so
heavily as they do on the testimony of enemies and critics, and a few
ambiguous passages in personal letters. Savonarola, the ascetic proto-
Republican of Florence, was right to harangue Alexander as a worldly

ruler who had bought the See of Peter, but it would be idle to deny this of a dozen other fifteenth- and sixteenth-century popes. In late 1999 it was announced that Vatican archives would be opened to a commission of 120 historians, who would assess whether Alexander's reputation was indeed merited. Their deliberations, it was said, would take into account an alleged smear campaign by his successor, Pope Julius II.

We have a good portrait of the Borgia features, although teasingly, we cannot be positive that they depict Alexander VI himself. The figure of a bejeweled, kneeling pope before a vision of the Risen Christ is part of the decorative scheme of the Borgia Apartments in the Vatican. Like so much else in the complex of rooms, it represents one of the artist Bernardino di Betto, a.k.a. Pinturicchio's finest works. The reason why we cannot be sure that it is a portrait of the reigning pope is that it is as likely to be a posthumous tribute to the previous Borgia to hold the office, Rodrigo's uncle, Calixtus III (1455–58). However, I cannot help thinking that Pinturicchio must have capitalized on his access to a living subject for such a vibrant portrait, even if technically it is supposed to be the earlier Borgia. The Borgia Apartments occupy the space within the apostolic palace immediately below the more celebrated *Stanze* of Raphael. They form part of the unavoidable route through the museum, but are often given scant attention by visitors because, unlike the rival attraction upstairs, they have to share the space with a tatty display of

uninspired and uninspiring modern art. There is, of course, modern art that is inspiring. It just doesn't happen to be represented here—the gems of the papal collection, by Bacon, Moore, Chagall, and Dali, are on display elsewhere. This arrangement is all to the good for the serious visitor, as the modern works scare most people away, and a reasonably unhampered view of the Borgia Apartment frescoes is usually available.

The palace was originally built by the scholarly Pope Nicholas V. On becoming pope in 1492, Alexander VI chose these rooms as his personal apartments, and commissioned their decoration by Pinturicchio and his school. The work took three years. The first few rooms are usually attributed to followers of the master, but still repay attention. The first, depicting the sibyls and prophets in the same juxtaposition that Michelangelo would use on the ceiling of the Sistine Chapel, is witness to the humanist idea that secular, even pagan, wisdom might be consonant with Biblical revelation. The sibyls, as the wise oracles of the pagan past, were reckoned in this scheme to agree with the Hebrew prophets in foretelling the birth of Christ. It was in this room that Pope Julius II imprisoned Cesare Borgia after his capture in 1503, and tradition chimes in with characteristically ghoulish relish that it was in the same room that Cesare had murdered his cousin Alphonso of Aragon, three years before. The Room of the Creed follows, in which all that is needed for the faithful to affirm about God (the words of the Creed) is written upon scrolls held by the twelve apostles depicted in the lunettes. A secular balance is again achieved by the addition of imagined portraits of the greatest ancient philosophers with attendant pithy quotations from their wisdom. The entirety of secular learning succeeds this expression of faith in the Room of the Seven Liberal Arts, as the personifications of Grammar, Dialectic, and Rhetoric (the *trivium*, or lesser course) give way to Geometry, Arithmetic, Astronomy and Music (the *quadrivium*, or greater course). As if heralding our entrance into a greater, more splendid world, this room gives on to the largest apartment, the room in which Alexander VI gave audience and probably ate dinner, the Hall of the Saints.

John Kelly, in his admirably comprehensive *Oxford Dictionary of Popes*, labels Alexander as "devout and a stickler for orthodoxy in spite of personal profligacy." His religiosity is well attested in the accounts of papal ceremonies and rituals exhaustively described in the diaries of his chamberlain and master of ceremonies, Johann Burchard. Although the manuscript of Burchard's journal seems to have been severely edited with pages missing and passages excised, whether by the author or by another's scandalized hand, it is at times surprising for what it includes. This is our only source for the notorious Tournament of the Chestnuts, during which red-hot nuts were scattered on the floor of the dining room to be collected in the mouths of prostitutes on all fours with courtiers astride them as jockeys. The girl who collected most won a prize. Who knows what? No doubt I am indulging in the prurience that I have already questioned as I wonder whether these scenes took place under the painted eyes of Pinturicchio's saints. Certainly, the frescoes are not without their sensual elements. In the representation of St. Anthony's temptations, the devils in semi-female form surely reproduce the attractions of contemporary Roman whores; and the lasciviousness of the two elders in the depiction of Susanna might well reflect the response of aging cardinals and courtiers to the scenes of debauchery unfolding before them. The whole artistic program seems to have a subtext of Chastity Besieged: Barbara in her tower, Sebastian pierced by arrows for refusing the emperor's advances, Susanna the target of peeping toms.

Schools for Scandal and Good Taste

If Alexander VI had his own seamier side reflected in Pinturicchio's decorative scheme, his typical and rather more admirable Renaissance love of learning, and the new humanist classicism, are also found in the frescoes. The masterpiece of the whole series is St. Catherine's disputation with the philosophers, set against the background of notable Roman monuments, principally the Arch of Constantine. Scholars have long debated whether the features of St. Catherine were modeled on Lucrezia; she certainly has the long golden tresses that the documentary evidence describes. An alternative theory suggests that Catherine was modeled on Giulia Farnese, one of the pope's mistresses. Emperor Maximian, in whose presence the disputation takes place, certainly seems to be a portrait of Cesare Borgia, whose features are known from other pictures. The models for the two figures dressed in Turkish clothes (one daringly riding a white horse usually reserved iconographically for the pope himself) have likely candidates in the hostage Djem and his closest intimate, the Duke of Gandia, who was the pope's eldest son. The very fact that these frescoes contain portraits at all argues strongly, to my mind at least, that we should take the saint herself as an idealized likeness of Lucrezia or Giulia.

The decorative scheme is broken up throughout by richly detailed borders, pilasters, and stuccoed frames. Here Pinturicchio, as in his other mature works, is heavily influenced by the archaeological discoveries of the time and the artistic fashions they inspired. Contemporary with the arrival in Rome of a large group of Umbrian painters to decorate the Sistine Chapel's walls for its builder, Sixtus IV (1471–84), was the discovery by accident of what are now known to be the remains of Emperor Nero's pleasure palace, the *domus aurea*, or Golden House. The pavilion on the Opian Hill (extensively restored from 1969 to 1998 and reopened to visitors in the Spring of 1999) is the main survivor of this much-written about complex of villas, gardens, water features, and art galleries constructed for the last Julio-Claudian emperor of Rome after the great fire of AD 64. Suetonius, Tacitus, and Pliny the Elder attested to its sumptuousness, and the unpopularity it aroused in both aristocratic and plebeian circles, taking up acres of central Roman real estate, was a factor in Nero's downfall. When, after a year of near-anarchy (that of The Three Emperors, AD 68–69), the Flavian dynasty was established by Vespasian, one of the symbols of Nero's tyranny, the *domus aurea*, was filled with ballast and used as the foundations for a public bath complex. Started by Titus, Vespasian's son, it was to be completed years later by Trajan. The Flavian dynasty cemented its public popularity by draining the large lake that had occupied a central place in the Golden House's esoteric pleasure scheme, to build a massive amphitheater, more suited to the bloodthirsty taste of the Roman public—the Colosseum. This structure took its name from the colossal statue of Nero, later with his features excised, which continued to stand close by during antiquity.

Late in the fifteenth century, just as Ghirlandaio, Perugino, Filippino Lippi, and our own Pinturicchio arrived in Rome, the painted walls and vaults of some of the *domus aurea*'s rooms were rediscovered as cave-like openings were made on the summit of the Opian Hill. They became a tourist attraction, then as now, and also a source of artistic inspiration. Termed the "grottoes," these rooms influenced the Renaissance painters, both from the point of view of technique, particularly color, and artistic design. We know that Ghirlandaio, Pinturicchio, and Raphael visited the grottoes from their autographs left there. The Grotesque style resulted from these visits, in which the Umbrian masters created friezes, patterns, and architectural features derived directly from the decorative scheme of the Neronic palace.

In Pinturicchio's Borgia *Stanze*, we see this influence most directly in the ornate framing of the pictorial panels, with candelabra of intertwining floral and animal designs, and the elaboration of fantastic creatures, winged griffins, and sphinxes: all calling-cards of the Grotesque school. The Vatican's coffered vaults, which were delineated (as in Nero's palace) by bands of gilded stucco, add a further refinement. Here, amidst the repeated leitmotiv of the Borgia family's crest—a bull—frescoes recounting classical episodes with bovine subjects (the rape of Europa, the story of Apis and Isis), recall the paintings discovered in the Golden House. They bear strong similarities to the eponymous frescoes of the rooms of Achilles on Skyros, and of Hector and Andromache. Pinturicchio's hallmark use of birds and small animals also recalls the liberal decorative use of these as motifs in the *domus aurea*'s wall decorations. Here then, Pinturicchio connects with an artistic tradition already a millennium and a half old, as he re-utilizes the vocabulary of an artist known to us only through these few surviving works and a half a sentence in Pliny the Elder's *Natural History*. According to Pliny, uncle of the writer of the better-known letters, Nero's artist was named Fabullus. As personally austere and formal as his painting was florid and fluid in style, Fabullus speaks only to us from the figurative panels now on display in the restored Golden House. In him Pinturicchio had a good master in dynamic realism and an ease of composition, and so in this particular lived up to the nickname given him by the jealous Vasari: Fortune's Favorite.

The painted panels of the *domus aurea* have been classified as a development of the so-called fourth Pompeian Style of Roman fresco. Their one flaw, however, is a miscalculation of scale. As Elisabetta Segala and Ida Sciortino have recently written of the paintings of the re-opened palace, they "are characterized by a taste for the miniature detail, which since it can only be perceived close-up, seems not at all worthy of the architectonic greatness of the rooms. Probably this meant that craftsmen used to decorating much smaller rooms had to extend their habitual decorative schemes over the vaster surfaces of Nero's pavilion."

Once again Fortune favored Pinturicchio; the scale of the Borgia *Stanze* lends itself to the artistic program on which he worked. Like Fabullus before him, he had only to decorate the upper portions of the rooms. In the *domus aurea* the walls were largely covered with colored marble slabs; in Alexander VI's apartments richly woven tapestries would have provided the rooms' lower decoration. Yet while the ceilings of Nero's palace extend in places to between sixty and ninety feet in height, the papal *Stanze* restricted themselves to less than thirty. The detail on the marvelously realized fabrics for the clothes of Pinturicchio's subjects seems close enough to touch.

Misunderstood Monsters

The fortuitous artistic conjunction of the Borgia *Stanze* and Nero's Golden House enables me to strengthen this already strong link between the pope and the emperor as we return to the subject of the Borgia family and the way history has judged it. The wits of the time clearly saw parallels between Nero and Alexander, as the *pasquinade* which heads this chapter shows. Writing of Nero, Segala, and Sciortino comment upon the universally negative image of the emperor which has come down to us: "The main sources for the history of Nero's principate— Tacitus (AD 55–120), Suetonius (AD 70–140) and Dio Cassius (AD 155–235)—all derive, directly or indirectly, from the political opposition and seem to be unanimously hostile to the emperor."

What is true of fleeting emperors, who now rise in public opinion and now fall, is even more true of fleeting popes. In a revisionist account of Nero's reign for his BBC TV series on "Villains," Brian Walden argued that the emperor was the first real instance of a statesman who employed political tools akin to those used by modern democratic leaders. Nero, according to Walden, reflected the tone, mood, and aspirations of the populace like a mirror. If he was cruel, it was because this was the spirit of his age; if he was an avid consumer of the good things of life, this was because the majority set such consumption as the criterion of success. Rodrigo Borgia, Alexander VI, similarly, was a successful pope in late fifteenth- and early sixteenth-century terms. He was genuinely interested in the new learning and the art that was its accompaniment, just like the still universally admired Nicholas V and

Pius II (1458–64). He was a reactionary defender of papal authority and the performance of the sacred pontifical duties which bounded his court's daily life, just as was the austere Dutch pontiff Hadrian VI (1522–23), the last non-Italian pope before Karol Wotija. He was a ferocious military defender of the Papal States through his son Cesare, just as was Julius II *in propria persona* (remember Rex Harrison in armor during *The Agony and the Ecstasy?*). He was as profligate a womanizer and as lavish a nepotist as Paul III, who still receives a reasonable write-up from the tribunal of history. The Borgia pope reflected the problems of the contemporary Church and secular society back on themselves. Reactions to these more than evident problems were violent: Savonarola's preaching and Bonfires of the Vanities; Luther's Wittenberg Theses; the Reformation itself and the protracted and bloody wars of religion that followed it. An audience with Alexander VI might be unnerving, not because of what it revealed about him, but what it revealed about you.

Patrick Smith, BBC correspondent in Rome during the 1960s, writes in his *A Desk in Rome* of his first personal encounter with the charismatic, much-loved John XXIII:

> *At the end some of us were presented to the Pope. I went up after the Italians, and the Pope, speaking to me in Italian, held on to my hand as he asked from where I came. He had a firm and comforting handshake, his eyes were a kindly blue, and his whole face was that of a kindly grandfather, to whom one could confide anything... For a few brief seconds Pope John had entirely concentrated on me; his was the great man's gift of making you feel that you alone were the person he had been waiting to talk to.*

Such an informal audience dispenses with the long traditions attached to its granting. The formal approach to the seated pontiff required a kiss of his foot, knee, and ring should you be a lay person, and knee, ring and shoulder for the lower clergy. Bishops and cardinals could omit the foot and knee altogether, make straight for the ring and, passing through the shoulder, reach the dizzy heights of the cheek.

It was the claim of a kiss on the cheek that so tarnished the reputation of Giulio Andreotti in the months following the *tangentopoli* scandal. Almost within days he went from heading the last "old style" government to being pelted with small change by the Roman mob, the traditional accusation of treachery, exemplified by Judas' pieces of silver. The Mafia informer, Baldassare di Maggio, claimed to have been present at a meeting in 1988 between Andreotti and the Boss of all Bosses, Totò Riina. At this audience Riina is supposed to have kissed Don Giulio on both cheeks, an indication of the kisser's seniority within *Cosa Nostra* and the dependence of the kissed. Thus the implication is that Andreotti was not only influenced by the Mafia, but was a member, even perhaps Rome's own Godfather. Andreotti has strenuously denied such accusations as preposterous and continued to appear in the Palazzo Madama's corridors and chambers as a Senator-for-Life even before his acquittal. History has judged Nero and Alexander VI harshly; we will have to wait patiently to see how the politicians toppled by *tangentopoli* fare.

CHAPTER NINE

The Popes
(3: In Private):
Velázquez's Portrait of
Innocent X

"...a stout old man with a white skull cap, a scarlet gold-embroidered cape falling over his shoulders and a white silk robe... his face was kindly and venerable, but not particularly impressive."
Nathaniel Hawthorne, *French and Italian Notebooks*

Whenever the world of the Vatican intrudes into the isolated existence of the priests on Craggy Island in the TV comedy series *Father Ted*, usually by means of a gold-plated phone in the languid hands of a chain-smoking cardinal, we are witness to the broadest of Roman caricatures. In the background of the shot you can see any number of fantastically garbed fellows indulging in an assortment of pastimes: a bishop seated at a drum kit beats out a throbbing rhythm, two others bend over the pool table, and another reads a lurid comic book. The satirist imagines a range of activity innocent in its content but ludicrous in its application. Such might be thought of the possession of a private life for any of the Roman Church's senior clergy, especially the pope, and yet private lives they have all more or less creditably managed to enjoy.

Pope John Paul II likes hill walking and mountain climbing, though the posed media shots of him engaging in these pursuits while still robed in his customary white soutane can have the effect of relegating these unremarkable and healthy pleasures to the ranks of satirical mockery. His interest in the theater, poetry, and literature in general are less easily mocked, especially when set in the context of a literature of protest against first Nazi and then Communist dictatorships. Perhaps their supposed innate seriousness is why these interests have often formed the staple of the pontifical unguarded hours. Even literature, however, has a tendency to stray from seriousness.

In the full flush of his humanistic youth, Enea Silvio Piccolomini, later Pius II, was the author of a best seller, *Lucretia and Euryalus.* This early example of a novel, based upon the amorous escapades of his friend Caspar Schlick, might have passed for nothing had the real-life hero not become Emperor Frederick III's chancellor, and the author the pope. It was as if the future secretary-generals of the UN and NATO were to be found out as youthful collaborators in an amateur soft-porn film. Although written in support of a serious theological change of mind, the pope's words used in a papal bull, to "reject Aeneas, and listen to Pius" might well be used to draw the world's attention to his personal, moral reformation in middle life, which all the sources assert to have been profound and long-lasting.

Comic Cuts

Pius II was not the last papal author in secular terms. The florid but uninspired poetry of Maffeo Barberini, Urban VIII (1623–44) survives, and although following the example of his early predecessor Pope St. Damasus (366–84) he turned it to sacred use in the composition of hymns for the new Roman Breviary, its quality did not increase. Rather more successful were the literary products of one of the Barberini protégés, Giulio Rospigliosi, later at the age of 67 elected as Pope Clement IX (1667–69). A student of Jesuit education and liberal affinities, he came to the attention of Urban VIII while still a young man, largely through his literary and artistic talent. He rose steadily in the Curia's cursus honorum throughout the middle years of the seventeenth century at the same time continuing as an author. His libretto for *Chi soffre speri* (The One Who Suffers Also Hopes), performed in the Palazzo Barberini in 1639, has been claimed as the origin for all subsequent comic operas, a form which until then had confined itself to the serious subjects of Greek mythology and the Bible. John Milton, who was visiting Rome at the time, was one of the 3,500 people in the audience, and the performance was clearly one of the highlights of that year's Carnival entertainments. The stage design was by Bernini, and dinner was served between the opera's acts. With such a bent for well-produced, ground-breaking comedy, had he been living now, Pope Clement IX would himself have perhaps been working as a scriptwriter for *Father Ted.*

Certainly Clement would not have had to travel far to get on set if he wanted to check that his scripts were not being perverted. It is only a journey of about thirty minutes from the Vatican's nearest Metro Station, Ottaviano, to the hub of the Italian TV production and film industry. Cinecittà, the sprawling complex of stages, studios, and lots, now also lends its name to a post-war suburb as bland but as cozy as most of Rome's commuter domiciles. Near to the end of the Metro A line in the direction of the Alban Hills, its location originally reflected the film producer's essential requirements: relative quiet and as much light as possible. Originally founded and massively subsidized by Mussolini as a Fascist propaganda weapon and an antidote to "corrupting" foreign films, Cinecittà was intended to be a vehicle for promoting national and patriotic values. It was in the 1950s and 1960s, however, that it lived its glorious heyday with US-co-financed epics such as *Quo Vadis* (1951), *Ben-Hur* (1959) and *Cleopatra* (1963). About one thousand films were made in this period, with foreign stars such as Robert Taylor, Charlton Heston, and Elizabeth Taylor adding to Rome's glamorous cinematic profile. But not all of Cinecittà's critical and commercial successes were transatlantic collaborations; Federico Fellini's masterpieces *La Dolce Vita* and *Roma* brought Marcello Mastroianni to international stardom while developing a neorealist and satirical tradition encapsulated by Roberto Rossellini's *Roma, Città Aperta* (1945).

Italy's film heritage is a proud one, and the domestic industry has maintained its comparative independence from Hollywood's globalizing tendencies, in spite of the compelling links between expatriate Italian movie men and their homecountry cousins. The culture of film going among Italians themselves picks up a thread laid down by the provincial touring opera companies; and the post-war boom in the former (chronicled so beautifully if rather sentimentally by Giuseppe Tornatore in *Cinema Paradiso*) marks the sure decline of the latter. The demand for a constant stream of indigenous features for every converted church hall and declining lyric theater from Udine to Bari, from Sciacca to San Remo, meant that the studios at Cinecittà were kept as busy with this as with their co-productions with English-speaking cinema. Marvellous series of comic films, highlighting the burlesque talent of Antonio Curtis, otherwise Toto, or the conflicts between the village priest Don Camilo and his friend the communist mayor poured out during the late 1940s and 1950s. Meanwhile the talents of Fellini, Pier Paolo Pasolini, and Luchino Visconti were being formed.

You can make a tour of the studios these days, but it bears no resemblance to a trip to Universal Studios in California, with its construct of movie-themed thrills. Rome's home of celluloid remains a functioning temple, but a temple all the same. It is with a sense of reverence that you approach its gates. Maybe it is only the second series of *Un Medico in Famiglia* (A Doctor in the Family) one of the latest and most popular TV soaps, which is being recorded on Sound Stage 3, but the atmosphere of the great present as well as the past is tangible. Anthony Minghella, with his Italian heritage and Anglo-Saxon education, seems set further to popularize Italy as a perpetual movie location—as if it needed any advertising. Opening in early 2000, his *The Talented Mr. Ripley* (Il Talento di Mr Ripley), takes us on a holiday whirlwind tour of the old country and its most glamorous sites, including superb shots of the Eternal City. A friend of mine, Alessandro Fabrizi, who worked on the film and presided over the dubbing of the original for Italian consumption, comes from a line of those Romans with their blood throbbing to the pulse of the movies. His grandmother was a regular feature of the Don Camilo films, playing the mayor's wife.

Cinecittà still also gathers around it a burgeoning colony of foreign hacks: screenwriters, technicians, *comprimario*-style actors. The Victoria Pub on Via Gesù e Maria acts as a meeting place for some of these on a Friday evening. If you want to tell a writer how you could have improved his last script or an actor how you might play Captain Corelli's musical assistant, then this might be your chance. It's odd how a couple of pints of the ever popular Scottish beer, The Devil's Kiss, can loosen the tongue.

Clement IX, with or without the aforesaid encouragement of liquor, brushed with another important genre in the history of comedy according to the extremely influential writings of the two Jonathan Richardsons, father and son. Their 1722 publication of *An Account of Some of the Statues, Bas Reliefs, Drawings and Pictures of Italy etc., With Remarks*, featuring Richardson Senior as the principal writer and Junior as researcher, was the first attempt in English to catalogue and describe the major works of art in Italy, but most of all in Rome itself. The Richardsons recount the tradition that some of the cruelest artistic caricatures by the Bolognese brothers Annibale and Agostino Carracci were inspired by one of the elderly pope's mistresses. Certainly the art of portrait caricature was continued by the Carraccis' followers and successors, Bernini, Maratti and Mole. An exhibition celebrating the British Museum's publication of Roman Baroque Drawings, c.1620–c. 1700, the sixth permanent catalogue in a series initiated in 1950 devoted to Italian drawings, was a recent opportunity to see first-hand the variety and inventiveness of those who set out to lampoon the papal court, often with papal sanction. Bulbous noses, animal-like features, items of court dress transformed into grotesque appendages: here was a tradition traced directly from ancient Greek satyr plays, and their visual representation on pottery.

Akin to the caricatures, but considerably more attractive, are the pastel portraits (also in the British Museum) of artists such as Ottavio Leoni, who enjoyed the extravagant patronage of Cardinal Scipione Borghese, nephew of Pope Paul V. Leoni probably established the practice of taking portraits in one sitting and he emphasized this by dating and numbering his subjects in strict sequential order. Thus, we have his likeness of Pope Gregory XV (1621–23), Number 182, dated to the month of his election and coronation (February 1621), and that of Urban VIII, Number 432, to September 1629. These slight but impressive works tantalizingly hint at a private side to the papacy that sometimes seems intellectually inaccessible. Who were these people, what were their emotions, how did they make a distinction between their public office and their private selves? In previous chapters considering the multi-layered nature of the papal office, we have looked at what was in essence public or semi-public art, planned to a theologico-political agenda. Here, we shall be examining the popes in private and focusing upon a work that is a product of its time and place and yet something else besides. An introspective baroque masterpiece, a personal statement and a profoundly private declaration by one of the seventeenth century's surest artistic hands: such is the portrait of Pope Innocent X (1644–55) by the Spanish Court painter, Diego Rodriguez Velázquez.

The portrait is now housed in the Doria Pamphilj Gallery, part of the palace of the same name, at the Piazza Venezia end of the Corso. It was painted in 1649 when the Spaniard was visiting Rome to select antiquities for the royal collection in Madrid, and during which time he was elected as a member of the Academy of St. Luke, the highest accolade for a Roman artist. The painting shows the 78-year-old pontiff at about half life-size in three-quarter view. It hangs in the Cabinet of the gallery and is startling in its complete dominance of this small room. Giambattista Pamphilj, an old man when elected in defiance of French disapproval, gazes unwaveringly from the canvas. The glance is sharp and implies severity, the sitter seems at once uncomfortable and yet thoroughly in control. The detail of the papal robes, chair, and tapestry hanging fades into an insignificance which even outdoes that achieved by Titian in his celebrated portrait of Julius II, upon which this painting is modeled and the original of which hangs in London's National Gallery. The face is everything, and it is a compelling face.

In this opinion, I (and many others) differ dramatically from the assessment of the painting by the Richardsons: "Infinite force and great variety of tincts, unmingled. A good picture, but less judgement than fire." More pointedly, the eighteenth-century critics unfavorably compare the effect of the linen/lace with that achieved in Guido Reni's portrait of Cardinal Spada, which was "more natural" catching its transparency and so "does not draw off the eye from the face." It is the contortion of face framed in wound-like red robes that inspires Francis Bacon in his *Screaming Popes*, a work which takes its inspiration directly from the Velázquez canvas.

Notwithstanding a divergence of critical opinion, the picture is the undoubted gem in what is now the best remaining private art collection in Rome, and so it would be simply in terms of the accomplishment of the painting were the sitter unknown to us. The addition of Innocent X's biographical details, however, makes this work something of a puzzle, or at least food for thought.

Career Prospects

In some ways, Giambattista Pamphilj's ascent to the papacy was totally conventional for the seventeenth century. He was a Roman, born there on May 7, 1574, and his studies were conducted at the newly created Roman College, the fruit of the educational reforms of the recently completed Council of Trent. He received financial support from a rich relative, which enabled him to continue his studies until he graduated as a Doctor of Laws. For perhaps obvious reasons, being an uncle and/or nephew seems to be the primary familial relationship in the history of the papacy. A curial legal career followed with a fairly long stint (1604–21) as a judge of the Sacred Rota, the principal papal judicial tribunal. His career then shifted into the diplomatic field, serving as Nuncio to Naples. Then, accompanying one of the three relatives Urban VIII (a major nepotist) had elevated to the Sacred College of Cardinals, he played a leading part in the 1625 legation to France and Spain. The pope's trust in him was confirmed by his appointment in 1626 as Nuncio in Spain at a particularly delicate time. A cardinal's hat followed in 1627, though for political reasons this was not made public until late in 1629.

The Thirty Years War had begun in 1618, and increasing hostilities between the Habsburg sphere of influence (the Empire and Spain) and the French Crown (at the time virtually worn by Cardinal Richelieu) made for particularly delicate papal diplomacy. As universal pastor to all

Catholics, Urban wished to be seen as neutral in the European power struggle between France and Spain, although in reality he was decidedly pro-French. A move in Spain's direction, such as making the Nuncio in Madrid a cardinal, could only be contemplated in the face of Richelieu's unacceptable intention of an alliance with Protestant Sweden. This became a shocking fact in 1631. Over ten years later, and with the catastrophic European struggle still grinding on, Pamphilj was elected as Urban's successor on September 15, 1644 after a conclave of 37 days, clearly indicating the Sacred College's reaction against the Barberini pope's support for France. Fortunately for Pamphilj and his pro-Habsburg supporters, the veto from Cardinal Mazarin, Richelieu's successor, arrived from Paris too late to prevent the election.

Roman superstition has it that certain things can be predicted at the time of a papal election. Custom says that a thin pope inevitably succeeds a fat one, and that the same pattern is shown in the rotation of pontiffs with the letter "R" in their name. As far as I can tell from their portraits, Urban VIII and Innocent X were about the same size, the well-upholstered norm for seventeenth-century dignitaries. The "R" rule, however, holds. And though often accused of being slow to make decisions, far removed from his predecessor's impulsiveness, the newly created Innocent X wasted no time in moving to punish the thoroughly unpopular surviving Barberini relatives. He arrested them and set up a commission charged with investigating the sources of their wealth. He was forced to a humiliating climb-down, however, when the Barberinis' chief ally, Cardinal Mazarin, exerted political pressure to have them reinstated. Innocent refrained from selecting a cardinal nephew from his family, as none could be found with sufficient capacity, though this had not been a restriction for previous pontiffs. He was in fact the first pope to entrust the Secretariat to a trusted colleague, Fabio Chigi, later to succeed him as Alexander VII (1655–67).

Nonetheless, Innocent did not entirely live up to his name as far as nepotism went, and he earned the opprobrium of the times by being subject to female family influence. The accusation ran that the Vatican was subject to the whims of his sister-in-law, Donna Olimpia Maidalchini, who, malicious gossip added, was also his mistress. This spectacular personage had managed to marry successively heirs of three aristocratic Roman houses, Aldobrandini, Borghese, and finally Pamphilj, increasing her personal fortune with each period as a widow. Following the well-established misogynist traditions of an almost exclusively male institution, commentators on the papacy have consistently represented her as a shrew "of insatiable ambition and rapacity" and described her influence as "sinister" (J. N. D. Kelly). Why her influence should be more sinister, say, than that of the fifteen-year-old street urchin whom Julius III (1550–1555) picked up in the streets of Parma and made a cardinal is difficult to explain, unless for the simple fact of her being a woman. Perhaps the outrage at Olimpia's apparent hold over Innocent says more about the commentators than it does about Olimpia herself. Her stark, anachronistically severe portrait bust, just a little down the Doria Pamphilj Gallery's corridor from the Cabinet of Innocent X, certainly shows the features of a determined woman, but her papal brother-in-law—at least as represented by Velázquez—looks like more than a match.

Accusations of nepotism in the papal court have too often had fulsome justification. Although from time to time popes have passed strict legislation concerning the non-eligibility of their own relatives for appointment as cardinals, and even banished their families from Rome to remove any shadow of a temptation, the standard practice for centuries was to use the papacy to make a name for those who depended upon you as well as for yourself. Throughout the high Renaissance, huge tracts of papal territory were alienated in order to provide hereditary duchies for the families of the most powerful popes. Pius VI (1775–99) caused considerable scandal when he revived seventeenth-century practice and did everything in his power to enrich his family, the Braschi, and furnish them with powerful positions. This trend was brought to a swift but temporary end by his successor Pius VII (1799–1823), who, under the influence of his liberally minded Secretary of State, Consalvi, exercised an equitable rule in the papal territories.

A marked difference in the policies of succeeding popes can even be seen in the last century. Pius XII (1939–58) permitted his brothers and their families to be promoted in the management fields of Italian secular life and although he refrained from giving them papal titles, his influence was important in providing them with honors from the monarchy. Pope John XXIII (1958–63) earned a surprising amount of criticism for his failure to do anything for his family. From Brescia farming stock, he commented that his concern for his brothers, who had lived happy lives at work in the fields for many years, was such that he would do nothing to take them away from that happiness. This characteristically humble thought has been the watchword for popes since.

Artistic Favorites

One of the minor, but still important, casualties of the sweeping change of Roman patronage when Innocent X succeeded Urban VIII was the sculptor and artistic polymath, Gian Lorenzo Bernini (1598–1680). Urban's particular friend, a native Neapolitan but the genius of Roman baroque *par excellence,* the artist was commissioned to decorate the interior of St. Peter's and the Barberini palace, and was reportedly given surprising signs of papal favor. A visitor to his studio is said to have found Urban holding a mirror for Bernini as he worked on a self-portrait. Similarly, Bernini had almost unlimited unannounced access to the papal presence. Urban might have made political mistakes, especially in his last years, but his artistic judgment seems to have been unerring.

The same cannot be said of Innocent. His hatred of the Barberini clan inspired him to reject Bernini out of hand and remove him from his important commissions, especially the work on the interior of St. Peter's. Papal favor is, however, as fickle as any other source of almost unlimited patronage. Bernini is said to have won over Innocent when the pope saw a silver model of his design for the Fountain of the Four Rivers intended for the Piazza Navona. This model, it is said, had been put in the pope's way by Donna Olimpia, who hated to think of such talent being neglected during her own ascendancy. The piazza was the location for Innocent's private palace, Palazzo Pamphilj (now the Brazilian Embassy), and received the majority of attention that he gave to the adornment of Rome during his pontificate. Not only was Bernini's baroque fantasy of the rivers transformed from the precious bait that had hooked Innocent into the triumph of marble that it still is today, but the exquisite church of Sant'Agnese in Agone by Bernini's contemporary and pupil, Francesco Borromini (1599–1667), was built next to the palace.

Much has been written about the artistic differences and personal rivalry between these two baroque masters. Can Borromini really have laughed when the north tower of St. Peter's facade, under Bernini's architectural direction, collapsed? Well, acknowledging that your friends furnish your worst enemies, and that professional envy is a powerful force, I suppose it could be true. The old tourist tale that the figure of the Nile in Bernini's Fountain of the Four Rivers is veiling his face because he cannot stand the sight of the facade of Sant'Agnese is simple nonsense, as the fountain was completed in 1651 before work had begun on the church. However, the inevitable juxtaposition of the two artists' work, and the different impressions that their varying sensibilities evoke, make for a nice opportunity to assess your own taste. A visit to two gem-like churches on the Quirinal hill will provide the evidence.

Opposite the so-called *manica lunga*, or long sleeve, a projecting wing of the Quirinal Palace, are the churches of S. Andrea al Quirinale and S. Carlino alle Quattro Fontane, the first designed principally by Bernini and the second by Borromini. They capture something of the different approaches the two men had to the baroque architectural vernacular. Internally, both are elliptical in plan, with the long side of the oval facing the street and providing the main entrance. Yet the facades of the churches could hardly be more distinct within their unifying terms. Bernini's simple solution of offsetting the daringly curved planes of the building's walls with a restrained portal, formed from a single order of Corinthian pilasters surmounted by a plain classical tympanum, reflects the soothingly sunny, reassuring impression his personality is often said to have had. By contrast the restless, almost squirming, character of S. Carlino's facade summons up the turbulent, depressive Borromini the writers love to diminish. In a bravura display of virtuosity within a constrained site, Borromini lavished this, his own *alma mater* (he had been educated in its school), with every mannerist conceit. The alternating use of convex and concave surfaces of the upper and lower fields of the church's front are held together by a solid, even stolid, entablature, while the pediment, following the undulating curves of the upper niches is pierced by a soaring medallion, borne aloft by angels.

The whole is given its final quirky touch by the bizarre *campanile*, a *pasquinade* on the traditional medieval type so distinctive to Rome, here half steeple, half cupola with concave drum.

Inside, the churches further illustrate the extremes of calm repose and frenetic activity. Bernini's church is a jewel-box interior in pink, gold, and white, a favored location for modern society weddings that demand the trappings of a formal past without too many of its difficult questions. S. Carlino, on the other hand, breaks up its elliptical plan with obtruding angles, using a triangular decorative theme to recall the dedication of the church and its adjoining convent to the Holy Trinity as well as to St. Charles Borromeo.

I like both churches, but forced to a choice, I would opt for Borromini's frantic radicalism. I first visited them in the early weeks of my student days in Rome and my guide was none other than a scion of the Piccolomini family, which had been decorated by the pontificates of Pius II and III. Charis Piccolomini, a person of profoundly international sympathies and experience, had landed, I know not how, upon the archdiocese of Westminster as his local church and was near the completion of his studies at Rome's Venerable English College. Roman Catholic seminarians must be "incardinated," sponsored by a diocese, which in the natural course of things will remain their "spiritual home," even if they end up working in Rome or elsewhere in the world. Charis, as a member of a papal family, was to be ordained deacon by John Paul II himself. Since then I have lost sight of him. On brief acquaintance he exhibited a good deal of the taste and discernment, a mark of his pontifical connections, even to the extent of risking an occasional risqué comment. The architectural walking tour that he led for a few of the "new men" also included Borromini's even more spectacular University Church of S. Ivo near the Piazza Navona. It is also really worth seeing. Sometimes you have to look hard for Borromini's buildings; it is simply impossible to avoid the prolific Bernini's work.

Time and Titles
Rome's Black Nobility, named either after the characteristic color of clerical dress or their mourning for the lost papal monarchy, is the fairly small group of families who have produced a pope. The four senior clans

who claim to trace their origins to the last days of the Roman Empire are the Caetani, Massimo, Colonna, and Orsini. As we have seen, the Borghese, Barberini, Chigi, and Pamphilj were the dominant houses of the seventeenth century, the last century in which every pope seems to have used his office to ennoble his family as a matter of course. It was largely these aristocratic families who provided Rome with its high society well into the nineteenth century. A terrible dilemma confronted them all, however, when the city became the capital of the united Kingdom of Italy in 1870. Dependent as they had been for their status upon a system that acknowledged no other earthly ruler than their spiritual Father, the pope, they had somehow to come to terms with the new order established by the Piedmontese monarchy of Vittorio Emanuele II. Some closed the doors of their palaces and turned the papal throne, which always stood in the antechambers of their principal apartments in readiness for a papal visit, to the wall. They also refused to attend the royal balls and galas at the Quirinal, to which they were inevitably invited as the most distinguished members of Rome's populace. Attendance upon Pope Pius IX, the self-styled Prisoner of the Vatican, and his reduced court became *de rigueur* for the loyalist nobles. A few, however, temporized, and gradual collaboration with the Italian state and disdainful toleration of Savoyard titles, as successive pontiffs softened their attitudes to the status quo, enabled the high-society survival of the Black Nobility.

If the papal families in Rome thought themselves superior to more recent dukedoms and counties, all is put into perspective by the claims and counterclaims of pretenders to imperial dignity. During the 1950s, a well-known figure in the city's *saloni* was someone styling himself His Imperial Highness Lavarello Lascaris Comneno, Heir Porphyrogenite of the Normania-Paleologue. His principal rival to the Byzantine "Roman" throne had the somewhat dubious advantage of also being the most popular film comedian in Italian history. Antonio de Curtis, known universally by his pet-name, Totò, was a kind of cross between Stan Laurel and Buster Keaton, but his nutcracker-jawed countenance could still smile benevolently upon the deep curtseys of society ladies who acknowledged him as Porphyrogenite of the Constantinian Descent of Phocis, Achaia, Imperial Prince of Byzantium.

Italians, even modern ones, can display symptoms of rather old-fashioned passion and respect for titles, which oddly runs counter to the general classlessness of society. I've personally witnessed the change in attitude a switchboard operator can exhibit upon discovering that his interlocutor is a *Contessa*. Generally speaking, status is now conferred by job, and so individuals are addressed by reference to the qualification that fits them for their employment. *Dottore* is the correct form of address for any graduate, even when they have not attained a higher degree, and *Professore* is the title granted to those who have passed the state exams to become qualified teachers. It is quite common also for industrialists to be called *Ingegnere*, and for your accountant to be addressed as *Ragioniere*. It seems unlikely that in English-speaking countries the title "Engineer" will ever confer the deference of respect. Reflecting on his own liberal distribution of honors within the new Kingdom of Italy, Victor Emanuel once remarked that there were two things that he could refuse no one: a cigar and the insignia of knighthood. It is needless to say that the old Roman aristocracy remained singularly unimpressed with these new creations. Such honors continued to be made, however, right until the last hours of the monarchy. On his way into exile after the plebiscite confirming a Republican government for Italy in post-war Europe, Umberto II conferred a string of titles on loyal supporters and retainers. These so-called *Conti di Ciampino* or Counts of Ciampino (Umberto left Rome for Cascais from the airfield of the same name) earned themselves considerable ridicule in the popular press by adopting and insisting upon their new styles.

Luigi Barzini in his book *The Italians* subtly illustrates the way the old Roman aristocracy survived, and survives, all this change. He comments upon the way the noble palaces of Rome are not closed environments, but hosts to public fountains and even on occasions to popular fruit and vegetable markets. Right into the twentieth century, the poor of the Ripetta district would regularly use the handsome fountain of the Palazzo Borghese, and access to the *Principi*, the Black Noble aristocrats themselves, was fairly general. Neighbors, even the most impecunious, needed only turn up to be admitted at the suitable hours. This treatment of all and sundry as *famuli* (dependents) undoubtedly implies a good deal of patronizing condescension, which would be embarrassing, if not downright offensive, to many recipients. Even so, it does also permit the urban environment to maintain its own specific ambience. As Barzini writes

One cannot easily escape an architectural imperative which so forcefully imposes memories, ways of life, a standard of taste, a special technique of living together, that even foreigners begin to feel different after having lived in one of our cities for a short time.

When Robert Runcie, as Archbishop of Canterbury, made an official visit to the Vatican for talks with Pope John Paul II in 1989, the reception he hosted in return for all the hospitality he received from the Curia was held in the Private Apartments of the Palazzo Doria Pamphilj, by kind permission of the Prince and Princess. An Anglican exchange student freshly arrived in Rome at the time, I was a little surprised, although disproportionately gratified, to be invited. The Palace was one of the grandest addresses in Rome, and this early opportunity for observing the Black Nobility "at home" not to be missed. Entrance was from the Corso, and access to the *piano nobile* up a broad flight of shallow marble steps. Liveried footmen stood at the bottom directing the guests to "go up higher." In the receiving line, the Archbishop was joined by the Director of the Anglican Centre in Rome and his wife, Howard and Celia Root (the Centre occupied rather cramped space at the top of the Palace, again by kind permission...). And then, at the end of the line, were the Prince and Princess themselves: he diminutive with a gentle face and an intelligent, almost shy, way of looking at people, she stately and straight, with her handbag clamped on her arm in the position that in British aristocratic circles spells "real class."

Meanwhile, the name of Innocent X's family keeps on growing. A later seventeenth-century dynastic alliance joined Doria to the Pamphilj, and brought the dignity of the famous Genoese clan to bear on Roman society. More recently, the surprising English surname of Pogson joined the list. The Prince, Don Frank, to whom we were presented at Lord Runcie's reception, was born and bred in Berkshire and had acquired his dignity simply by falling in love with a young Italian woman he met during the allied occupation of Italy. She, Donna Orietta, was the only child of the then Prince and his Scottish Princess (the family had a well-established taste for British spouses), who unlike many of their peers had been staunch opponents of Mussolini and his Fascists in the run-up to war. The Prince was repaid with popular acclaim for his principled stand against the tide when he emerged as the first post-war *sindaco* of the city. The story goes that when the family had to "disappear" from the Palazzo Doria Pamphilj in the darkest days of the Nazi ascendancy in Rome, Orietta carried family jewels with her into hiding in Trastevere in a plain shopping bag. It is also said that the Prince did not actually leave the palace, but simply kept on the move through its more than 2,000 rooms, aided by a few trusted servants. The war over, Orietta married her English naval officer, who adopted her name and rank, and for the next fifty years they and their children became a focus for the unique mix of English-speaking diplomatic and church circles to be found in Rome.

Don Frank died in 1998, and received lengthy obituaries in the English dailies. The management of the extensive Doria Pamphilj property in Rome has been assumed by his son, Don Jonathan, whose excellent recorded commentary to the gallery recalls the unmistakable tone and accent of the fully British aristocracy, themselves brought to the point of having to open their houses to the public. The Doria Pamphilj Gallery, however, has been a "must" on any tourist's list for well over a century. A daughter of the Earl of Shrewsbury, Mary Talbot, married into the family during the mid-nineteenth century, and together with her husband, the then Prince, enlarged the collection's range and taste. The arrangement of the gallery is such that the star exhibits of each century, other than the Velázquez, are now highlighted in a recently opened wing, just beyond the celebrated mirrored hall. My last visit was in January and although the external temperature was comfortable it was icy in the gallery. Roman princely splendor, with its thirty-foot ceilings and draughty corridors, has a downside. These palaces must be the devil to heat! Perhaps Innocent X's intriguing expression could be explained by the fact that Velázquez just kept him sitting too long in the cold.

Too True

A well-established tradition relates that when he saw the finished portrait, Innocent commented that the work was *troppo vero*, "too true." He was not a stranger to overt criticism of artistic works that touched him personally, as an anecdote in the Richardsons' handbook relates. Guido Reni painted a St. Michael triumphing over the devil in the Capuchin church, and society was not slow to note the similarities between Satan's features and those of the well-known Cardinal Pamphilj. When questioned about it by the offended cleric, the artist commented that "he only designed to make the devil as hateful and disagreeable as he had made the angel amiable." But, he added, if the picture happened to resemble the Cardinal, "twas not he that was to be blamed, but the Cardinal's deformity." Such forthrightness might have been expected to earn a heavier punishment than a simple loss of patronage, but Innocent seems to have had a lighter side. The rehabilitated Bernini made a bust of the pope, also on show in Doria Pamphilj Gallery, which shows a remarkably different view of the man from Velázquez's power politician or, indeed, Guido Reni's devil incarnate. Smiling and full-faced, the pontiff seems the model of seventeenth-century affability, ready to bless and shower favors on any petitioner.

Which is the most characteristic aspect of the man who had served as an ecclesiastical judge for twenty years, and Nuncio to the stiffly formal court of Spain for just as long, but who was equally the alleged slave of a woman's sharp tongue? I leave you to decide. As the truly private, "internal" life of anyone, let alone any pope, remains ultimately beyond our reach, we shall never know for sure.

CHAPTER TEN

Seventeenth- and Eighteenth-Century Visitors: Canova's Stuart Monument

> *"[Rome] where every stone almost is a book: every statue a master: every*
> *inscription a lesson: every anti-chamber an academy."*
> Richard Lassels, *An Italian Voyage, or Compleat Journey through Italy*
> (1670)

At the press conference, the journalist asks the soft-spoken princess, indisposed throughout her entire Roman stay, which of all the cities on her tour of Western Europe she has most enjoyed. Dressed in demure but fashionable 1950s chic, given the royal "thumbs up" by the UK's

Princess Margaret, Princess Anne begins a considered speech to please all her host nations and offend none, but suddenly her well-modulated tones falter, and she is unaccountably struck dumb. After this heart-stopping hesitation she announces clearly and unmistakably, "Rome... by all means, Rome."

This Oscar-winning performance by Audrey Hepburn in William Wyler's *Roman Holiday*, with her co-star, the dashing (even if awardless) Gregory Peck, is one of the twentieth century's most enduring and widely accessible celluloid icons of Rome. Dealing as it does with the changes that any monarchy has had to face during the last century, whether forced upon it by the cataclysm of war, revolution or media hounding, the film's theme fits the location well. Rome has always found a place for stray kings and queens. Hepburn, as Princess Anne, manages to break free of royal constraint by climbing out of the back of her nation's embassy, and engaging in a three day Roman romance with Peck's meltingly masculine American stringer. He sacrifices his journalistic scoop, the photos of the Princess engaged in a nightclub brawl, in his consideration for her as a young and vulnerable woman.

The film was famously "fun" to make, and it is easy to see why. The locations have all the freshness of Rome at the height of its fashionable ascendancy. Peck's bachelor pad, No. 51a on the then and still fashionable Via Margutta, can now easily be visited as it houses a pizzeria (good if a little over-priced). The scene in which Anne, in her assumed identity of Smitty, the American college girl, is given a haircut by an enamored Roman hairdresser, results in a vision of gentle, sensitive beauty. And, by all accounts, she really was the unaffected, innocent girl she appears to be. The rapport between Peck and Hepburn is at its best in the celebrated moment when, unscripted, the actor puts his hand into the Bocca della Verità and mimes a fight with an internal monster, only to draw out his arm with his sleeve hiding his hand. Hepburn is genuinely shocked, and then retaliates with mock anger, raining blows upon his manly chest. Oh, to be young, beautiful and Hollywood stars! All this, and money too. However cynical I try to be, this film touches something deep inside me, especially in the poignantly conveyed resignation of its otherwise fairly conventional ending. The Princess, her blameless fling over, has been transformed into a mature woman, able to accept her high calling more successfully. The journalists, too, are shown to be human after all. Grace Kelly and Diana Spencer's stories ended rather differently.

Rome, the city of the popes and ideological world capital of reaction, has received royalty for centuries. The journeys, actual and postponed, by claimants to the Holy Roman Empire, so that their *de facto* government might be authenticated by imperial coronation, were many. Napoleon, ever the innovator, succeeded in devising an ironic trope on these proceedings by abducting Pope Pius VII and including him in the Parisian ceremonies of December 1804 which made him emperor (though notoriously declining coronation at the pope's hands). A number of Anglo-Saxon kings, including Alfred the Great, visited Rome in the ninth and tenth centuries, so that they might be invested in their office, and Cnut the Dane even assisted as a lesser king at the coronation of a Holy Roman Emperor, that of Conrad II in 1027. (Incidentally, the ceremony was performed by John XIX (1024–32), one of the few persons to be elected pope as a layman; his ordinations as deacon, priest, and bishop in a single day shocked contemporaries.) When the Habsburg Charles V visited Rome following his sack of the city in 1527, the Sacred Way through the ruins of the Roman Forum was re-paved so that he might make a traditionally triumphal entry to the Capitol. Shortly after her 1953 coronation, Elizabeth II of the United Kingdom made her first state visit to Italy and landed at Ciampino airport, from where she was driven directly up the Via Appia Antica rather than the more usual and better paved Appia Nuova so that she might be impressed by the antique ruins more than by the modern ones.

Perhaps the city's most extensive preparations made for a royal arrival were those at Pope Alexander VII's instruction for the welcoming of Christina, former Queen of Sweden. The whole Sacred College waited at the second mile stone on the Flaminian Way to accompany the abdicated monarch into the papal presence in the Piazza del Popolo. The square had undergone a preparatory face-lift, not unlike that it has more recently enjoyed for the millennium, and was lavishly decorated with awnings, pavilions, and platforms from which the separate courts might, quite literally, pontificate.

Politically, Christina's conversion to Roman Catholicism and decision to settle in Rome was a major coup. The daughter of Gustavus Adolphus, King of Sweden and the most successful of Protestant generals in the Thirty Years War, Christina had ruled her patrimony from an early age following her father's untimely death in battle. Her intellectual capacity was amply reflected in the interest the great French theologian and mathematician René Descartes showed in her tutoring, and she proved herself again and again a creative and maverick force in the rigidly controlled world of courtly etiquette. Sexually permissive and experimental (she was almost certainly bisexual), her court in exile in the Palazzo Riario (now Palazzo Corsini) was both an embarrassment to and an adornment of the Chigi pope's city. Alexander had to support her financially, as well as give her protection, and she was a growing burden for his later seventeenth-century successors. Interested in everything from science, through alchemy, to fine art, Christina attracted a wide circle of aristocratic and clerical stars to her salon. A fascinating memorial to her Roman sojourn are the cabalistic inscriptions covering the tiny gazebo of her former pleasure garden, the Villa Palombara, up on the Oppian hill. She believed these indecipherable words to hold the truths of rejuvenation and of transforming base metal into gold; they still puzzle scholars. Her bedroom is the only room in the Palazzo Corsini, now housing part of the National Gallery of Ancient Art and the Academia dei Lincei, which has been left in the style of the earlier palace. It isn't a large room, and is covered in Renaissance frescoes, giving it the quality, somehow, of a particularly luxurious gypsy caravan; grand, eclectic but just a little garish, the perfect setting for an enormous state bed, sadly no longer *in situ.* This decoration seems to chime with the character of the woman who died here, and whose intellect and daring added spice to the Rome of the early Enlightenment.

The Challenge of Science

Papal Rome had often found itself at odds with the trends produced by its own peculiar advantages, especially in the field of scientific research and philosophical theorizing. Strange anomalies arose from the Counter Reformation's imposition of heavily policed religious conformism and a corresponding received orthodoxy in the natural sciences set against the intelligent patronage of the worldly clerics who wished to see human knowledge grow. A fine case in point can be seen in the acceptance of the Gregorian Calendar promulgated throughout the Catholic world by Pope Gregory XIII (1572–85) in 1582. Here, new astronomical techniques had been employed to correct the shortfall of days which had accrued through the inaccuracy of the old Julian calendar, then in operation for over fifteen hundred years. This initiative (which was a great improvement on the old) was rejected by Protestant nations, in some cases for centuries, as the fruit of despised superstition. And who could blame them, when the same Roman Church wracked itself over the famous trials of Galileo Galilei.

Galileo, the pioneering astronomer and physicist, a life-long friend of Urban VIII, and the man whom Stephen Hawking described as being "most responsible for the birth of modern science," was twice arrested by the Inquisition and forced to renounce the Copernican System as the best way of understanding the universe. He was persuaded to recant by worldly friends, including the pope, who wished to save themselves from the enormous embarrassment of having to burn a man who was well known as the leading scientist of his day. House arrest for life and an enduring Catholic faith did not stop him smuggling his second and greatest work, *Two New Sciences*, into Holland for publication. The same efforts had proven unsuccessful in the case of Giordano Bruno, the speculative Dominican thinker, who went to the stake in the Campo dei Fiori in 1600. John Paul II's 1980s "apology" for Galileo's treatment may have seemed a little belated, but the fact that the Vatican thought this worth issuing is a pointer in the direction of the whole problem. When an institution thoroughly believes itself to be the guardian, under God's guidance, of the whole revealed truth about the world, then it would act disingenuously if it did not consider its pronouncements to carry definitive weight even after four centuries. Following the erection by the new Italian state of a memorial to Bruno on the site of his execution as a martyr to papal intolerance, one early twentieth-century priestly commentator still could not bring himself to admit any fault:

> *His life would have been spared had he been willing to repent and retract his errors. But he remained obstinate and impenitent to the last, and when the crucifix was presented to him at the stake, he turned*

away and refused to kiss it. (P.J. Candlery, SJ, Pilgrim Walks in Rome, 1908)

Leo XIII (1878-1903), in an encyclical of 1890, had clarified the point for the faithful:

The erection by the sect (Freemasons) of the monument to the notorious apostate of Nola (Bruno), was, with the aid and favor of the Government, promoted, determined and carried out by the Freemasons, whose authorized spokesmen were not ashamed to acknowledge its purpose and to declare its meaning. Its purpose was to insult the papacy; its meaning that, instead of the Catholic faith, there must now be substituted the most absolute freedom of criticism, of thought, of conscience.

These hard words were written at a particularly difficult time for the papacy. Leo XIII was committed to the political restoration of the Papal States, even though, ironically, he was to restore some standing to the battered institution by moderation and common sense. It has taken almost a century for the Vatican to begin to allude in public pronouncements to the ways in which the papacy has been vastly benefited by the loss of the temporal power in Italy and the accompanying higher prestige enjoyed worldwide as a spiritual and moral arbiter. The belated rehabilitation of Galileo was a token of this change, and there has even been speculation that Bruno might be thoroughly rehabilitated by beatification or canonization.

The Vatican is often the victim of its own principled stands. What seems undoubtedly right at the beginning of a century can bear a different face at the same century's end. This chapter, which looks at Rome as a travel destination during the Enlightenment, is underpinned by the contention that Rome has for centuries also been behind the times. One more visit must be made to St. Peter's Basilica, but for the last time in this book.

On entering the church the general movement seems to bend you to the right, (compass north, but liturgical south) in the direction of *La Pietà* by Michelangelo. The natural expectation would then be to proceed past the first great pier of the basilica's aisle. Look up and under the first arch you will see the Memorial to Queen Christina, designed by Carlo Fontana and set up in 1689. In an equivalent position in the opposite aisle stands the monument to which we are making, so go against the crowd and cross right over the immense nave. (Attentive readers will now note that I have never required them to go further into St. Peter's than the first pillar; you must judge yourself whether this is a mercy or a deprivation). The elegant tombstone, for such it is, has been designed in the neoclassical style so characteristic of its sculptor, Antonio Canova (1757–1822). A simple, though grandly proportioned Greek *stele* in pure white marble stands as the facade of an imagined mausoleum, its doors guarded by sleeping angels. Above the lintel runs a Latin inscription:

IACOBO III
IACOBI II MAGNAE BRIT REGIS FILIO
KAROLO EDUARDO
ET HENRICO DECANO PATRUM CARDINALIUM
IACOBI III FILIIS
REGIAE STIRPIS STUARDIAE POSTREMIS
ANNO MDCCCXIX

FOR JAMES III
SON OF JAMES II OF GREAT BRITAIN
CHARLES EDWARD
AND HENRY DEAN OF THE COLLEGE OF CARDINALS
SONS OF JAMES III
THE LAST SHOOTS OF THE ROYAL HOUSE OF STUART
1819

Above these words, portrait busts in bas-relief of the three named Jacobites are almost casually sketched in. Crowning the *stele's* pediment in a small medallion, are the Royal Arms of England, Scotland, France, and Ireland.

Pretenders and Pretensions

Romantics of all sorts will tell you that there is often a single rose deposited upon the cenotaph's shelf. I've yet to see one, although I wouldn't put it past the extravagant whimsy of someone to keep a light burning for the hope of a Stuart revival, even after the self-declaration of the monument that no further claims be made. After all, the papacy treated the exiled Stuarts as rightful wearers of the three crowns (England, Scotland, and Ireland) for almost a century, while successive British monarchs had been claiming the crown of France, vainly, since Henry VI had lost it in the middle of the fifteenth century. After the Treaty of Utrecht (1713) Louis XIV of France was forced to withdraw his protection of his princely cousins who had kept up their court at Saint-Germain, despite their claim on his own throne, in the years following James II's abdication in 1688. He had been succeeded by Act of Parliament, not by his Catholic son as he had hoped, but by his Protestant daughter, Mary, and her husband, William of Orange. The Jacobite pretender, styled James III since his father's death, sought refuge with Pope Clement XI (1700–21), who knew all about exiled monarchs. He had been an *habitué* of Queen Christina's salon while still Cardinal Albani, and was even rumored to have been her lover (giving us one of the few pieces of evidence that anyone thought she had any heterosexual inclinations). He certainly benefited from a sizable bequest in her will.

Perhaps the Swedish queen's generosity inspired his liking for the exiled English/Scots. He placed a substantial palace, that of the Muti (now known as Palazzo Balestra) in Piazza SS. Apostoli, at their disposal, and recognized the legitimacy of the titular James III and VIII. The Royal Arms of the Stuarts were erected above its principal entrance, and the formalities of a fully recognized court were granted to the Jacobites. James was given the privilege of nominating consuls to act in his name at the main ports of entry into the Papal States, causing some difficulties for British travelers during most of the eighteenth century. The nearest "legitimate" Hanoverian minister was the Resident to the Great Duke of Tuscany, for many years Sir Horace Mann. Some members of the Jacobite court also found employment in the pope's armed forces, like the Irishman Parker who commanded the tiny papal navy. The marriage of James III to a Polish princess, Clementina Sobieska, was conducted in Rome with much pomp, and despite the failure of the 1715 rising in the wake of the death of Queen Anne, the last Protestant Stuart, the birth of sons to the Pretender in 1720 and 1725 gave hope that the Stuart cause was not yet lost.

During the period of the titular king's residence in Rome, the city became an increasingly important destination for those gentlefolk who traveled. The Grand Tour originally specified the French part of the journey undertaken by many British aristocrats in the periods of peace that relatively infrequently interrupted the European hostilities of the eighteenth century. The Transalpine section of the Tour was properly designated the *giro d'Italia*, but this name gradually fell into disuse, the first part of the trip coming to stand for the whole.

The dangers of the journey were considerable. John Raymond, the principal influence on the more famous John Evelyn's Roman diary, lists three in particular, which were the same for the eighteenth as well as the seventeenth century: "The first is the heat of the climate; a second that horrible (in report) Inquisition; the last, hazard of those merciless outlaws Banditas." Raymond adds that moderation and discretion should save the traveler from the first two of these "evitable" dangers; the third should be looked to by the police authorities of the states through which the traveler passed.

The route of the journey from Britain to Rome seems to have changed very little over the centuries, although there were significant variants. The favorite British Alpine pass was that of Mons Cenis, after a journey through the majority of mainland France. If a sea-journey were undertaken at all, it was most often from Genoa to Rome or Naples. A splendid account of the waves of British tourists from the earliest times to the period just post-war is given in Brian Barefoot's elegant and exhaustively researched book *The English Road to Rome* (1993). In both seventeenth and eighteenth centuries, the principal pretext for the journey was education. It seems that no one just went on holiday. Milton had come to study Bembo and Tasso, and to meet Manso. The Italianate English that he was to use in his mature verse was the fruit of time well spent abroad. Architects like Inigo Jones had come to Italy and taken the principles of Palladio and his master Vetruvius home with them. It became the received wisdom of well-furnished pedagogy that an education was unfinished until it had taken in the sites of the ancients' habitation. British noblemen and women came most often to Italy to view the Roman ruins and acquire some of the antiquities for themselves. To begin with at least, there was very little appreciation of contemporary art or that of the comparatively recent past. British curricula were crammed with Latin and Roman

history, not with classes in Renaissance art appreciation. Thus, it is with reference to the classical remains that Robert Lassels, the originator of the technical term "Grand Tour," pointed out the educative qualities of the stones and statues.

If the Jacobites and aristocratic tourists formed two distinct English-speaking circles in Rome during the eighteenth century, a third was made by resident artists and antiquaries who came to study in earnest and to practice where they could. Joshua Reynolds, Richard Wilson, George Romney, and Robert Adam each had significant stays in Rome, which were to influence their work on return to London or Edinburgh. The class of artist was difficult to define for British society; the painter occupied an intermediate position between gentleman and servant. Robert Adam, for example, had to play down his studies with Piranesi in order to maintain his place in the socially rigorous expatriate circles of Piazza di Spagna. The matter was not so cut and dried for native Italians; artists were frequently rewarded with papal orders and petty titles, a custom which was adopted at the court of Charles I of England, but not adhered to in the early Hanoverian years. The title "Chevalier" is that most usual with those native artists who enjoyed papal patronage, and the Cross of St. John is frequently glimpsed upon the breast of an artist's self-portrait. Clearly, Italian attitudes to art were more self-confident than elsewhere in Europe, and it was only in the wake of the founding of Royal Academies and National Galleries in the northern countries that anything like the same respect was given to painters there.

A British traveler who deigned to condescend and endeared himself hugely to the artistic community in Rome, while remaining in the highest circles of society, was Frederick Hervey, 4th Earl Bristol and Bishop of Derry within the established Church of Ireland. So inveterate a traveler was he that the multitude of "Bristol" hotels throughout Europe are named in his honor. This eccentric, but apparently generous, connoisseur enjoyed many adventures during his travels. He once arrived at a Swiss convent and having been announced with all his Episcopal dignity, he entered to find the religious inmates of the house prostrate and waiting for his heretic blessing. Not wishing to disappoint, he obliged with considerable panache and then had to continue the masquerade of being a Roman Catholic ecclesiastic. Fortunately, on that occasion he was not traveling with his wife. My favorite story about him comes from the time he was resident in his Irish See. The Bishop suggested to a group of his clergy who were eager to be considered for a rich living that they should race each other for it, indicating a muddy field as the course and a deep ditch as the finishing post. He proceeded, Solomon-like, to appoint the one priest who refused to join the contest.

Hervey commissioned paintings and urged his friends to buy from the Roman artists. The collection he amassed with the intention of bringing it back to England to furnish Ickworth, his country house in Suffolk, was confiscated when Napoleon's troops occupied Rome in 1798. Many of his artist friends petitioned the French authorities to release the works of art, and the Bishop himself even had the ingenious, though vain, notion of being designated "Minister to congratulate the

Roman People on their emancipation" by the British government, so that the occupiers might look more favorably upon him. In due course, some of the paintings were restored to him, only to be impounded again shortly afterwards. Few ever made it to Suffolk. When he died in 1803, making a short journey from his villa at Albano back to Rome, his funeral in the city was attended by more than 800 grateful artists from all nations. His body was shipped back to England for burial in a package that purported to contain works of art.

Foreigners with titles or a taste for them have often found Rome a congenial environment. The longevity of the aristocratic claims of some Roman families has been alluded to elsewhere in this book, and my researches have made me aware just how much writers about the city like to be fulsome in their thanks to anyone with an extravagant name or exotic sounding title. Duncan Fallowell thanks a bishop, a priest, a baronet, a baron, a knight, a professor, an Honourable, a princess, and someone rejoicing in the name and title "Baronessa Pucci Zanca" in *To Noto*. But let me cite Christopher Kininmonth as my prime example:

> *I would like to record my gratitude to Countess Sylvia Piccolomini, Giacomo Pozzi-Bellini, the Hon. Edmund and Mrs Howard, Signore and Signora Emilio Cecchi, Dario Checchi, J.B. Ward-Perkins, Ronald Botrall, Edwin Muir, Mr and Mrs Cecil Sprigge, Baroness Cotta, General Helbig, Signora Serra-Salvo, Count Massimo Filo della Torre di S Susanna and Signore and Signora Gaspero del Corso... In conclusion I would like to dedicate this book to Princess Marguerite Caëtani whose kindness has borne such fruits as will make me ever beholden to her.*

The conjunction of such dignified names with high-sounding titles reminds me of the annual list of the departed read out as part of the All Souls' Day rituals of Catholic and Anglican churches. I will never forget some of those annually commemorated among the benefactors of my own university college, where in the midst of Humphrey Duke of Gloucester, Helena, the Marchioness of Milford Haven, and Maria Attatagraff Johnson, the rather incongruous Ruby Doe used to make her appearance. I have no idea who she was or what she did (she sounded more like a college cleaner than a noble patron), but I cherish her memory and would like to thank her all the same. She may stand for all those who never get thanked in the acknowledgements of books, and yet who do most of the work in keeping places like Rome worth visiting.

Music for a While

A common cause for comment by the Grand Tourists was Rome's music. John Evelyn during his winter visit of 1644–45 paid the obligatory visit to the Oratorian church of S. Maria in Valicella, otherwise known as the *Chiesa Nuova*, where inspired by the example of their founder St. Philip Neri the members of the community provided "rare music." Next door to the church is the exquisite oratory itself, in which the performance of musico-religious dramas, closely related to the new genre of classically based operas, took place. These oratorios, as they came to be known, were usually performed in Latin and based upon biblical stories. Well-known examples of the type are Carissimi's *Jephtha* and *Jonas*. The singing of the papal choir, which contained the endlessly fascinating *castrati* voices not so commonly heard in northern European countries, reached its annual high point with the performance of Psalm 51 during the Ash Wednesday liturgy in the Sistine Chapel. Set to music by Allegri, the *Miserere* was not published, so the story goes, until Mozart attended the ceremony and transcribed it on arriving back in his lodgings. When the Earl Bishop of Bristol and Derry attended this spiritual closure of the Carnival season, he chose to wear the gaiters and apron of his Anglican prelacy. As a result, he was looked on with such puzzlement by the ushers that he was placed to stand among the commoners, rather than seated among the Sacred College with his other distinguished compatriots.

Sacred music has a long Roman history, starting with the psalms and spiritual songs which St. Paul commends as part of Christian worship to the readers of his letters. Pope St. Gregory the Great is credited, almost certainly erroneously, with the creation of the monastic chant that dominated the cloister for seven centuries. But it was the rise of European polyphony in the fourteenth and fifteenth centuries that opened the creative doors to Rome's greatest genius. Giovanni Pierluigi da Palestrina served as organist and choir-master to both St. Peter's and

S. Maria Maggiore during the sixteenth century, and so highly regarded were his motets and mass settings that a legend telling that he took down heavenly musical dictation direct from angels became current. It forms the principal scene in Hans Pfitzner's 1917 opera, *Palestrina*. Another major church with strong musical traditions is S. Maria in Trastevere. Frescobaldi was organist here at the beginning of the seventeenth century, and the organ, designed in 1701 by Philippo Testo for the then organist Pasquini, has recently been the subject of a major restoration. Conducted by Prof. Giuseppe Basile and the students of the Rome School of Restoration, the reconstruction works have enabled the organ to be played in a totally authentic manner, recalling precisely the tone and style of the seventeenth and eighteenth centuries.

Sadly, I was not the beneficiary of such careful study and authentic reconstruction when I attended the annual celebratory vespers at S. Cecilia in Trastevere in 1989. St. Cecilia is the patron saint of music because she reputedly constructed an organ in the *peristyle* of her Roman suburban villa before her martyrdom. (A second-century Roman organ is one of the most interesting genuine exhibits in the Museo della Civiltà Romana in EUR—see Chapter Thirteen). Formed from a mixed group of university students, the choir who sang the seventeenth-century polyphony was really excellent, with an authentic intonation drawn from recent researches into "early" music. Unfortunately, the choristers' clerical musical director had rather less creditably abandoned some of the twentieth century's conventions about conducting. During the sacred performance he actually clicked his fingers to signify the beat and scurried between a music stand and the chamber-organ console with the air of a demented bluebottle. Whenever he struck cords from the keyboard, the music tipped up from its stand and fell down upon his hands. The ludicrous effect was not helped by the presence of the Sistine Chapel Choir (colloquially known to English-speaking visitors to 1980s Rome as the Sistine Squealers), who blasted their way through the plainsong as if it had been composed by Verdi.

During the Enlightenment, opera proper was an ornament of Carnival, the wild preparation for the austerities of the Lenten fast. Rospigliosi's *Chi soffre speri* formed the highlight of the 1639 Carnival, and each year brought its new works to tickle the public taste. Although *opera seria*, massively conceived mythological or historical pieces with a string of arias to libretti by Metastasio and his like, formed the staple of princely entertainment, the controlling feature in popular works was comedy. *Opera Buffa*, with characters taken from the earlier *comedia dell'arte* traditions, abounded. Perhaps the best known late example of this *buffo* tradition was the first production of Giacomo Rossini's *Il Barbiere di Siviglia* at Rome's Teatro Argentina in 1815. Ironically, like so many other operatic masterpieces, it did not succeed with its first audience, and Rossini had to take it to a carnival audience more familiar with his work, that of San Carlo in Naples, to get the reception which the piece so richly deserved.

Rome's operatic life has not always been happy. Although it has hosted other notable premieres such as that of Giuseppe Verdi's *Il Trovatore*, the strict papal censorship exercised right up until 1870 ruled out many plots suitable for opera. Verdi himself had planned *Un Ballo in Maschera* for Rome, but the subject of a successful plan to assassinate a monarch proved impossible for the clerical censor. Strangely, Rome's opera house does not live up to expectations, even though I write as one who has attended many enjoyable performances there. In his novel *Other Lulus*, Philip Hensher records his own impressions of a trip we made together to Il Teatro dell'Opera, while attributing them to his heroine, Freidericke:

> I asked Charlotte about Archy and this is what she told me... He was a very great singer who had performed at Covent Garden, which was an opera house in England... Despite frequent telephone calls from the great opera houses of Milan and New York and San Francisco and Paris and Berlin and Rome... he gave the whole thing up to create singers greater even than himself. I think that Charlotte got this bit slightly wrong, as I had been to the opera in Rome and it was not a great opera house, but a theatre filled with ladies in furs singing along to Bulgarian Sopranos in Madame Butterfly.

Rome's opera has had managerial shortcomings to match its shaky artistic standards. A victim of the parties' unofficial state colonization scheme, *lottizzazione*, its control was handed in 1991 to a nominee of the Christian Democrats, Giancarlo Cresci. During a brief but "creative" two years as *Intendant*, Cresci bankrupted the theater, which previously had enjoyed a small but happy annual profit. Paying hugely inflated fees to star singers, and commissioning exorbitantly priced uniforms for the front of house staff, he had hoped to raise the house's international profile. It was a lost cause, and it has been a slow road toward recovering even its former modest standards for his dedicated and commonsensical successors. For the dawn of the millennium the baton was to have been wielded by the artistic director, Giuseppe Sinopoli, whose taste for the German Romantic repertoire promised to convert the Romans into Wagnerians. The moderating influence of the General Manager, *Sovrintendente* Francesco Ernani proved too much for the Maestro, however, who resigned even before starting work. This might ensure that the paying public gets the Verdi it wants. With a name like his, Ernani ought to insist upon it—not everyone has an opera named after him!

Rome has frequently dedicated itself to lost causes. Look at the Stuarts and the Jacobite Court during the eighteenth century. Long after they had been given up by the principal Catholic powers of Europe, France, and Spain, the popes continued to award them dignities, shelter, and sometimes even money. There is, of course, something strikingly noble about such loyalty. The younger of the two Jacobite heirs, Henry, (the one preferred when observed by Horace Walpole, visiting in the 1740s) came in due time to be made a cardinal, and ultimately Cardinal Dean of the Sacred College and Bishop of Ostia. The Cardinal Duke of York even had his chance at the papacy itself, but like Cardinal Wolsey before him, political problems stemming from England denied him the Church's highest office. After the death of James III in 1766, even the papacy began to temporize. Bonnie Prince Charlie had never returned to his father's court after the tragic fiasco of the '45 Rebellion. But when he did reappear in Rome, styling himself Charles III, the pope refused to give him royal recognition. Only his brother, Henry, made the ceremonial point of waiting for him in his carriage at the first milestone on the Flaminian Way. Fat, gross in conversation and manners, the not so Young Pretender died virtually friendless in the Palazzo Mutti in 1788, nursed only by his natural daughter, the Countess of Albany. The Royal Arms had been removed by order of Clement XIII (1758–69) long before.

The touching pendant to the whole story, however, is that the Hanoverian George IV provided a handsome pension to Cardinal Henry Stuart following the catastrophe of the Napoleonic occupations of Rome. The vastly wealthy prelate had been stripped to the bone by the revolutionaries and accepted the old enemy's generosity, driven to it by the acquisitive thoroughness of the new. He died in 1807, and it was Pius VII who commissioned the Stuart Monument in St. Peter's from Canova. This same victim of Napoleon's egoism also received the princely exiles of the House of Bonaparte to Rome with characteristic gentle open-handedness. The nineteenth-century royal pretenders fared better than their eighteenth-century predecessors, however, as Napoleon III was ultimately to regain his uncle's crown. The Stuarts had been destined to enjoy only a prolonged "Roman Holiday." Perhaps they could take some comfort in its providing the best education the world can offer.

CHAPTER ELEVEN

Nineteenth-Century

Visitors:

Babington's Tea Rooms

"I am young, beautiful and live in Rome; dear Mr. Proust, what does your book mean?"
Female American Correspondent of Marcel Proust

If we view this book as a series of conversations which, if I was fortunate enough to meet you, dear reader, we might enjoy during the course of a single Roman day, I've permitted us to get quite a long way through our time together with very few references to food. This, I have to admit, and as my friends would surely tell you, is out of character. I am what the Romans call *una buona forchetta*, "a good fork"; that is, I like my food. In fact, since we are a good deal further along than halfway, we seem to have missed a lunch stop altogether. Since the last chapter is going to focus on my own particular favorite restaurant and the period since its establishment in the 1950s and the present day, I propose that we *cenare*, dine, as our closing activities, and at the same time take our *pranzo*, lunch, retrospectively.

This scheme of things suits my palate, since had we followed our chronology and got stuck with ancient Roman food early on, we would have been lacking all sorts of good things to eat. No tomatoes, turkey, or potatoes, deriving from South America; no aubergines (eggplant), rice or pasta, these being introduced by the Saracens and Marco Polo (by tradition) much later; no refined sugar products. Yes, we could have enjoyed most of the salads and all the combinations of beans and pulses with garlic and onions that still form a significant and delicious part of the Italian diet. But even I would have balked at sucking pig or larks' tongues in aspic and honey for breakfast. Then again, perhaps not...

As a student I prided myself on having learned all the Latin vocabulary for the various kinds of lettuce that appear in Virgil's *Georgics*; my favorite was *intiba*, endive, which actually came up in the exam, although I've yet to meet it in a Roman salad bowl. There again, if we had been faced with all the roast meat that graced a medieval table, I think the majority of us would have had the reaction I first experienced together with a group of friends, having ordered a Florentine steak when all other *carne* was "off." As far as I am concerned, this particular cut can stay by the Arno and away from the banks of the Tiber. It was a little bit too much like being introduced to the cow.

So what sort of refreshment at this late afternoon hour (which Chapter Eleven represents) might we take? Though I'd love to be able to pretend that I could ever be thoroughly integrated into the Italian way of living, I know that I should fail instantly on one major count at least: I could never give up tea entirely for coffee. I've never liked milky coffee, and so the banishing of the *cappuccino* and *caffè latte* that takes place in Rome after 10:30 AM has never been a hardship. *Espresso*, known simply as *un caffè*, has always provided my mid-morning stimulant. But I'm afraid to say that whatever other recommendations Roman bars possess (there are many, my favorite being *tramezzini*, sandwiches), they singularly lack the know-how to prepare a reasonable cup of tea. A single Lipton tea bag served alongside a tiny pot of lukewarm water for the patron to dunk personally is never going to supply the cup that cheers. Now, I can't judge for you, but *I'm* ready for a proper cup of tea.

Babington's Tea Rooms occupy just about the prime position in what used to be the old English quarter of Rome, the Pincio side of Piazza di Spagna. Though it would be wildly pretentious to make any claims these days for there still being a recognizable *quartiere*, the frail shadows of the myriad British gentlewomen and men who passed their winter seasons here or settled as more established expatriates during the nineteenth century are cast exceedingly long. The Pensione Smith, at 93 Piazza di Spagna and run by that ideal of quiet respectability, three spinster ladies, gave lodging to many of these. It would have been here that Charlotte Bartlett and Lucy Honeychurch fled from a Fiesolean kiss in E. M. Forster's *Room with a View*, although, like Duncan Fallowell after him, Forster declines to give us "his" Rome. Tangentially, the actor Julian Sands, who appeared to advantage in the hugely popular Merchant Ivory film of the book, was often a worshipper at the nearby English church of All Saints during the flowering of his subsequent Italian movie career.

The continuing presence just across the piazza of the British legation to the Holy See (only raised to full embassy status as a result of John Paul II's visit to Britain in 1982) and the Keats House on the opposite side of the Spanish Steps are testimony to a tradition dating back to the arrival here of the eighteenth-century traveling carriages that had carried their passengers, road-weary and dusty, all the way from Calais. The Landmark Trust of English Heritage owns a flat for rent above the Keats-Shelley Library, and though exceptionally atmospheric both for lovers of Romantic poetry and those with a taste for an archaeological tourist tradition, I wouldn't recommend a stay there except in the coldest, wettest months. First, this would correspond to Keats' own brief stay (November to February 1820–21). Second, it is the only time of year that can be sure to restrict student partying *lungolanotte* on the steps, beloved of "youth culture," beneath. A Rutelli notice proclaims that there should be no demonstrations or noise on the steps between midnight and 3 AM; personally, I am not convinced that this would guarantee a quiet night's sleep.

The Archaeology of Tea Time

There had been facilities specifically aimed at an English clientele since the middle of the eighteenth century. The *Caffè degli Inglesi* just off Piazza di Spagna was the accustomed haunt of the students and jobbing artists who clustered around there looking for patrons. It was described by one of them, Thomas Jones, in 1766:

> *The English coffee house, a filthy vaulted room, the walls of which were painted with sphinxes, obelisks and pyramids, from capricious designs of Piranesi, and fitter to adorn the inside of an Egyptian sepulchre, than a room of social conversation. Here seated around a brazier of hot embers placed in the center, we endeavored to amuse ourselves for an hour or two over a cup of coffee or glass of punch, and then grope our way home darkling, in solitude and silence.*

Although I don't think the description actually counts as an advertisement for the place, it does express some of the expatriate's grudging loyalty to what has become familiar.

For most of the nineteenth century it was the Caffè Greco on Via Condotti which claimed the loyalty of the visiting and resident artists. Byron had established himself at a favorite seat there during his relatively short stay in 1817, while Liszt, Goethe, and Wagner were the German tokens of its abiding popularity with visitors from immediately north of the Alps. One visitor in the middle of the century complained that the Greco was always full of artists and German tobacco! The Nazarene School of German painters, devoted to a Canovan neoclassicism and rather insipid religious subjects, were Rome's gift to the fussy drawing rooms of *Biedermeier* Vienna and Munich. H. V. Morton was able to make the claim in 1960 that you could get excellent tea at the Greco, a memorial to its cosmopolitan past. It certainly hasn't been true in the twenty years I've been coming to Rome. For my generation there has been no choice but Babington's.

The English Tea Rooms were founded in 1893 by Miss Anna Maria Babington, a collateral descendant of the Catholic noble who planned to assassinate Elizabeth I and replace her with Mary Stuart. Working with a friend, Isabel Cargill, they started in Via dei due Macelli and soon had another establishment near St. Peter's. It was in 1894, however, that their definitive premises were acquired in the very heart of the English Quarter, and there they have remained, even through the months of Rome's Nazi occupation. An English-language journal of the time was full of the commodious accommodation, gas lighting, reading room, and other conveniences provided by the two maiden ladies. It also comments upon the "modicity of the prices charged." In this particular, everything has changed. Babington's is ridiculously expensive. But what do you get for your money? And is it worth it? Answering the second question first, I would reply that in certain circumstances it is, and explain myself by going on to answer the first question.

The room is high-ceilinged (it was once the carriage floor of the whole Palazzo) and dark; the shuttered and curtained windows remove any sense of your being in the throbbing, and in summer boiling, heart of modern tourist Rome. Discrete, but effective modern air-conditioning compliments the traditionally cool environment. There is a cumbersome cake counter near the door, the wares of which glumly defy you to consider them appetizing; but this is nothing but a ruse. My experience has always been that a Roman *pasta* or cake proves to be tasty in precise inverse proportion to how good it looks. These sludgy-looking offerings taste divine. A small, middle-aged woman in a neat cotton uniform shows you to a table, and you sit on rush-seated chairs. The decorative scheme was originally Japanese, and some small screens and decorative fans still hint at it; but the underwhelming impression is of wide expanses of polished wood and subtle gray-green paintwork. The menu presents you with a wide selection of teas, and a variety of what I think a properly English village tea room would describe coyly as "savouries." You can personally go to choose a cake; remember to go for the ugliest.

The tea itself used to come in low-slung green pottery, but these nods in the decorative direction of Nagasaki have been succeeded by silver plated Sheffield ware, with tiny cats as the crowning lid-handles. Frequently, an example of the live variety, sleeker and better fed than most Roman felines, stretches on top of a radiator shelf (the premises are accommodatingly warm in winter). There is always a hot water jug as well as the teapot itself, and lemon *and* milk are served as a matter of course. The customers can also be diverting. The last time I went, I had two French couples of a certain age sitting on my right, and a very elderly aristocratic-looking Italian woman eating her solitary Welsh rarebit on my left. The conjunction led me to reflect how much more glamorously French women age than their Italian cousins. They abandon the revealing recklessness of their youth, and assume filmy and soft-edged clothing and make-up, while Italian women persist in their sometimes aggressive *décolletage*. The bird-like *Contessa* on my left, clothed in a sleeveless and simply too red dress, still sported jet black hair in an uncompromisingly hat-like arrangement, although she must have been nearer ninety than eighty. When she left, after much dabbing with a napkin and the prolonged use of a powder compact, she grasped her bag and umbrella (as it was August, could it have been a sun-shade?) with the determination of one who has to summon up reserves of energy even to complete the simplest and most regular of habits. This tea at Babington's looked like a ritual she was set on preserving, and I admired her for it.

Morton still found tea here reasonably priced in his 1950s visits leading to the publication of *A Traveller in Rome* in 1960. He did, however, have a very respectably middle-class traveler's memory reaching back to the 1920s, and was more accustomed to the increasingly costly administration of servants at home and in public than most people are in the current century. He catches the tone of the place and its oddly overlapping contacts with different periods nicely, although I have some doubts as to the accuracy of his description of "modern" clothing:

> *Babington's has been preserved to make tea in a world so different from that of 1893. It is doubtful whether Miss Babington would have approved of the modern tourist in their open-necked shirts and chromatic Miami beach jumpers who go there these days. You will often notice little groups of contesse and marchesi taking tea together and speaking the English taught them by those great ambassadors of England, the English governesses. The late King Alfonso of Spain liked tea and was a keen Babingtonite.*

Morton clearly was always dressed in a collar, tie, and tweed suit, and had a better eye for *marchesi* than "chromatic Miami beach jumpers."

According to Luigi Barzini the kind of British internationalism that Babington's represented was viewed as a kind of fetish for the Roman bourgeoisie of the inter-war years, who "lived their lives according to patterns of behavior borrowed from abroad": the French novel, English governesses, Swiss schools, American films. The mood is recreated perfectly in Alberto Moravia's novel *The Age of Indifference*, and more recently in Franco Zeffirelli's sentimental, but still hugely enjoyable, autobiographical film *Tea with Mussolini*.

American Arrivals

If the seventeenth and eighteenth centuries had been the occasion for the leisured classes of the Old World to make their *giro d'Italia* with its almost obligatory wintering in Rome, then the nineteenth century was to allow a turn to their social equivalents from across the Atlantic. Americans certainly got a head start on their British cousins in the first years of the new century, as the still fledgling United States remained neutral in the Napoleonic Wars. It was only in the later years of the century, however, that Rome might be said to have developed an American quarter to rank alongside the English, taking advantage of the post-Unification expansion of the city. It was further up the Pincio and Esquiline and the valley that divides them, following more or less closely the line of the present Via Vittorio Veneto, where the US Embassy can still be found. Most notable among those who stayed on was the sculptor William Wentmore Story, the author of one of nineteenth-century Rome's most iconic of contributions to travel literature, *Roba di Roma*. He lived, with his family and ever-growing guest list, according to national type regarding location, taking for many years a large apartment within the Palazzo Barberini. It was here that he entertained on a grand scale such European luminaries as the Brownings, Hans Christian Anderson, and Edward Lear. Nathaniel Hawthorne visited the Roman colony of his compatriots after his stint as American consul in Liverpool, and his novel *The Marble Faun*, set in the city, became one of the favorite reads of his time. Among the single American women who could cause considerable scandal by insisting on liberties which had become acceptable stateside but still remained shocking in Rome, such as walking or indeed riding out alone(!), was Margaret Fuller, a friend of the Carlyles in London and an enthusiastic supporter of Mazzini, the Italian patriot. Her letters and journal of the winter 1848–49 provide an important source for foreign reactions to the political turmoil of the Year of Revolutions.

One of the most unusual American visitors to Rome at this time was the repudiated wife of Napoleon's brother Jérôme, Elizabeth Patterson. A Baltimore heiress, she had met the young Bonaparte after he had been serving a term in the US navy. Her brother-in-law, the French emperor, would have none of the marriage in spite of a son being born, and it was only after Napoleon was banished to St. Helena that she appeared in Rome among the exiled remains of the imperial dynasty. Princess Pauline Borghese, the emperor's devoted sister, immortalized by Canova's naked statue of her as Venus, received her kindly, and Napoleon's mother, Madame Mère, made a space for her at the family table in Palazzo Buonaparte, crowded with ex-kings and even a cardinal (Napoleon's uncle, Fesch). Elizabeth Patterson left Rome in the middle years of the century to settle, a rich miserly old woman, in the Baltimore of her birth. A line of American Bonapartes stretched into the mid-twentieth century, a descendant being made attorney general under Teddy Roosevelt.

Despite the ups and downs of the House of Bonaparte, France herself, though only temporarily annexing the whole Papal State (1809–14) under the rather spurious title of the Italian Republic (with

Napoleon as President), managed to gain permanent possession of two fabulous, and fabulously sited, Roman buildings. The Palazzo Farnese had been the French Embassy since 1635, but during the eighteenth century's games of political winner-takes-all had been used by the Neapolitan Bourbons as their principal residence in Rome. The Bonapartists reclaimed it and, when forced to return property commandeered during the wars, kept their gain by swapping it for a suitably grand *hôtel* in Paris.

Also from 1802, the French government had instituted the Académie Française in the villa built in 1540 for Cardinal Ricci, but universally known as the Villa Medici, since it had been occupied by Ferdinando and Cardinal Alessandro dei Medici in the late sixteenth century. Here, artists designated as winners of the *prix de Rome* have been housed, engaging themselves with whichever plastic art has so distinguished them. At first restricted to painting, sculpture, architecture, engraving, or music, and presided over by such dominating talents as Ingres, the list now includes dress-design and cooking. The villa, like Palazzo Farnese, has recently undergone a lengthy period of restoration. Its magnificent garden-front, covered in antique statues and bas-reliefs, is now returned to its pristine grandeur. Yet more needs to be done internally to make a visit rewarding than to trot out the rag-bag of pieces produced by the 1999 prize winners. Dwarfed and in some cases imprisoned in the cavernous rooms of the lower floors, some of these works were difficult to distinguish from the builders' rubbish which, accumulating during the restoration, surrounded them. I suspect that this was intentional, adding the necessary post-modern gloss on the vanity of the millennium, but it was a peculiarly dismal experience all the same.

Literary Giants

British tourism was almost completely suspended between 1797 and 1814, but after the Hundred Days of Napoleon's return and Waterloo (which fell rather considerably between the Roman Winter seasons of 1814–15 and 1815–16), it was once again the fashion to head off to Italy. William Makepeace Thackeray indicates as much in *Vanity Fair* by sending Becky Sharpe and Captain Crawley to Rome in the wake of her triumph in Brussels and his unexpected return from the field of battle. Thackeray himself followed his characters' example later in the century. The advantages which now opened in Rome for those who though of gentle birth had insufficient incomes to live comfortably at home is exemplified by this literary arrival. And whereas the two preceding centuries had attracted painters to Rome, the predominating flavor of the well-known "arty types" who came in the nineteenth century was literary. The opinions these visitors expressed were not, however, always to Rome's advantage.

As well as Thackeray with his two motherless daughters came the whole Dickens family, traveling together in a gargantuan coach. This colossus of British fiction in the making was decidedly unimpressed with what he saw, likening the city to London in its picturesque points and disparaging it for lack of modern conveniences. A little later in the 1830s Lord Thomas Babington Macaulay (another distant connection of the Elizabethan plotter and thence the Tea Shop) set the tone for British historians and critics by being disgusted by the behavior of Italian officials on the road. William Hazlitt joined him in voicing negative opinions, and as if to complete the Trinity itself, John Ruskin, too, rejected Rome's attractions for his celebrated advocacy of Venice. In this sense, he proved the exception to the nineteenth-century expatriate rule of awarding the palm of preference: the English visitors always made a choice between Florence and Rome, the Americans between Venice and Florence. Robert Browning and Elizabeth Barrett were here, as we have seen, intimates of William Wentmore Story's household, the American exception to the same rule. Robert encouraged Story's writing, just as his host praised Browning's models in clay. Even so, it is his literary portraiture that has endured. Although Ferrara is the city which best recalls *My Last Duchess* (1842), Rome must delight in being the scene for the mono-drama *The Bishop Orders his Tomb*. Although set in S. Prassede on the Viminal, the tombs described best seem to fit those in the first chapels of S. Maria del Popolo, conveniently close to the Piazza di Spagna and the English Quarter; no Babington's yet, but plenty of other sources of tea.

In fact, Babington's did appear specifically in response to what was thought of as an opening in the market. The year 1893 was one of some considerable distinction among Roman society (although that really should be "societies"). The papal court celebrated the Jubilee of Leo XIII's episcopacy still firmly and exclusively behind the walls of the Vatican, while the Quirinal and its royal inhabitants marked the silver wedding of King Umberto and Queen Margherita. It was getting on to 25 years since the city had been incorporated in the Kingdom of Italy, and how much the city had changed in so short a space of time.

Only fifty years before, the reactionary Pope Gregory XVI (1831–46) was rapidly burning up the last political capital deriving from the Congress of Vienna and the post-Napoleonic conservative restorations. Supported throughout his reign by the force of Austrian arms, this narrow-minded monk from Venetia forbade the construction of the telegraph or railways in the Papal States, referring to the latter, whether with conscious or unconscious wit, as *chemins d'enfers*. Though pressed, even by his political supporters abroad, he refused to listen to calls at home for limited representation in assemblies or indeed the appointment of laymen to positions of direct authority. His Rome was that which was constantly described as dirty, dark, and squalid, where the impoverishment of the peasantry was at times medieval, and in which Jews were still confined to the Ghetto and forced to wear distinctive clothing. The political atmosphere was close and suffocating, with the numerous secret societies supporting spies, *sbirri*, and double-agents everywhere, in Rome and abroad. It was the real world of Giuseppe Mazzini, political exile and ideologue of the *Risorgimento*, and the fictional one of Wilkie Collins' Count Fosco, the evil genius of *The Woman in White* (1860).

Although unshakable, Gregory's was to be the last-ditch defense of a system that simply could not survive. He was succeeded by a young man (for a pope), just past his 54th birthday, Giovanni Maria Mastai-Ferretti, who reigned as Pius IX. A reputed liberal in that he supported moderate changes to the administration of the Papal States and showed some limited sympathy with the growing aspirations for Italian unity, his election and proclamation of a political amnesty were received ecstatically in the capital. He was feted as he drove in his open coach, and countless children were held out to him for a blessing. How quick things were to be reversed, however, in 1848. George Macaulay

Trevelyan in his romping good read, *Garibaldi's Defence of the Roman Republic,* has but faint praise for him:

> *All that Pio Nono could contribute to the solution of the impossible problem was a stock of mild benevolence toward everybody, which was not completely exhausted until he had been some two years on his uneasy throne.*

Brave Days

From the date of his flight from Rome to the Kingdom of Naples, the Romans attributed the evil eye to poor *Pio Nono*, and after his restoration turned their backs as he passed in a closed carriage. He had finally taken fright in November 1848 after the assassination of his moderate, but still anti-democratic, chief minister Rossi, as he went to the opening of the new chamber of deputies housed in the Palazzo Cancellaria. By February 1849, Garibaldi was in Rome as a leader of irregular troops and deputy for Macerata, followed, after his naturalization by the Roman Assembly, by Mazzini in March. The short-lived but heroic Roman Republic of 1848–49 was born.

Mazzini himself, with the typically strange mixture of religious mysticism and political level-headedness that stayed with him throughout the long years of exile, wrote of his entry into Rome:

> *I entered the city one evening with a deep sense of awe, almost of worship. Rome was to me as, in spite of her present degradation she still is, the Temple of Humanity. From Rome will one day spring the religious transformation destined for the third time to bestow moral unity upon Europe. As I passed through the Porta del Popolo, I felt an electric thrill run through me—a spring of new life.*

And although he, Garibaldi and others in the city continued to "act like men who have the enemy at their gates, and at the same time like men who are working for eternity" (Mazzini in the Assembly), even these political dreamers knew that they were doomed. The combined military might of Naples, Austria, and France was leveled at them, and there was almost a competition between the Powers to see who might be first to topple the revolutionaries and return the pope. The cruelest cut came when it ultimately proved to be that home of liberty, France, under President Louis Napoleon and General Oudinot. The fighting in and around the city during May and June 1849 has left many retrospective monuments, especially on the Janiculum, as the successfully united Italy celebrated its history twenty years later.

During the Republic many expatriates left the city, some from political sympathy to the authoritarian rule of the papacy, others simply concerned for their own skin. The Brownings, though eager for Italian unity, observed proceedings from the relatively peaceable distance of Florence; William Story and Margaret Fuller remained in the city and lent moral and some physical support to its defense. Miss Fuller went daily to the hospitals to comfort the wounded and wrote:

The Palace of the Pope on the Quirinal is now used for convalescents. In those beautiful gardens I walk with them—one with his sling, the other with his crutch... A day or two since we sat in the Pope's little pavilion, where he used to give private audience. The sun was going gloriously down over Monte Mario, where gleamed the white tents of the French light horse among the trees... It was a beautiful hour, stolen from the midst of ruin and sorrow; and tales were told as full of grace and pathos as in the gardens of Boccaccio, only in a very different spirit—with noble hope for man, with reverence for women.

Rome fell to the French on June 30, 1849. Mazzini returned secretively to exile in London ("Italy is my country, but England is my real home, if I have any"), and Garibaldi left with his heroic two battalions to make the mighty retreat through central Italy to the neutral territory of San Marino and the Adriatic Coast beyond. The pope returned from Gaeta across the border in Naples, and a more repressive regime, backed by the French, was instituted. The Republicans had been wildly romantic, and occasionally brutal. Even as hardened a Garibaldian as G. M. Trevelyan finds himself struggling to justify the assassination of Rossi, who was at heart an honorable, liberal-minded reformer. It is no surprise that clerical reactionaries such as P.J. Chandlery were to memorialize their losses too:

The piazza of S. Maria in Trastevere was the scene of the massacre of several priests by Mazzinian soldiers in the revolution of 1849. A human fiend, named Callimacho Zambianchi, presided over this deed of blood... Their only crime was their priesthood; no other charge was brought against them, and even the show of a trial was dispensed with.

However, Chandlery reserves his bitterest outcry for the desecration of the church of S. Pancrazio by the defenders of the siege:

> They broke and profaned the sacred altars and monuments of the saints, desecrated the shrines, tore to shreds the sacred vestments, and covered the walls with blasphemous inscriptions, vile caricatures and indecent sketches... Such disgusting outrages sent a thrill of horror throughout Europe, and caused intense pain to Catholics all over the world. These fiends of the 19th Century were far more brutal than the barbarians of old, more impious than the pagans, for the pagans had respected the Christian tombs as sacred and inviolate.

Pius IX himself never came to terms with the loss of temporal power in Italy, even if his assumption of doctrinal and moral infallibility following the First Vatican Council might be assumed to have been some consolation. His words addressed to Italy on the occasion of his Jubilee (1873) carry the strong import of a wronged man:

> I bless Italy, but I do not bless the usurpers of the Church, the enemies of God! I do not bless the spoilers of her churches, those who lead scandalous lives, the profaners of holy images; no, I cannot bless either these sacrilegious wretches, or those who take little or no care to keep such within the bounds of duty. I bless Italy, not those who oppress it; I bless Italy, not those who lead it astray.

Needless to say, P. J. Chandlery did not stay long on the Janiculum to admire the statues of the heroes of the *Risorgimento*.

Marcel Proust, it may be recalled, found inspiration and remembrance in a cup of herbal tea, although the exact implications of so doing remained opaque, even to some residents of Rome (see chapter epigram). Although I like the odd *tisane*, give me the old British cuppa any day. Babington's takes me to a place where the anxieties of both the present and the past seem distant and trivial. People who have known Rome for many years (that usually means thirty) always seem to be telling you that it has changed, that it isn't the place it used to be. No doubt I'll be doing the same too, when I chalk up the requisite score. If it is ironic that Babington's expensive haven now comes at the pleasure of its Japanese owners, rather than from the direct commercial descendants of Misses Cargill and Babington, I am not going to make any complaints. When the tea rooms were founded, Japan was still more a place to inspire chic decor than supply political or industrial competition. The world, even the Roman world, in which we now live is a foreign, though in many ways better, place.

CHAPTER TWELVE

Unified Italy: Palazzo della Rinascente

"If fashion dictates that a skirt be long, no guillotine can shorten it."
Mussolini's advice to Hitler on how to deal with a Parisian couturier

On March 5, 1998 the London *Times* reported the extent to which secular values had successfully invaded the Roman religious enclosure. Wafers used in the celebration of mass have been made for centuries by nuns, as part of the fruit of their prayerful industriousness. A European Union directive had finally caught up with this niche product and specific market by insisting that in future the communion wafers display sell-by-dates. L'Avvenire, the popular Roman weekly, held up its worldly hands in a pantomime of sacrilegious outrage: "It seems nothing is sacred anymore where European regulations are concerned, not even the body and blood of Christ."

The degree to which Italian public institutions, including the press and increasingly the electronic media, have stepped over lines set by the Church in the last century or so illustrates most succinctly the passage of Rome from religious capital of the world to seat of government in a modern state. The fact that Rome surely still represents the highest *per capita* consumption of communion wafers worldwide only goes to underline that the religious life of the city is now often paradoxically a reflection of its secular counterpart.

Modern Rome, it sometimes seems, is a monument to consumerism. Very few of its nearly three million people work in manufacturing industry, perhaps ten percent at most. Over half work in the state bureaucracy of national and local government and its administration. This does not imply, however, that they are unable to contribute to the local economy. Many civil service posts operate on extremely short hours and leave their holders time to occupy themselves with family businesses in the afternoon and evening. The service industries of shops, hotels, bars, and restaurants depend upon this totally respectable "moon-lighting." But even this burgeoning tertiary sector cannot hide the fact that Rome is heavily dependent upon the industrial zones of the country, particularly the northern towns, for what it remains frantic to buy. In the same way, it looks to the agricultural regions of the center and south to provide the food it devours. So much, it appears, is shipped into the capital; so little flows out.

This phenomenon of a dependent, luxurious city, kept by its hardworking, if somewhat rustic, neighbors, is a common theme in criticism of Rome down the centuries. Even the European Union, acting like a beneficent relation has been open to the charge of having "spoiled" Rome, its favorite child. The effect of European legislation has had some amusing outcomes within the city. The system of subsidies developed by the Common Agricultural Policy encouraged one enterprising Roman to go into cattle farming. His herd, large enough to generate an annual subsidy of over $1.5 million, was officially housed in his own fifth-floor apartment near the Piazza Navona. No doubt he took his cows out daily to be watered at the Fountain of the Four Rivers and milked them in the back room of the Tre Scalini bar. It's a shame no one ever saw him while spooning up the best *tartufi* ice creams in Rome.

On a shopping tour of modern Rome you are, in fact, more likely to meet with cats than with cows. Providing there's a bit of sun and a little shade, and also the visitation of a shabby old lady to leave messes of butcher's scraps bursting from greasy papers, Rome's cats, *i gatti di Roma*, are ready to pose for the photographic calendar dedicated to them each year. Just over a century ago, however, your shopping would perhaps have taken you to a farm within the walls of the city, or a market nearby, giving plenty of opportunities for bovine encounters. The *rus in urbe*, countryside in town, character of pre-Unification Rome was one of its principal delights for those of its residents who prized charm above modern utility. The Roman Forum itself had for centuries been known as the *campo vaccino*, the cattle pasture, until during the French occupation of the early 1800s systematic archaeological excavations were initiated, and a field was turned into a series of small walls and cracked pavements. There were dairies, vineyards, and vegetable plots all over the city, but especially on the slopes of the Viminal, Caelian, and Oppian hills. And suitably enough, it is only now in one of these quarters that a ghost of this former atmosphere can be sensed. On the Caelian, with its still extensive monastic sites and larger villas, trees and gardens proliferate and, yes, there is still the odd vineyard. Walking down to the Porta San Giovanni or Porta San Sebastiano can give you a hint of Augustus Hare's rural rambles within the walls; but you'll have to dodge the cars that tear up and down the deep-set lanes with no respect for the spell they are breaking.

Immediately before the Unification of Italy (1860–71), the myth of countless clerics and religious being wantonly supported by the papal government at the cost of ever increasing taxation was a tool frequently employed by the demagogues of the *Risorgimento*. The peasant farmers of Umbria and the manufacturers of the Romagna rallied to the call to strip the city of her unearned wealth. The loss by simple annexation of the larger part of the Papal States on November 4, 1860 to the newly created Kingdom of Italy was a crushing blow to the city's economy. If the town was already shabby at the beginning of Pius IX's reign, it was to be in virtual ruins when the Italian troops, under the leadership of General Raffaele Cadorna, finally burst through the walls near the Porta Pia on the morning of September 20, 1870. The City of the Popes was gone forever; the thoroughgoing secularization of Rome was a task just started.

A Modern Capital

The first capital of Unified Italy was Turin, but Count Camillo Cavour, the political architect of the *Risorgimento*, knew that the rest of the peninsula would not put up with such a clear sign of Savoyard colonialism for long. He failed, however, to persuade his monarch, Victor Emmanuel II of Sardinia, that henceforth he ought really to renumber himself "the First," since he was now the king of a new country. Florence provided the intermediate seat of government, causing turmoil in that relatively constricted city for the few years of the ministries' sojourn. The arrival of national government in an "empty" Rome generated the same kind of boom, especially in the construction industry, which a decade before had bankrupted Vienna during the wholesale expansion of its cityscape. In ninety years the population of Rome increased tenfold. Some of the old established Roman landowners suffered in this speculative free-for-all to provide the necessary accommodation; the Borghese family lost their massive park and villa as the bottom eventually, and it seems inevitably, fell out of the market.

The principal monuments to the building boom are now to be found in the apartment blocks of the Prati district near St. Peter's, and the Umbertine city epitomized by the long drag of the Via Nazionale. It is possible that the institutionalized anti-clericalism of the period is represented by the design of the streets in the Prati. As their name implies, these were formerly unencumbered meadows by the Tiber, and so could have been the site for any preferred planning scheme. The one that was chosen permits no monumental, in fact, not even the most discrete vista of St. Peter's and the Vatican from its streets. This may, however, simply reflect the established urban environment in which no view was presented from the medieval Borgo. The fact can still be something of a puzzle, though, to those who arrive as tourists at the Ottaviano Metro station (the official name of which has only recently acquired the prefix, San Pietro). Those unfamiliar with the area have to follow their noses or struggle with unwieldy maps to find the largest church in the world hidden within the labyrinth of nineteenth-century high-rises. This considerable task was made even more complex, and worthy of congratulation if successful, during the complete closure for re-paving of Piazza Risorgimento during the summer of 1999. The temporary signs pointing to the basilica seemed to direct you in every conceivable direction simultaneously. Among the few to profit from this arrangement were the more obvious cafés and restaurants, already notorious in this district for their high prices and poor quality, which acquired a larger number of victims in the shape of exhausted and disillusioned tourists, foiled in their attempt to see what they had come to see.

Before Unification, papal government had most recently been housed in the immense Palazzo della Cancelleria, and so the secular authorities, in a conscious attempt to break with the past, looked for new premises in this town of a thousand palaces. The Palazzo Madama (named after Margherita, the illegitimate daughter of Emperor Charles V) near Piazza Navona was made the seat of the Senate, while the Chamber of Deputies was located in the Palazzo di Montecitorio, just off Piazza Colona. Designed by Bernini for the Ludovisi family in the middle of the seventeenth century, this palazzo was substantially altered in 1918 when it was given its red brick art-nouveau facade by Ernesto Basile, although it preserves the slightly concave plan of the *maestro*'s original. The most imposing of Rome's entirely new constructions for the Italian state was the so-called *Palazzaccio*, officially Il Palazzo di Giustizia. This vast and ugly building, constructed entirely of grotesquely ornamented travertine stone, housed the law courts until 1970, when it was found to be in serious danger of collapse. And so it provided another opportunity for the extensive repairs so beloved of party bosses and their scam-hungry clients. Channeling billions of public lire into a project that has never been completed, the "naughty" palace (for such is the implication of the suffix -*accio* added to give it its popular name) fittingly proved itself a source of regulated naughtiness. In the meantime, other accommodation has had to be expensively provided for the law courts in one of Rome's further flung quarters.

Although representative of the wide-scale changes brought by the Unification of Italy to Rome, it isn't the government palaces that best symbolize the secularization of the city for me. If you turn away to your right of the Palazzo di Montecitorio and leave to those inside the ponderous, slow-motion dog-fighting that is the character of Italian political rhetoric, head for the Corso and cross over carefully. There, just a little further in the direction of Piazza del Popolo, and on the corner with Via del Tritone, stands the shrine to Roman commercial values and the culture of consumerism, the Palazzo della Rinascente, a truly palatial department store.

Palatial Shopping

La Rinascente is the Harrods and, at the same time, Marks and Spencer's of Rome; its name simultaneously signifies bourgeois luxury and pedestrian good sense. In a town where shopping habits still largely reject the under-one-roof principle increasingly common elsewhere, it really is the only department store that can hold its head up among the best of the independent boutiques. Here on five floors (the basement housing *intimo per le donne* or lingerie; the fourth floor stocking ladies' fashions; perfumes and gentlemen come in between) you can find clothes reflecting the real trends of the inventive fashion houses outside, but at a price and quality that appeal to the Italian, and you could add, universal, pleasure in good value. Rivals in the big store market are spread quite thin in the town, and come in three guises: Standa, Upim, and Coin. None is as good as Rinascente for the clothes that form its staple. Standa (once called Standard, but changed at Mussolini's insistence in his drive to re-Italianize institutions tainted with foreign influences) is more directed toward household goods, of which it has a wide variety of reasonable products, and Coin is rather similar. Upim is on the whole the poor relation, its clothing and other goods being cheaper and perhaps just a little bit too cheerful (or somber) depending upon the prevailing trends.

One of the two flagships of the nationwide Rinascente empire (the other, naturally enough, is in Milan), the Rome store seems to have been created with someone like me in mind. It is quietly calm, cool and perfectly composed. Walking toward its stately bulk, with *rinascimento* flourishes, soaring arches and a loggia-like elevation, you could kid yourself that you are on your way to an engagement of considerable importance with a dignitary of some noble and ancient institution. If it's true that London railway stations have been mistaken for churches, then this shop could most certainly double as an archiepiscopal residence. On a hot day its air-conditioning comes as the more sedate equivalent of throwing yourself fully clothed into the nearby Trevi Fountain.

It's my belief that La Rinascente was created to satisfy the needs and taste of those who hate shopping. Unlike some of my friends, I don't like shopping, but I do like La Rinascente. The main reason for this is that whenever I go to buy something there, I find what I am looking for *and* I find it quickly. I've bought three different overcoats from Rinascente over the years, and the only reason I've had to buy three is the fact that the first two were successively stolen from British cloakrooms. I suspect this infuriating fact provides the best advertisement for the place that I could think of. Before you begin to suspect that I'm in receipt of some sort of bribe from the store (for example, a lifetime supply of coats), let me move on to my Rinascente reservations.

Although the fact that the store always seems sinisterly empty suits me and my aversion for shopping, I can't help wondering whether this consumer void points at a well-kept secret: that there are far better places to buy nice clothes even more cheaply. And that these places simply will not reveal themselves to the mere visitor or temporary resident. The area just off Via Arenula is a definite candidate for such shops. Then again, the shop assistants are not what I would call eager to please. They stand around somewhat vacantly, backing off from any intrusion upon your view of the perfectly color-graded racks of the very long socks (beloved of Italian men), ties and sweaters that form a material rainbow across the walls. Nor do they appear happy when having to process a credit card payment. I prefer this stand-offishness to any nod in the direction of deference, but it can be just a little unnerving.

The opposite service ethos is employed in the clerical tailors which, from time to time, I have used to make my cassocks. There, respect for the cloth is taken to such a level of abasement that making purchases becomes a trial of endurance. The story goes that one shop always grants a title of religious honor to its clients a station higher than the one they possess. And so the seminarist is flattered to be entitled, somewhat prematurely, *Reverenza*; the simple priest is addressed as *Monsignore*; the monsignor himself is given an Episcopal *Excelenza*; the bishop granted a cardinal's *Eminenza*; and the red robed cardinal awarded the pope's unique *Santità*. This leaves only one option open should the tailor receive an order in person from the pope: he has to be addressed as *il mio Dio Signore*—God Himself!

As I've already indicated, Romans themselves prefer to shop at small outlets, the smallest of these, I suppose, being the stall-holder in a market or at a street corner. Vegetable and meat markets spring up every day across the city, from the celebrated Campo dei Fiori to the almost unknown (try finding it in a hurry) Via di Tor Millina. The largest meat market is found in Piazza Vittorio Emanuele, not far from Termini, but it's worth making a detour or traveling across town if these things fascinate you or you are preparing a special dinner party. Should you have a taste for songbirds in season, this is where to stock up your skewers. *Edicole*, newsstands, are local institutions which earn lifetimes of patronage, as are the *Alimentari,* grocers, which lurk, like Aladdin's cave, behind a beaded curtain and a narrow frontage. Even the humblest lottery-ticket vendor on the Via Magna Grecia has his well-defined place in the scheme of things. In a hurry to buy a bus ticket from just such a vendor, I learned the value of patience. By permitting or even encouraging the garrulousness of such simple functionaries, you can assist in making even a tedious and menial job slightly more fulfilling. There is nothing worse for the human spirit than sitting at a checkout and simply being expected to perform actions in the way a machine would perform them. Rome has an unwritten law that honors its salespersons by protecting them from this fate worse than death. It can make for slower shopping than elsewhere, but it ensures a better life for the majority of people, a truly noble end. And now let me leave my sententious tendencies behind and pursue another consumerist Roman icon: the nun's underwear shop.

Why nuns need a special shop for the purchase of these items remains something of a mystery, and why their windows should so wantonly advertise that Tax Free Shopping is practiced might appear venal. All clerical and religious dress began as plain, ordinary clothes, also possessing some feature to identify the wearer as belonging to a particular order or ministry. Gradually, as fashions changed, habits remained retrogressive, until now the everyday clothes of the late Middle Ages have become entrenched as the traditional religious choice.

Undergarments are, however, another matter. At one of Rome's well-known religious stockists, nuns and priests are carefully funneled in opposite directions once through the door to avoid any embarrassment

on behalf of customers or staff when dealing with plain priestly jockey shorts or flesh-colored brassieres suitable for sisters. As strict observance as to wearing black has increasingly come to imply a priest's traditionalist stance in doctrine and other teachings of the Church, one student in my Roman days was considered so ultra-rigorist that he was suspected of wearing black underpants. No one dared to check.

Since Giorgio Armani was brought in to redesign the uniforms of the senior branch of the Italian police, the *carabinieri,* about ten years ago, perhaps someone should suggest a designer makeover for clerical dress. Vivian Westwood with her taste for post-modern glances at the past would perhaps be the traditionalists' choice, whereas the more flamboyant clergy might prefer Versace. In the meantime, we will have to put up with the sacred equivalent of Marks and Spencer's; at least that way we can ensure dependable, if somewhat unimaginative, foundation garments...

Village Mentalities

Local shops define the local character of the *rione,* or district, in which they are found. This division into districts of Rome is a very ancient one, and dates back to Augustus' principate, when he expanded the Republican quartering of the city into a system of fourteen *regiones*— eight within the walls, six outside. In his delightfully light and carefree account of his period as a British diplomat to the Republic, *Rome Sweet Rome,* Archibald Lyall writes amusingly of the individuality of the city's shops, whose particularities as far as stock is concerned mirrored the localism of districts in the late 1940s and 1950s:

> Since they are all government monopolies, salt, tobacco, playing cards, lighter flints and postage stamps are sold together in what is usually, except in smart districts, a general shop selling anything from toffy to toothpaste. It takes an old hand also to know exactly what you can get in a drogheria *which sells not drugs but groceries, condiments, household soap and so forth; a* profumeria *which sells perfumes, cosmetics and scented soaps; and a* farmacia *which is a chemist's shop proper but like our own, handles a number of sidelines such as deodorants. Some kinds of paper can be bought only in a* carteria *and others only in a* cartoleria. *For some reason* abbacchio,

the young lamb which is a Roman specialty and is so excellent roasted, is not to be bought in a butchers' shop but only at a poulterer's. Similarly liver, kidneys, brains and offal generally may be found only in a frattaglie *shop.*

The enduring identity of specific districts can still at times support the claim that modern Rome is a series of villages. Strongest and most

obvious in its particularities is Trastevere, where the accent is distinctly different from that used in other parts of the city (even harsher, more curt and more nasal). The inhabitants of Trastevere are traditionally supposed to be proud of their working-class history, and view themselves as the Romans *par excellence*; but both these qualifications are also claimed by the neighboring districts of Testaccio, just across the river, and the Borgo, further upstream near St. Peter's. A district likes to be able to point to a particular dish in its restaurants that comes from somewhere more specific than simply "Rome," and all like to be able to allude with pride to their local poets and dialect historians. Attractive modern monuments have been erected to a number of local bards in Trastevere. Meanwhile, a simple and unobtrusive plaque high up on a wall, noting that the greatest nineteenth-century Roman poet, Giacchino Belli, traced his origin to the tiny central *rione* of Sant'Eustachio, compliments the large statue in his memory just across the Ponte Garbaldi at the entrance to Trastevere proper. Few would realize that he was a "foreigner" in the district he best exemplifies.

In Alberto Moravia's short stories, characters have the ability to change their lives by changing the district in which they live, usually from one right across town, say from Prima Porta to Re di Roma (far north to southeast). This sort of shift implies a complete change in fortune, from miserable penury to comfortable employment, or vice versa, and from free and easy youth to responsible middle age. The different *rioni* also used to take on characteristics of specific personality according to their patron saints, their *feste* and associated foods. The Trionfale district at the foot of Monte Mario, for instance, would keep the (old) feast of St. Joseph on March 19 by the eating of *bignè*, deep-fried tubes of batter filled with confectioners' custard. The Nativity of John the Baptist (June 24), on the other hand, brought the delicacy of snails cooked in tomato sauce to the district around Viale Carlo Felice. Trastevere itself celebrated its festival on July 15 with the rather less objectionable (unless you are vegetarian) *porchetta*, spit-roast pork. This *festa's* name, *noialtri*, "us other lot," epitomizes the district's belief in its uniqueness.

Although these displays of localism are not as universal as they were, they are the treasure still guarded by the really old people you see in the city. It's worth remembering that Italians are the world's longest-lived people after the Japanese, and their store of communal memory is correspondingly large. Some start to say that there are no local distinctions anymore, since Trastevere and the like began to be fashionable and gentrified. It is true that smaller distinct communities like the tiny area centered on Via Frangipani near the Colosseum are in danger of losing their *alimentari* as the proprietor is nearing ninety and there is no obvious, nor even available, successor. But such worries are in a way groundless; Rome will continue to be diverse simply through the force of the individuality of its inhabitants and their desire to find roots even in the most unpromising soil.

Even if walking Rome's streets insures that you get the most complete sense of the ways in which the different localities of the city ripple with various smells, colors and atmosphere, a good way to get a reasonable taste of the immediately post-Unification suburbs is to board a tram. Dirtier than those in Vienna and Manchester, Rome's trams are more spacious and cleaner than their truly decrepit cousins in Lisbon. While riding them you can take in the long, wide streets of the Umbertine city at a slow enough pace to appreciate the grandeur of its tall buildings without tiring of their pomposity. My first tram ride was half of the line, which more or less traces a 180° circuit of the city just inside and at times well outside the Aurelian Wall, from Piazza Ostiense to the Gallery of Modern Art on Viale delle Belle Arti. You'd never want to trudge along the entire length of the drearily worthy streets named in honor of Queens Elena and Margherita, but they make quite a nostalgic jaunt on the suitably Umbertine trams.

Cemeteries

My object on this occasion was the city's main cemetery, Campo Verano. As it was on the Feast of All Souls' (November 2), I joined the thousands of Romans tending the graves of departed relatives with an appealing mixture of seriousness and festivity. Large bunches of bronze chrysanthemums and scarlet carnations were much in evidence, as each proud family did the equivalent of spring cleaning at their grave, vault, or plot. Burial in the Campo Verano is the nearest thing to not having to leave your own local "spot," and this enormous rambling necropolis, with its formal avenues broken up by the unexpected construction of almost precarious family mausoleums, represents the ultimate district of Rome. Its defining color is a quiet warmth—these are most definitely not unvisited tombs. In this way, Campo Verano, although officially "full" for new burials, feels strangely lived in, a character which it shares with the more usual sepulchral destination for visitors, the resoundingly entitled Cimiterio Acatholico al Testaccio, more often known inaccurately as the Protestant Cemetery.

A walled garden shaded by pines and overshadowed by the bulk of the Pyramid of Gaius Cestius, this beautiful place is where Keats is buried, and the heart of Shelley is interred. It is also the resting-place of Antonio Gramsci, founder of the Italian Communist Party and revered Marxist theorist. Few people can have come to Rome to die as certainly as did John Keats. Accompanied only by one of the remoter satellites of his male London coterie, the would-be artist Joseph Severn, Keats arrived at Rome untypically from the south, after six weeks of quarantine aboard a ship in Naples harbor, and far gone in the advanced stage of consumption. His written reflections on Rome are scant, for normally a prolific journal-keeper and letter-writer, his illness robbed him of his literary facility. It is Severn's account of his last days that gives us the details of the unhappy months spent in Rome. One of the last things which the poet himself took note of was the spectacle of a Cardinal and his party hunting in the Campagnia as they approached the city. It was as if the grand romanticism of Rome held out just a taste to the man who no longer had the energy even to try the pleasures to which he would have been so responsive. Despite the gloomy Italian fate of both Keats and Shelley, they remain part of Rome's mythology, if only from the foundation of the Museum and Library dedicated to their joint memories in Piazza di Spagna. Joseph Severn, on the other hand, settled in Rome, married, produced a large family, and acted as British Consul for many years. Perhaps it should come as no surprise that present-day language schools for English teaching, when choosing names, universally neglect Severn, the real Roman Englishman, in favor of the poets with lesser local, but infinitely higher international, credentials. As always Romans know what will sell, and what will not.

Unity and Conformity

The Unification of Italy was famously dismissed by the Austrian statesman Metternich when he claimed that "Italy" was nothing but a geographical term. The political troubles that have afflicted the state in the wake of *tangentopoli* have sometimes argued in the same way. The truly new parties approach unity differently. The separatism of the Northern League, led by the crudely populist Umberto Bossi, has attracted huge support in Lombardy and other regions of the north. Contrariwise, in their different ways the neo-Fascists and supporters of Forza Italia desperately attempt to recoin a myth of Italy threatened by disintegration. The first are hampered by such difficult ideological baggage from a discredited history that in spite of their leader Gianfranco Fini's popularity, they look to play, thank goodness, only a peripheral role in direct government. Some would say that even this is too much, but it could simply be the price of a genuine democracy.

More interestingly, Silvio Berlusconi, the media mogul who founded Forza Italia, focuses on making his party the sounding-board for the nation's aspirations and tastes.

Forza Italia (literally, Go for it, Italy!—what you might shout at an international football match) has been analyzed as a mirror, devoid of the obstructions of any political creed, created simply to reflect back to the electorate what they admire and approve of. Berlusconi's guiding star in this project has been business success in his multimedia empire. Publisher, newspaper baron, and TV proprietor, with the presentational skills of the cruise line crooner he once was, Berlusconi knows how to "tickle" the public, and his phenomenal success in the 1993 elections which made him the "instant" prime minister was testimony to this ability. Style undoubtedly won him power, but a total lack of experience and policy left him useless in delivering the most pressing of the public's demands: better standards of living on the tail of the early 1990s recession. Although still undoubtedly focused on presentation above political content, he is now, following his premiership, serving an apprenticeship in the real political world. In the light of this, serious politicians like President Ciampi have recently given him the opportunity of earning some respect by drawing him into the mainstream of inter-party cooperation. Once again Italian politics looks to be fashioned on a reworking of the old —*trasformismo* for the twenty-first century.

The phenomenon that brought Forza Italia into government is controlled by the same principle that raises and lowers the hem lines of dresses and pronounces that the new black is yet again going to be gray. Fashion in Italy appeals to a quirkily conservative response to anything new: the conservatism lying in the uniformity with which it is adopted throughout the country. This cultural conformity consists in the wholesale adoption of the new, or its complete rejection. Either everyone changes to the new fashion or nobody does. What is most strange in this tendency is that it seems to happen simultaneously. There is no introduction of whatever is going to be accepted with a period of reception; suddenly and simply, everyone adopts it. Fashions arrive, fully formed, in the same way that other Italian social conventions are adhered to. The day upon which one Roman woman decides that it is cold enough to wear a fur is the day upon which every Roman woman does the same. "Political correctness," unlike couture, attracts few dedicated followers in Italy.

The growth in numbers of mobile phones (*telefonini*) over the past few years in Rome illustrates the way in which a commodity is universalized. In the summer of 1997 two teenage lads out in a Testaccio pizzeria flourished their handsets with considerable pride as they laid them alongside their plates, so unusual were these accessories at the time. Needless to say, they did not ring during the meal, as they were only used for their mothers to contact them and for them to contact each other, and their mothers must already have been informed that no dinner was needed that evening (in fact, they may even have needed to give permission for the outing...). Two years later, their mothers and even grandmothers, or women like them, were to be seen brandishing the infernal toys during the *passeggiata* and everyone was ringing everyone else constantly. Radio advertisements were almost exclusively dedicated to the latest refinement of personalizing your phone, from clip-on covers to individualized ringing tones.

Talk like this might seem patronizing—lumping "Italians" together as if they form a single, easily identifiable social grouping, and an "oh, so funny" and quaint one at that. It was the cheap trick of the eighteenth- and nineteenth-century visitors to Italy to treat all inhabitants of the peninsula as if they were servants or children, and I am well aware that I am dangerously near to doing the same. But I defend myself by claiming that "being Italian" most definitely implies more than simply finding yourself located within arbitrary geographical boundaries. Not even being buried in Rome can achieve the transformation. It is a kind of sixth sense, which however long foreigners stay within those boundaries, cannot be acquired. It is the true unity of Italy, and it inspires in me at least admiration rather than condescension.

CHAPTER THIRTEEN

The Fascist Era:

EUR

"*Adesso è in boccio; presto si aprirà.*
Now it's only a bud, but it's soon going to bloom."
Roman street hoarding 1999

It felt like a dream, or more properly a sci-fi nightmare. I was looking out from an elevated gallery over the ruins of an empire: bridges, towers, and engines of war, discarded and left to collect dust within the crepuscular shade of a huge over-arching vault. Rank upon rank of chipped portrait busts leered at me from the gloom. In every corner placards and informative notices languished, their days of explanation and scholarly attention relegated to a hard-to-imagine past. So much effort, physical and intellectual, seemed here to be transformed into the refuse it was ever destined to be. Like a disillusioned and wounded emperor, a dictator no longer absolute, I leaned heavily upon the cracked and dusty balustrade better to see the ruin of my dream, that of holding the city within the limitations of my poor head and transmitting it into words. I shuddered and knew a feeling directly contrary to the one I'd experienced on the Janiculum, described in Chapter Three. This was of the smallness of things and of the ultimate vanity of human labor, the reverse of so much of what I had been wanting to say about Rome. It was a quantum leap, a Roman *Götterdämmerung*; all it lacked was a Wagner soundtrack.

Outside this momentary fantasy, back in the real world, I must have been one of only about three visitors early that morning to the vast, echoing halls of the *Museo della Civiltà Romana*. I was certainly alone in my contemplation of its weird staging-area, where literally thousands of scale models and plaster casts, exhibits which had once formed the didactic life-blood of the place, had been taken to die. They had been made for two major exhibitions in 1911 and 1937, investigating every aspect of ancient Roman life, the second also being the occasion for the building of the Piazza Augusto Imperatore and the unveiling of the reconstructed *Ara Pacis* (See Chapter Two). I had stumbled across them while trudging, mesmerized, along the extensive length of the entire set of casts from Trajan's Column, immensely worthy but failing completely to fire my imagination. No, it was to be the disarray, the tragedy even, of the decline and fall of a collection that provided a thematic germ that day.

Like so many Roman museums, this one was undergoing a major restoration; like so many others, this was not a work of years, but of decades. Rome was not built in a day; her museums were not reordered within one season. Nor even was EUR, the suburb of Rome in which the museum is located, finished to schedule. Begun in 1938 to hold the planned 1942 World Fair which its abbreviated name memorializes (Esposizione Universale di Roma), the modernist suburb to Marcello Piacentini's design was incomplete as war broke out in Europe and Fascist Italy belatedly followed in Nazi Germany's belligerent footsteps. The successful target of allied bombing during the Italian Campaign of 1943–4, many of EUR's showpiece *palazzi* were virtually destroyed, and it was only in 1952 that a full-scale reconstruction was undertaken, with the repair of damage and the completion of what had never been started. The still nearly-new *città ideale*, ideal city, purged of its Fascist era overtones by trendier, brutalist rehabilitation, was deemed suitable to provide the accommodation for many of the new Republic's ministry buildings and was chosen as the site of major sporting facilities for the 1960 Rome Olympics. Its originally modest, but worthy, housing scheme, on a "homes for heroes" basis, has gradually become a place of fashionable domiciles, the smartness of the local shops identifying the district as one of Rome's most gentrified. It is on this whole area that I now want to concentrate.

EUR is about four miles due south of the Aurelian Wall's Porta Ardeatina, and straddles high ground and an adjacent valley on the right hand bank of the Tiber. The only significant site of antique interest close by is the Abbazia delle Tre Fontane, the traditional location of St. Paul's martyrdom (See Chapter Seven). The suburb is a mix of public and private buildings set in a monumental plan with wide boulevards, an open-air theater, and a large ornamental lake. Many commentators have found it pompous and cold. I insist on liking it in spite of myself. I can easily imagine how it once must have resembled the bare marble bones of Fascism's ugly skeleton, but visiting it on a graciously beautiful early autumn day, I was struck by the current effectiveness of site, buildings, and vegetation. Before the trees and shrubs which now give shade along every street had matured, this would have been an unforgiving place of sharp angles and over-long perspectives, a de Chirico dreamscape of nightmare proportions. Now, oleanders, bay trees, limes, and neatly trimmed hedges of holly make it far more worthy of the title "park" than either the tired and dusty Villa Borghese or the overgrown Villa Doria.

If you know of garden cities only in their provincial English forms (Welwyn for the 1930s, Milton Keynes for the 1960s and 1970s), then you won't get the scale right. But the principle seems the same: the placing of attractive residential units within a landscaped environment and yet comfortably close to public buildings of distinction. EUR does not have the absolute grandeur of Washington's Mall, perhaps the most celebrated of these "created" urban spaces, with its attendant monumental display, but it has a far happier mix of the domestic set within the institutional life of an apparently vibrant community. Here, the hefty marble tread of public stairways is scented with a scattering of giant pine cones and needles. A simple curving lawn holds a bronze and granite memorial to Gandhi, outlining the remodeled sympathies of EUR's 1950s designers. The apartment blocks have mellowed within their own garden plots, and their balconies and terraces, wider and more prominent than their neighbors in other suburbs, abound with the planted color and fragrance of mimosa and bougainvillea. Not usually an enthusiast for what Ivy Compton Burnett scathingly termed "excellent descriptions" in the works of her rivals, I hope that my enthusiasm for the place sufficiently excuses this unwonted purple passage.

Ugly Stains

Elsewhere in Rome, the relics of Fascism have not always been so attractively rehabilitated. Christopher Kinninmonth describes the furore over monuments with the *Duce*'s name inscribed upon them with the immediacy of someone personally involved, even if only as a visitor in the early post-war period:

> In the forecourt [of the Campo della Farnesina, Mussolini's sports center] stands a monolithic obelisk that has been cheated of grandeur by some unnecessary twistings of that essentially simple form. On it is still cut the name and title: "Mussolini Dux." The Allied armies were so anxious to efface all trace of the dictator that anyone who knew Italy during those days of conquest, or liberation, will find this sight a painful, sacrilegious one. Why was this presumptuous monument spared? Because it would be a pity further to spoil a good piece of stone or because someone woke up one day to realise that Mussolini had his place in history, since history is as indifferent as rain to moral worth? Did that someone remember previous and equally futile attempts to annihilate all recollection of Caligula by removing his images and palaces?

One of the *Duce*'s sadly most enduring civil engineering projects, the Via dei Fori Imperiali, cuts a disfiguring gash across the magical territory where medieval Rome, tumbling down the Esquiline hill, meets the ghosts of her antique past in the valley of the Roman Forum. Running from the Colosseum to Piazza Venezia, the street was constructed on Mussolini's orders to provide a sufficiently grand triumphal way to impress the visiting Adolf Hitler and prepare for military victory abroad by provision for its celebration at home. It was a project of childish vanity, reflecting well the cruelty and bullying of the conquest of Abyssinia in 1936. The city's planners have toyed with the idea of making the road permanently closed to traffic (it already is on Sundays and some holidays), allowing for some sympathetic planting and the addition of street furniture less trapped in a pompous formalism. The archaeologist's dream is to reclaim the whole area and fully excavate the series of imperial forums currently bisected by the broad roadway. Since 1997 extensive digs on both sides of it have been improving the fragmentary remains of these monumental squares which celebrated successive reigns and dynasties. As the work has continued, excellent public notices have provided not only detailed descriptions and illustrative reconstructions of what is being uncovered, but also the added cultural trope of modern poetry in a variety of languages, celebrating "the grandeur that was Rome" with a knowing melancholy. An extract from Ezra Pound's *Personae* meets the delicacy of Chinese characters in the form of a stanza by Ai Xing, while the more ancient Greek culture pays tribute to the evocative quality of the Roman ruins in a wistful verse by Yannis Kokkos.

Were the archaeologists to get their way, no doubt overall knowledge of the substance of Rome's antique heart would be greatly enhanced. I am not convinced, however, that there would be a corresponding improvement in the information that the visitor actually would receive. The British comedian Eddie Izzard lampoons the search for historical truth and its exhibition through archaeological remains by asserting that whatever impressive claims are made for a historic site, it always emerges as "a series of small walls." Whether these bits of masonry are Troy, Sparta, or the imperial forums of Rome, they all end up being less than fascinating. This charge, of course, can easily be countered here simply by turning around and gesturing to the eponymously colossal and impressive remains of the Colosseum. But the sad truth of the matter lies in the acknowledgment that even the imperial forums are never going to be anything other than "a series of small walls," however well explained.

Tangentially, let me add that a visit to the Roman Forum itself could be disappointing if you go expecting to see lots of ancient buildings standing in their pristine glory. The *curia hostilia*, or Senate House, was reconstructed under the Fascists as a political gesture, and the Basilica of Maxentius and some remains of the Domitianic palace on the Palatine hill are sizable and grand. Otherwise, you need a guidebook of specialist depth to make the ruins speak of the ancient

Rome which I, at least, dream of. You cannot do better than Amanda Claridge's *Rome* in the Oxford Archaeological Guides Series. As I've tried to indicate in this book, there are plenty of ways to access and appreciate the most distant levels of Rome's culture. It's just that they are not always to be found by dutifully trudging around some builder's debris with your nose in a book.

Restructuring the past as a kind of political theme park was what the Italian Fascist movement aspired to in commissioning art and architecture. The frieze of maps outlining the extent of the ancient Roman Empire and its wished-for successor state, Fascist Italy, which lines Via dei Fori Imperiali is almost Disney-like in its synthetic, but aggressively bright simplicity. However, an ugly pride lies just beneath the surface. Moving back from this would-be Triumphal Way to a whole quarter given to such a sick dream, the most grandiloquent of EUR's buildings is the so-called Square Colosseum. This squat marble skyscraper with row upon row of mighty Roman arches designed by the trio Giovanni Guerrini, Ernesto Bruno La Padula, and Mario Romano, was finished, ironically enough, just in time for the collapse of Fascism in 1943. First called the Palazzo della Civiltà Italiana, it was renamed after the war in the left-wing influenced enthusiasm of the new "new" order, Palazzo del Lavoro, The Palace of Work/Labor. The towering inscription, repeated on each facade in a direct challenge to established architectural precedent and good taste, seeks to idealize the Italian people's achievements under every flavor of government:

Un Popolo
di poeti di artisti di eroi
di santi di pensatori di scienziati
di navigatori di trasmigatori

A People
of poets of artists of heroes
of saints of thinkers of scientists
of navigators of explorers

Nearby and sharing the same height above the river is the ecclesiastical version of the same idealization, the gargantuan church of SS. Pietro e Paolo. Taking almost the whole period of EUR's gestation to

reach completion (1938–54) this tribute to Michelangelo's first plans for St. Peter's itself is based on a Greek Cross. Designed by Arnaldo Foschini the church has a cupola almost as large as its more eminent model, the dome of which, together with the campanile of St. Paul's Basilica, is clearly visible from the northern colonnade immediately flanking the church. The interior is disappointing after the cliff-like facade and impressive external bulk. Decorated with mud-hued panels bearing huge but mystifying religious symbols, it lacks the light and color for which the space cries out. The bronze doors, with attractive modern panels recounting scenes from the lives of the two saints including their martyrdom, allude specifically to Filarete's work in the Vatican. From the terrace at the western end of the church, and at the top of a monumental flight of steps, the whole of EUR, sloping gently from left to right, can be viewed from above.

Most of the architectural designs in the suburb employ a modern neoclassicism. Symmetry is not always adhered to rigidly, but hinted at. So, having entered the complex as intended from the north, Via Cristoforo Colombo sweeps into its antechamber, Piazzale delle Nazioni Unite, where two *palazzi* mirror one another in their seeming acres of plate glass, forming graceful hemicycles as they do so. The form resembles the exedral structures of ancient Roman baths, best represented in the curvature of Piazza della Repubblica and S. Maria degli Angeli near Rome's Termini Station. Then, to right and left, the Viale della Civiltà del Lavoro, leads the eye or the traveler to the square Colosseum or the Palazzo dei Congressi respectively. The latter, the second of EUR's grand palaces, was designed by Adalberto Libera and again not finished until 1954, but this time takes the form of a modified basilica, a plan suiting its original purpose as meeting place, conference hall and exhibition space. Continuing, you enter the true heart of EUR in the massive Piazza Marconi, named for the Italian pioneer of radio, the scientific and stratospheric equivalent of Columbus whose *via* is bearing us on in our exploring. The space is articulated traditionally in Roman terms by a central monolith; this time not an Egyptian obelisk as so often in the city, but a modern, carved *stele* of white Carrara marble, 130 feet high. The work of Arturo Dazzi, it was finished in 1959 in time for the Olympics, and in its high relief depicts aspects of Marconi's technological breakthrough.

Now, on either side of you the impression of symmetry is given by the two colonnaded Palazzi dell'Esposizioni and off to the far left at the end of a receding perspective, the Museo della Civiltà Romana, providing the architectural closure. Like their neighbor in which we started, the museums the exhibition buildings house have long been subject to campaigns of restoration. Their collections seem determined to reflect the modernism of the place in living up to the theory of entropy implied by the second law of thermodynamics: that disorder has the tendency to overwhelm order through time. Displays of both traditional handicrafts and ethnography have never held much fascination for me, so not even the research for this book could tempt me to venture inside these imposing structures. However, I really enjoyed the Museo Storico delle Poste e delle Telecomunicazioni, with its Marconi memorabilia and relics of the papal postal service, just a little further down the main street on the right. Also unvisited was the distant dome of the Palazzo dello Sport, which elegantly closes the prospect to the south, rising athletically above the lake and surrounding trees. The effort exerted in the walk there would easily have qualified me for participation in some sporting event, and as I am resolutely an armchair competitor, I stuck to my predisposition (or should that be indisposition?).

If Catholicism is the principal cult of Romans, sport is their religion. And for many individuals participatory competition in local soccer teams or in a cycle club provides the "works" to balance the "faith" of simply being the fan of a particular team. When there's a big match on, the city goes noticeably quieter, and even the Italian Grand Prix will empty the streets and fill the bars provided with a TV. Attendance at the games, be they the gladiatorial shows of the ancients or the Lazio/Roma derby, has been an overwhelmingly consistent element in the life of most Romans. The realization of this centrality was made manifest in the preparations for the 1960 Olympics, when a ten-mile road, the Via Olimpica, was constructed joining the EUR facilities with those of Foro Italico (home of the big football stadium which we will visit in the next chapter), and the Centro Sportivo dell'Acqua Acetosa. Physical exercise, proverbially noted as the key to the bonus of a healthy mind, is well served by the large numbers of gyms, *palestre*, in the city. These institutions seem to have little to do with the servicing of fads and the body-beautiful needs of the over-worked and over-paid executives of London or New York; they rather provide a perceived need among the most ordinary people that they take some healthy exercise. If that enables them to promote their own *bella figura*, then all well and good, but it does not seem to me to be the driving force behind the exercise.

Unified Society—a Good Thing?

Strangely, this realization makes me reflect on something that is evident everywhere in Italian society: its lack of well-defined and enduring class structure. Taking reasonable care of yourself, eating healthily, following fashions, and aspiring to the good things in life are truly common concerns in Rome. Although it is possible to identify richer and poorer districts in the city, and observe more and less affluent persons in the street, the factors uniting the population seem more defined and firmly established than those separating them. Such social factors are clearly the cause of the conformism that I began to outline in the last chapter. They also explain, to some degree, how an entire nation lived for over twenty years within a one-party state both fairly peaceably, and without veering into the most extravagant brutalities. The success of the Fascist myth of Italy was that it was fashionable. Mussolini's early career as a journalist and editor links him firmly with the principle that the best way to succeed, politically or in any other field, is to give the people what they want. EUR bears an unnerving testimony to this, especially in its post-war reworking and its attractions, which are even more evident today.

Like the Via dei Fori Imperiali, Mussolini had another significant road to build during his ascendancy. Relations between the Italian state and the Catholic Church, as we have noted before, were strained at the best of times and non-existent at the worst. The Fascists knew that *rapprochement* with the pope and a solution to the Vatican problem would not only remove a potential thorn in the flesh, but also earn them political credibility and even a powerful ally. The Lateran Treaty of 1929 guaranteed the autonomy of the Vatican Sovereign State, and delivered a cash reparation in millions of lire, and billions of state bonds, to the Church for the loss of its temporalities. The physical expression of the new relationship can be seen in the Via della Conciliazione, the street which apologized for the slight inflicted on St. Peter's in the building of the Prati district, and destroyed the ancient Borgo quarter in so doing. A broad vista of the basilica is now afforded from the river bank in front of Castel Sant'Angelo where once a teeming ancient maze of streets had ambled toward the sudden startling revelation of space provided by Bernini's vast colonnade and piazza. The architectural effect of the street is, strangely, to belittle the church. It is a long, long drag up the Via della Conciliazione, and yet it gives the impression of being just a stone's throw in length, and in so doing diminishes the scale of St. Peter's. Sometimes pavements seem harder than they actually are; this is just such a one. It was paved with an unworthy compromise.

Given a guarded papal blessing, Mussolini's regime could and did acquire a conformist veneer denied to every secular government since

1860. More respectable even than the king, *Il Duce* reveled in popular support at home and threw his weight around internationally. His withdrawal from the League of Nations after flouting its sanctions in support of Abyssinia was the high-point of his grasp of diplomacy. He took risks on the understanding that he had no real political capital upon which to rely. Popularity, even he realized, was a spectacularly weak base for government, but should be exploited fully for as long as it was found to last.

Mussolini came to prominence in Milan following the First World War. His dissatisfaction with the socialism he at first supported led him to found a radical party of direct action, backed up by *squadre*, literally teams, of thugs. Beatings and enforced doses of castor oil were the rewards for political opposition. Taking inspiration from the maverick Italian nationalism represented by the poet and adventurer, Gabrielle d'Annunzio, who successfully occupied the city of Fiume, the Fascists bemoaned the small pay-out to Italy determined by the Treaties of Versailles, and set themselves to win more territory and more standing for their country. Their assumption of power depended upon a well stage-managed confidence trick, the so-called March on Rome, which precipitated the collapse of the last pre-war democratic government.

With Mussolini safely out of the firing line in Milan should the coup fail, the Fascists descended upon the capital in a much-publicized wave (October 26–29, 1922). Overseen by party officials in Perugia (maybe representing that city's bitter hatred of Rome for the imposition of a crippling salt tax in the sixteenth century—grudges last a long time in Italy), most of the marching was done by trains not yet running on time. To make them do so was one of Mussolini's vaunted promises. *Il Duce* arrived two days later wearing a natty suit and bowler hat, just in time to be summoned by the king to the Quirinal and asked to form a government. Sartorial propriety in the presence of the king was to become a matter of considerable annoyance for Mussolini. Each Tuesday, the day allotted for the weekly audience, the President of the Council of the king's ministers had to take off his pompous Fascist uniform and don the morning dress required by formal etiquette. He could not even wear a military uniform of the Italian forces, as the king himself did on these occasions, as he bore no rank within them.

The veteran politicians of the old dispensation still thought that Mussolini and his Fascists could be brought around to see sense and so be molded into their way of doing things. Giolitti, the master of *trasformismo*, never doubted his own powers of persuasion and political finesse until it was too late. First came the murder of leading opponents, most notably the socialist Giacomo Matteotti. Then came the proscription of political parties other than the Fascists, briefly resisted by the brave Aventine Secession (June 1924), where a few independent politicians left the chamber of deputies to set up a rival body on the hill of that name. Had the Head of State, Vittorio Emanuele III, acted decisively to end the unconstitutional behavior of *Il Duce* and his minions by ordering the army to arrest them, as was suggested during the government's panic at Rome on the eve of the Fascist March, things would have been different not only for Italy, but for the world. But this

was not to be a service provided by the House of Savoy, and was chief among the charges leveled at it after the war, underwriting the end of the Italian monarchy and the establishment of the Republic.

Mussolini met an unpleasant end. Italy was invaded in 1943 and his government fell. After his rescue from allied custody by a daring group of German paratroopers, Hitler used him as the puppet head of Northern Italy under Nazi occupation in the so-called Republic of Salò. As the partisans' and Allied strength increased, and German troops were chased out of the peninsula, Mussolini prepared for flight. Disguised as retreating Austrian soldiers, he, a few stalwart supporters and his mistress, Clara Petacci, were captured by Communist partisans in April 1945. Somewhere and somehow they were all executed. There followed a gruesome exhibition of their corpses hanging upside down from a petrol station awning in Milan's Piazzale Loreto, and a violent mutilation of their bodies. All of this was caught on film by a US serviceman, and its finding and showing in 1994 after years of neglect in Washington's Library of Congress film archive was a crucial moment in the change of tack Italy's politics was then undergoing.

Ignored almost totally in the post-war teaching of history, Mussolini's legacy now had to be faced. This was done most directly and damagingly at the ballot box with Gianfranco Fini and the neo-Fascists garnering a huge increase in support. More generally, the Italians had to be more honest about the past. Mussolini was no Hitler, but he was not a suitable role model for aspiring politicians or for a hero-hungry coming generation. He was a charlatan who had some big ideas, not all of which were bad. He appealed to the times during which he was successful; putting him in proper historical context would make certain that he would not do so to any other period. The film of his lynching ends with a shot of his dead body now abandoned, propped up against that of his mistress, on the empty platform of a nearby train station. Pinned to his clothing is a label with his name and a number scrawled upon it.

Hanging Tags

Labels and descriptive placards are common in Rome. There has long been a tradition of satire and political comment emanating from the so-called *statue parlanti*, or talking statues. The most famous of these is Pasquino, the very battered remnant of an antique figure-group (maybe that of Achilles and Patroclus, or Aeneas and Anchises) to be found at the back of Palazzo Braschi, just south of Piazza Navona. Poems, articles of political support, and more frequently denunciation, jokes, and puns were, and sometimes still are, hung around the neck of the figure. At times Pasquino would enter into a long discussion with another such talkative monument, such as Marforio, the river-god on the Capitol, or Babuino, the monkey-bodied man on the street of the same name. Questions and answers would pass between the statues, and ever more scurrilous accusations might be made against popes, emperors, kings or dictators. Chapter Eight's epigram comes from a *pasquinade* against Pope Alexander VI. More modern ones have attacked Fascist party officials, like the one that once again puns on the acronym of Rome's civic government, SPQR: *Sa il Podestà Quanto ha Rubato* – "Only the governor knows how much he has stolen." The Fascist Party initials themselves (PNF) were readily converted into a commentary on their acquisitiveness: *Pasqua, Natale, Ferragosto* (Easter, Christmas, the August Holiday), the feast days customary for the payment of annual tips and bribes. Spring 1999 brought a fresh crop of *pasquinades*, this time aimed at NATO and American aggression in the Balkans. *Pasqua in Serbia*, Easter in Serbia, was a neatly delivered, if rather crudely expressed, poem denouncing US imperialism and belligerence:

Con morte e distruzione la pasqua si festeggia....
Sotto la macellazione della America selvaggia.

With death and destruction Easter is kept....
Under America's saving butchery.

Street hoardings are worth reading in Rome. They are often funny, sometimes provocatively sexy, and anything but drab. Restoration work proceeded at Stazione Termini for what seemed like an age during 1998–9, making any passage through it an even more unpleasant experience than normal (it is literally just about the only place in the city I've ever felt intimidated). But I loved the huge blow up of a rose just about to bud accompanied by the legend with which I headed this chapter plastered all over its scaffolding and chip-board. Termini, we were assured, was just about to flower in time for the millennium. I had amused difficulty in imagining a less appropriate metaphor for the giant-sized station, reveling in the modernist architecture of the early 1960s, than a tiny delicate rosebud. Maybe it was a deft reference to Citizen Kane's last words. If so, no doubt Bugs Bunny would have been pleased, as nearby his own image was promoting the re-opening of the formerly pornographic cinema in Piazza della Repubblica as a Warner Village complex, safe at last for all the family. Truly it seemed that Rome was coming up smelling of roses.

EUR has been transformed by its sensitive planting and the fulfillment of God's good time expressed in the maturing of its trees and shrubs. My visit to the Museum of Roman Civilization, one of the suburb's temples to didacticism, was itself transformed by its ultimate and parting exhibit. This was the great *plastico di Roma,* or the Rome model, the ante-type of the ruins I had seen in the desolate storage area of the museum. The model reproduces the city at the time of Constantine at a scale of 1:250. It is spectacular. Frightened of the carnage which might result should I or the three elderly German school teachers in the museum at the same time be allowed to see the *plastico* close up, we were restricted to a view from above. My earlier nightmare was once again made dream-like. Here, on the tiny scale, order was returned to Rome and her culture. Viewing it as from the heavens, we could forgive and forget her ugly moments, even to the extent of letting it slip from our memories that this very model was made for an exhibition designed to puff up the Fascist state and its vaunted links with ancient Rome. Here, our rose-tinted spectacles firmly in place, we watched entranced, as the bud slowly broke into flower.

CHAPTER FOURTEEN

Timeless Rome:

Trattoria Dell'Omo

Gino

Quando hic sum non jejuno Sabbato; quando Romae sum jejuno Sabbato...
"When I am here in Milan I don't fast on a Saturday; when I'm in Rome I do..."
St. Ambrose to St. Augustine, St Aug. Ep 36, p.62

It seems that the ancient Romans did not make extravagant claims for themselves when demanding that visitors toe their line of behavior. Their own version of our proverb "When in Rome" paid tribute to the need to conform to the habits of Crete (*Cretizandum est cum Crete*—"We must do in Crete what the Cretans do"). Nowadays, the full force of Roman disapproval is launched at the unwary when it comes to questions of food and drink, their appropriateness to the occasion and the proper time of their consumption. I've already touched on the disdain with which a milky coffee can be served if ordered after a very specific time; authorities disagree on whether the point of no return is

10:30 AM or 11 o'clock. Matt Frei in *The Unfinished Revolution* defines it precisely:

> There is nothing chaotic or haphazard about Italian society... take the enjoyable and deceptively simple act of drinking a cappuccino. This ritual is a minefield of regulations.
>
> Rule number 1: never have a cappuccino after eleven in the morning
>
> Rule number 2: never order a cappuccino after lunch or dinner
>
> Rule number 3: never have a cappuccino sitting down.

Another somewhat intractable problem is how to organize a meal. Menus all list *Antipasti, Pasta, Carne, Pesce, Contorni, e Dolci,* but faced with this choice, where do you literally start? The classic Italian meal consists principally of only two dishes, known deceptively simply as *primo,* first, and *secondo,* second. Most often the *primo* is pasta or risotto, but you might have had some *crostini,* little pieces of toast with pâté, or a selection of meats or pickled vegetables even before you get to the first course. Then you might choose your *secondo* from the *antipasti* or even the *contorni,* vegetables, passing over the temptations of fish and meat. Confused? You will be when you get to *dolci,* sweets; they are a minefield. You ought not really to have one at all. The proper conclusion to a Roman meal should be fruit, whatever is in season and is ripe. Like most Italians, Romans only permit a pudding on a feast day or personal celebration, and then you sometimes wonder why they bothered. Invariably bought from a confectioners, even when served in a restaurant, all Roman cakes and pastries follow the general rule I laid down as a warning to customers at Babington's: the better they look, the worse they are. Of course, Romans will indulge their visitors like spoiled children who know no better, and provide them with these spun-sugar disasters. But why not simply do the right thing, and have a pear instead?

Nothing can beat a Roman pear in mid-autumn. Perfectly plump but not too yielding to the firm caress of the finger, these golden-green globes speak of the shortening days and the blowing of fallen leaves along the *Lungotevere.* Sweet, but not too sweet, their charms perfectly compliment the obligatory half-liter of *Castelli Romani* wine that should be drunk at lunch. A one-time Rector of the Venerable English College used to summon students to his study if he observed them failing in this bibulous duty.

As you will have gathered, as far as food is concerned at least, I want to conform, recognizing within this surrender of self-will the most enduring of Roman traits. Why trouble yourself to choose when what is best has already been established? Many of my friends, like so many other visitors, insist on going against the current and having what they actually want rather than what Rome thinks appropriate to provide. Luckily, when I was a student there simply was no choice, and we ate better than I had ever done or probably ever shall.

The food at the Venerable English College was prepared by three local ladies of the parish of S. Lorenzo in Damaso, the basilica incorporated in the design of the Palazzo della Cancelleria. They were supervised by a small community of Elizabetine Sisters who lived in a tiny convent within a wing of the college. As the Second Vatican Council had insisted, this religious order had closely examined itself to identify specific charisms, or gifts, to offer to the broader Church and the broadest world. The Elizabetines, it seemed, had come up with their defining three-fold mission: to increase the comfort and successful convalescence of patients in their hospitals; to increase the quality of life and loving care given to the residents in their homes for the elderly; and, last but not least, to increase the waistlines of the students of the Venerable English College. Whenever the college went out *en masse*, for example to observe the conclusion of a Forty Hours Devotion at S. Lorenzo, the sisters would accompany us and point out to the local women with swelling pride that they were responsible for the cassocks straining around the middle. When I went to be measured at Gammarelli for my soutane, the assistant commented that I couldn't have been at the college for long as I was far too thin. I've made up for this deficiency since.

It has been said that Romans are more enthusiastic gourmands than fussy gourmets, and the best of the city's food reflects this. Plates are loaded fairly high, and the use of substantial sauces, based upon animal fats, compound the solid feel to most dishes. Elizabeth Bowen neatly describes the general effect: "Roman food of the kind to which I sat down is for the hungry, the healthy and those in humour... finer palates than mine find it unsubtle."

The rustic, or at best bourgeois, feel to this cuisine is reflected even in the most expensive restaurants, like Alfredo and Ranieri, where Rome's commitment to offal, particularly liver, tripe and brains, finds notable advocates. The dominant motivation in the most typical Roman restaurant always seems to be one of coaxing the diner to have something which someone in charge, probably "Mama," knows will do you good. That in fact it turns out to be tasty, even perhaps delicious, almost seems like a piece of luck. Evelyn Waugh, in a neat aside within *Brideshead Revisited*, records the horror with which Lord Marchmain and his mistress, Cara, witness the vulgarian Beryl forcing food upon her matrimonial prey, Bridey at the exclusive Ranieri, "the height of bad taste." But what the aesthetically aristocratic sensibility of the Marquess fails to grasp, is that such vulgarity is at the heart of Roman food. Much of this weight and stodginess finds its origin in the Jewish influence in the specifically Roman dishes (some of the best restaurants are still to be found in the former Ghetto area), where the outrageous idea of deep-frying an artichoke receives a culinary apotheosis and total vindication.

Table Talk

But the restaurant I want us to visit is not in the Ghetto, nor in any other part of the *centro storico* come to that. Its proud claim that it has been established in a street hardly spitting distance from Stazione Termini since 1950 roots its aspirations in the simplest of social strata. Those who eat here are local business people, tourists who hit lucky, and those who live on the otherwise unprepossessing streets around. By its cherishing of the Abruzzi culinary influences which show up on its menu (particularly the house specialty, *Bucatini all'Amatriciana*), it also points firmly to the post-war expansion of the city and the accompanying mass immigration to the capital of Italians from all over the peninsula. The Dell'Omo family may have been foreigners, rustic country folk from the hill villages looking down upon Amatricia fifty years ago; they are now established Romans, as much so as the most *noialtrian* of Trasteverans.

I've never been to this *trattoria* knowing which street it is on. I had to follow my nose until I firmly established a sure way of finding it. To the east of the vast piazza in front of the station rises the leaden nineteenth-century basilica of the Sacred Heart, crowned by a massive gilded statue of Christ displaying the characteristic internal organ specific to this devotion. It was here that Don Bosco performed a miracle by celebrating a mass in which there was an unlimited supply of the host, the sacramental bread of Holy Communion. To me at least it does not seem sacrilegious to thank Don Bosco for bringing me so close to so many marvelous meals. You take the street immediately to the left side of the basilica, and Dell'Omo is the second restaurant you come to. I've never been to the first one; it may be as good as Dell'Omo, it may not be. Having found what I now know to be my perfection I don't choose to try something which might disappoint.

Dell'Omo never has tables outside, and even in summer the street door is often shut, and nothing that a first glance could reveal would recommend the place. The decor may indeed date from the restaurant's opening in 1950: lower level paneling in a dirty chocolate brown, and, at something just a little uncomfortably above eye-level, faded prints of nineteenth-century Rome handed out as free gifts with a weekly magazine (I know this because the self-same pictures have decorated my own study since I collected the set fifteen years ago). Most disconcertingly, perched on a beam running across the archway dividing the front part of the restaurant from the more intimate back, a huge pair of cow horns (the famous Abruzzi cattle?) are garishly beribboned and yet casually ignored by everyone. I only noticed these distinctive ornaments when I knew I had to write about them. In spite of the lack of inspiration expended upon its decoration, the restaurant's dark and shady recesses can be refreshingly cool in summer even without the assistance of air-conditioning, while the door closed against the draughts and drizzle of December can insulate the coziest of atmospheres. A huge refrigerated *armadio* or cupboard, with brown melamine veneer, squats across the entire rear wall, and seems only to serve the functions of providing a prominent ledge for bottles of *amari* to jostle each other, and a station for the *caraffe* to be cooled before filling with the pee-green (no spelling mistake here) *vino bianco* from the *Castelli Romani*.

Gino dell'Omo is an old man who looks like he's worked here for twice the fifty years exacted by reality. In a short, crumpled (and not too clean) waiter's jacket he sidles around the confined space flicking his tea towel at non-existent flies. He may give you a menu, or bring a little basket of *rosette*, the Roman bread rolls, disconcertingly hard on the outside, rewardingly soft if peeled like a tangerine. Overcharging for an obligatory serving of *pane* per head was a feature of Roman restaurants until the early 1990s, when the city council regulated the practice. This bread charge had customarily taken the place of a tip, very rarely granted in Rome, except by romantically inclined tourists. More traditional eating-places like Dell'Omo still seem to operate as before, but it seems a price worth paying for the wealth of culinary excellence it provides in return.

For the most part, Gino has given place to his young relative, Antonio, who is now the one to greet you at the door, to ask if you are ready to order or indeed to recommend what you should have. Wearing casual clothes, but not too much gold jewelry, Tonio has matured from the petulant youth forced to serve in the family business, through his year's military service (air force), to the point where he is clearly proud of what the restaurant does. But Gino is still in charge of the bill; he has successfully identified the true source of power, and kept it for himself. But I was quite startled not so long ago to see how Gino can still rise to the occasion. On a particularly busy lunchtime in summer all hands were summoned to the fray. Gino was almost running to get someone their *insalata*—no more than some lettuce and a whole, fresh *mozzarella*—and taking and delivering orders as in the old days.

Ordering here can be fun. If things don't immediately draw you from the menu (and it has to be admitted that it might strike you as uninspired: the usual half-dozen dishes which appear everywhere, *saltimbocca, scalopini, spedini*) ask if you can see what there is. Just by the kitchen door is a set of tables groaning with ugly galvanized cooking-dishes transfigured by their edible content. Aubergines, artichokes, and peppers reveal their depth of color through a rich, oily sheen. Cuts of veal stand ready to be grilled or pan-fried, and a joint of beef, broiled in water heavy with a pound of butter, prepares to be thinly sliced. And then there is the fish. Maybe there are deep fried whitebait, swordfish steaks from a haunch of pink *spada*, or the whole sea-bass, *spigola*, offering its bright eye as a sign of freshness. A trip to this dragon's horde of priceless food properly accompanies lunch, and might inspire you to order nothing more than a perfectly cooked artichoke as *secondo*.

Dinner is slightly different. Gino will push the *lasagne* (I think it's his favorite), and it is good; but as I've already stated, the *amatriciana* sauce remains the most typical of the house's offerings for pasta. When I first visited this restaurant as a back-packer with a group of friends, we variously tried to order different *primi* listed in the menu, only to be informed solemnly by the obviously bored teenage Antonio that it was off—*non c'è.* We rose to the challenge by finally asking what there *was.* Antonio, with his girlfriend or football dominating the foreground of his mental attention, shrugged and announced the *bucatini* dish with the air of having to answer a silly question. It was on the very same occasion that the lights failed and I glimpsed for the first time Signora dell'Omo, the culinary magician of the establishment, as she emerged from the kitchen in a flurry as lamps and candles were swiftly lit. Flapping around and shouting on her part seemed to do the trick as power was restored within minutes and she could return to her realm confident that nothing would be wasted. In the evening, *involtini,* very superior beef olives, stuffed appropriately to the season make their appearance, and heavier, hearty meat dishes seem to emerge especially during a cold snap in spring or the rain of early December.

Getting to Know You

Although I've always loved eating here, it is only recently that I've felt like a patron, to be recognized and welcomed, and to be offered a complimentary *digestivo* on departure. Maybe I'm a slow developer, but I also recognize that previously I have not wished to stray over a certain line of reserve apparent in myself and the *padroni.* Keeping a restaurant requires you to be courteous to your customers, and friendships formed from such everyday pleasantries ought surely to be reckoned as exceptional. The fear that condescension is implied from one or both parties does not feel groundless. In Rome, however, generations of a certain kind of visitor have established themselves fairly quickly at their chosen bar or restaurant, sometimes being drawn directly into the organic life of a neighborhood through this loyalty. I wonder if what has kept their interest has always been food. Christopher Kininmonth's 1950s sojourn in Rome refers to his patronage of a number of eating establishments, usually on the "low" side, and his fascination with the lively banter and horse-play of the young male company indicates a subtext of gay desire in the general atmosphere of homosociality. Am I reading too much in to this? I think not:

> *The tavern door burst open and a half-dozen lads, scrapping like demons... belched into the street. The largest of them was forced to the parapet of the bridge where he cried for mercy. Laughing they all returned indoors, propelling us with them, and the whole company sat down to a large table scattered with cards at which two elegant and not-so-young men, heavily beringed, were impatiently waiting... One never quite knows whether such an encounter, in Miss Bankhead's words "constitutes a social introduction," and it was not until later we found that, in this case, it did.*

Kininmonth's camp tone becomes more sinisterly visceral as he recounts an encounter with a young car mechanic beneath the arches of the Colosseum on another moonless night. Nothing happens, or at least 1950s attitudes did not encourage him to divulge anything even if it had. Kininmonth constantly chooses the Rome of the night hours as his controlling theme, as the precise obverse to H. V. Morton's early rising and making the most of every brisk morning. If Kininmonth is the slow inhalation of a strong cigarette, then Morton is freshly squeezed orange juice:

> *As I have said, I liked to be out before six in the morning, when the air is fresh and before Rome is properly awake... In the early hour the sun is low, touching first the domes, towers and chimneys of Rome, then flooding downward over the walls until one half of the street is gold and the other in shadow.*

Morton is the monk of travel writers—devoted, chaste, and just a little pedantic. The Rome of post-war chic, night clubs on the Via Veneto, the more generally acceptable face of a heterosexual culture belongs to the third in the post-war trio, Cecil Roberts. The opening of his chapters usually find him accompanying an attractive female to some pleasure spot with an aperitif very much in view, knowledgeable witticisms ready on his lips:

> *"I want to go to the Via Vittoria," I said one morning to my companion, who had the merit of being a tireless walker.*

"How odd! that's exactly where I want to go," she exclaimed. "What takes you there?"

"Bonnie Prince Charlie."

"What has he to do with the Via Vittoria?*"*

"And what have you?"

Oh, to be so suave and to have such charming companions! If you find yourself alone, however, Rome still provides you with plenty of street theater in the form of a perpetual playing to the gallery by myriad "characters," with love and romance as a recurring theme. In a humble bar the girl behind the till is delighted to see her boyfriend come in for his mid-morning snack. As she carefully wraps his *panino* in its obligatory and hygienic paper napkin, she lifts the pastry tongs to her lips to place a kiss ostentatiously upon the sandwich soon to be consumed by the beloved. It has grace, a teasing sensuality and, at the same time, a degree of unaffected playfulness. Not all lovers on the Roman streets are so artless, among whom I would number the increasingly visible gay couples braving the conventions. I enjoyed a fascinating *tartuffo* at Tre Scalini on the Piazza Navona one balmy September evening watching the bar's clients watching two young men engaging in the most theatrical of grappling, in what had to be one of the most public places in the town. A youngish mistress-type was enormously amused, whereas her distinguished-looking sugar daddy simply shrugged in the most resigned of ways. A middle-aged French couple tutted rather too obviously, only to spend ages repositioning their chairs subtly so that they could get a better view.

It does not strike me as odd that operas often contain scenes where the first tentative suggestions of love between hero and heroine occur in church. For centuries it was one of the few public places where the sexes even got a glance of one another. The baroque excesses of some of the Roman churches seem to tease at this stereotype, with seats resembling opera boxes and decorations, which although clearly not erotic in tone, have an undeniable sensuality. Most notorious in the city are the two swooning statues of female saints by Bernini, St. Teresa of Avila at Our Lady of Victories, and St. Frances Gonzaga in her own church. Here the mystical state of union with God in prayer is graphically made plastic in poses and expressions which resemble nothing less than orgasmic physical rapture. Some commentators have remained insouciant, and deny any subtext in the artist's purpose:

If the visitor finds this group startling (St Teresa transfixed by the love of God)—almost blasphemously so—he will not be the first to react in this way. One viewer was immediately reminded of a bedroom scene. The saint's attitude has been described as the ultimate of sensuality, and the smile on the face of the beautiful young angel has been seen as a malicious grin. If this is your reaction, you had better not admit it, because here the evil is almost surely in the mind of the beholder.

Sadly, much as I trust Barbara and Richard Mertz as companions around the medieval parts of Rome, I have to abandon them when they express their doubt that anyone could see the Ecstasy of St. Teresa without being minded of what they coyly refer to as a bedroom scene. That's the point of it; within the sculpture religious passion is shown as meeting human sexuality and finding an expression that transcends it. If it wasn't about sex, it would be cheap. The bas-reliefs of male voyeurs to either side of the main group only contribute to highlighting its use of a public sexuality, which remains part of Rome's stock-in-trade. If you doubt it go back to Piazza Navona and reposition your chairs.

Performance of all types is part of the city's tradition, and yet it remains a living feature. Piazza Navona plays host to puppeteers, jugglers, and acrobats most nights of the year, extending the traditional periods of special license in carnival and during the Advent and Epiphany markets. Foremost among the regular performers for the past few years has been Marcel, the "finger dancer." This exiguous art form, which you might think too intimate for the grand spaces of the Navona, consists in the prodigiously mustachioed Marcel using his gloved hands to create diminutive characters which pirouette, waltz and can-can if in historic mood, only to leap into upbeat modernity with break-dancing and mambo. He is odd, but like so much in Rome, his oddness is in no way threatening. People often comment that Rome, though truly a tiring and at times infinitely frustrating city, is above everything safe.

Bread and Circuses

Even the gangs who variously support Rome's twin soccer teams seem to exhibit genuinely good-natured high spirits, generally steering clear of the hooliganism that so taints the British game. A trip to the Olympic Stadium on a Saturday or Sunday afternoon leaves the impression that you are engaging in a festive activity, a variety of local performance, which although it may not involve every family member (grannies are conspicuous by their absence) still enjoys a popular respectability. The teams, Roma and Lazio, who share the stadium, have traditionally drawn their support from different areas and social groups within the city. Founded in 1900, Lazio is immensely proud of its position as the aristocrat of the *calcio* world, and has celebrated its centenary in style. Typically the richer suburbs of Parioli and Prati have been the recruiting ground for its bourgeois support, and being a Lazio fan for many years implied a political stance right of center. Ironically this position led to a conflict with the Fascists in the 1920s, when Mussolini planned to give his capital city the football team it deserved, and capable of facing up to contests with the large clubs from the cities of the north, by uniting all the small clubs into a single Roman team. In 1927 Lazio stood out for its independence, as three other clubs united to create Roma. Trastevere, Testaccio, and other working-class districts have usually associated themselves with this idealized "popular" club. However, to describe Roma as leftist and Lazio as right-wing would nowadays probably seem anachronistic, were it not for a perceptible difference in their fans' attitude toward race. Lazio games still seem to produce more overtly racist comments from the crowd, and the selling of neo-Fascist literature before the game and the display of far-right insignia on banners during it seem more prevalent than at Roma games. However, in an age when soccer allegiances are made as much from exposure to media coverage as local and family traditions, or indeed ideological posturing, these sharp distinctions cannot really be maintained.

The Olympic Stadium was built for the 1960 Games, but was substantially modified and improved for the 1990 World Cup. It holds around 80,000 spectators, and the principal change of the remodeling was to provide an architecturally freestanding awning that projects over the majority of the seating. Not far from the old Flaminia stadium, which still houses the poor relation, rugby, soccer's current Roman home is an immense arcaded ellipse, close to the Mulvian Bridge and enjoying the monumental approach designed by Mussolini's architects for his sports complex, the Foro Italico. Approaching the stadium on a bright winter's day by following the Tiber as it winds its way northward from the city center, you might catch sight of a few unseasonal sunbathers on the riverside terraces of the Italian navy's officers' club. Certainly it will not be long before you come across other fans sporting scarves of either the light blue and white of Lazio, or orange, black, and maroon of Roma. A bit nearer to the ground, you will pass the self-appointed parking attendants who patrol the Lungotevere and its parked cars, selling tickets for the benefits of this dubious duty. Still nearer, you will be able to buy a scarf to make sure that you fit in with whichever team is playing. (Friends of mine have both scarves and wear them appropriately, displaying a fickleness in partisanship but a true love for the game). Getting a ticket at the ground is relatively easy for Lazio games (although their success in the 1999/2000 season has made it harder), but, with the exception of the twice-yearly Rome derby between the clubs, tickets for all games are bookable in certain bars by means of vending machines. In a city which has only just managed to arrange that most banks provide an automatic till, this convenient provision of tickets for the match underlines the essential nature of Roman football.

Snacks for the game can also be purchased outside the stadium. No match is complete without a couple of shots of liqueur coffee, served in tiny canisters about the size of a camera film container. This *café borghetti* is just what you need to maintain your ability to leap from your seat at each goal and its electronic repetition on the enormous screens high above the *curve nord e sud*, the short north and south curves of the elliptical stadium. During Roma matches the *curva sud* provides the home terraces, while Lazio fans prefer the north end during their local games. Both teams rejoice in catchy popular-style songs (*Grazie Roma* is especially and annoyingly memorable), and in the run-up to the game fans greet the announcement of the teams with deafening choruses of their heroes' names.

In more than one way, attending a soccer game at the Olympic Stadium probably gives you the best insight into what it must have been like to go to the public games held centuries ago at that other monster amphitheater that the city boasts, the Colosseum. Certainly the holiday atmosphere is exactly what would have been felt by ancient Romans as strongly as it is enjoyed by their descendants. Gladiatorial games formed chains of entertainment in a period of festival, with each day given over to different types of skill and slaughter. Taking its origin from the rituals that accompanied the death of an important personage, in which a number of slaves would be sacrificed on the funeral bier of their master, gladiatorial spectacle was as big a business in the ancient, as soccer is throughout most of the modern, world. Although running considerable and obvious dangers, individual competitors (all of whom were slaves) might grow personally rich and exchange ownership for vast sums. The prize for a particularly glorious career was freedom and comfortable retirement; the fate for a failure was the blood-soaked dust of the arena.

Built as we have noted by the Emperor Vespasian to reward the Roman plebs with a prime piece of the site formerly and very briefly given over to Nero's Golden House, the Colosseum (or more properly the Flavian Amphitheater) was the largest of its kind in the Roman Empire. Built with considerable elegance, its four tiers of arcading display the passage between the principal architectural orders: Doric for ground-level passes to Ionic on the second and Corinthian on the third—the fourth is crowned with Rome's own Composite order. A huge ellipse like the Olympic Stadium, although with its tiered seating set at a far more extreme rake, it seated more than 60,000 spectators. Scholarly debate ranges over considerable distances in trying to analyze the sociological function and practice of the entertainment. We have to reconstruct what we know about the customs associated with the games from a wide range of fragmentary literary references, as perhaps not that surprisingly no serious author has left us with a detailed account of what went on. Although it is certain that the Vestal Virgins, together with ex-consuls and the high priests of various state cults were given important seats of marble near to the arena, it is not even certain that women were regular spectators. Food was sold to the audience by hawkers inside and outside the stadium, and it could be emptied like its modern counterparts in less than eight minutes. When the weather was hot and the games continued into the late morning and afternoon (they started early), sailors from the navy stationed at Ostia were drafted in to hoist huge awnings made of sail-cloth over the seats.

For centuries the Roman church has held the Colosseum in special awe as a place of martyrdom, although as we have seen in earlier chapters, archaeological and documentary evidence suggests that persecutions of Christians may have more often been held in the circuses of the city. Today, other than being the biggest tourist draw in Rome (and giving ample opportunities to have your photo taken with a big guy posing as a Centurion), it also hosts the Pope's annual Good Friday observance of the Via Crucis, or Way of the Cross. Its association with death is underlined in literary sources, often being used as a particular exemplar of the dangers of catching the deadly Roman Fever. It is here that Henry James' Daisy Miller is bitten by the malarial mosquito, thus cutting short her adventurous career. And all eighteenth- and nineteenth-century visitors who knew that no trip to Rome was complete without a moonlight excursion to the Colosseum were equally well aware of its attendant dangers.

If the modern football stadium recalls something of the physical experience of attending the gladiatorial shows of the arena, the partisanship of Roma and Lazio fans is more akin to that which was lavished upon the competing chariot teams of the circus, the reds, blues, whites and greens. Rival gangs would patrol the city causing spasmodic havoc after heavy drinking and on encountering an opposing faction. This was the most direct sporting legacy that Old Rome bequeathed to its successor in the field of government, Constantinople, where riots sparked by a defeat of the greens could cause a national crisis in the seventh century. Through this Byzantine channel fan behavior has been passed down to a modern, but still occasionally barbaric, world.

Underground Culture

Now that Termini Station has undergone such a startling face-lift, with the promise of zero tolerance of anti-social activity which shows every sign of being lived up to, the most obvious outlet for the principal irritant to Rome's visitors, pickpockets and aggressive begging, will be the Metro itself. The woefully inadequate lines A and B, which roughly quarter the city, are insufferably full most of the time, and opportunities for theft are ample. Originally planned as early as the 1890s, Rome's Metro was postponed until the 1960s due to the scale of work that threatened archaeological treasures along every few feet. The lines as they now exist are deeper than most underground railways to alleviate this problem, but negotiations for the beginning of a line C rapidly degenerate into flat refusals from the heritage lobby every time they are begun. Line A has managed to be extended through Monte Mario in the direction of Lake Bracciano, thus providing a link to an otherwise isolated but busy commuter destination, but little else seems probable for the near future. What the Jubilee year could not achieve seems impossible for lesser dates.

Though the Metro and buses can offer opportunities for thieves, mugging as such seems relatively rare in Rome. That does not mean that you will not fall victim to the gangs of gypsy children who haunt the popular sites and move toward tourists holding out newspapers and cardboard trays the better to cloak their dexterous and intrusive fingers. But even they, if confronted sharply, know better than to try—or if the worst comes to the worst you can pick them up and shake your wallet or passport out of their pockets without hurting even their pride. However, it is good to reflect that few places in Rome communicate a sense of menace. The poorest suburbs are not as poor as they were forty years ago, and Romans do not really go in for interfering in other people's business. Many is the time I've seen a group of Japanese girls hopelessly lost, heading in the opposite direction to the center of town on some lonely bus, only to reflect that the worst that will happen to them is that they might be sold some over-priced cold drinks and have to pose for snaps with the overweight proprietor of some seedy suburban bar before being sent on their way. London or New York seem infinitely more dangerous, for all their lack of obvious sexual harassment.

Rome-sick

St. Anselm, Archbishop of Milan in the fourth century, advocated following the religious observances of Rome when he was making a visit there, and disregarding them when he was back at home. This, I suppose, is the theological equivalent of owning both a Lazio and a Roma scarf. It is impossible to recreate a Roman life anywhere other than at the fountainhead itself. I need only reflect briefly on my attempts to recreate the dishes which I have enjoyed in the Venerable English College, at Dell'Omo's *trattoria*, or even at the simplest of *Tavole Calde* within a bar, and the singular failure which results. Dinner party conversation will bore us with the truisms that the ingredients we can get here (in London, New York, Manchester or Moscow) are simply not the same. But there is more to our case of Rome-sickness than this straightforward deprivation. Not being in Rome is a state of mind only to be remedied by its opposite, being there. Nothing else will do, if it's that which is at the heart of your expectation or desire. It's been at the heart of my desires for some time now, and as I stand on the precipice and prepare to be fulfilled once more, my innate Protestant fear of getting what I actually want gives me some cause for concern. Luckily my guide in this matter is that practical saint whose words head this chapter—note that he will conform to Roman practice in terms of its fasting rather than its feasting—I can reassure myself by undertaking to do both. Now, I wonder just how often my stipend will run to a good meal at Dell'Omo. Maybe I'll see you there.

EPILOGUE

Leaving Rome

During this book our world has been bounded by Rome's walls and the suburban pavements and gardens that stretch a couple of miles beyond them. That is its purpose, so I don't mean to apologize. But, as we've followed our tortuous route through time and space, maybe you've asked yourself if Romans ever leave the city. We've heard how plenty of people have arrived to visit or stay, but what about jaunts out, free time to be enjoyed away from the hard work and real world which is Rome? Time away for Romans comes in two main varieties: the *gita*, which is usually a day-trip, and the *villeggiatura*, which implies an extended stay away, traditionally in a house you or your family owns at the sea or in the mountains. I was party to both while a student here ten years ago, and I am busily planning how best to maintain the tradition when I firmly establish myself as a resident.

At the Venerable English College there was a further subdivision of the *gita*: the "slug" and "hearty" varieties. The first of these consisted in rising late on a Thursday morning (the free day from lectures in seminarist Rome), lingering over a coffee, and heading off to take a short train journey or bus ride to a pleasant town with interesting sites and, most importantly, an excellent restaurant. Lunch would last two or three hours and there would be the prospect of a light(ish) supper on arrival back in college in the early evening. The "hearty" *gita* was a very different beast. Rising before dawn, its participants caught a bus to some far flung village in the Apennines, and fueled only by a couple of *mortadella* sandwiches hiked over a brace of mountains, forded the streams, followed every rainbow, until they found their bus home from some other tiny hamlet. They often arrived back so late that supper was over, and the cupboard (almost) bare. I sampled both types of trip during my short time at the college, and acquired a taste for each, vainly hoping that the effects of one sort would cancel out those of the other.

Most native Roman *gite* are to the seaside, and in his story *The Vow*, Alberto Moravia successfully characterizes the excitement which they can generate:

> When the fine weather came, I began to long for the sea again, and for trips to the seaside. I had been ill all the winter and part of the spring... Meanwhile the months were going by, and I, shut up in my little car-accessories shop, kept thinking of the sea, the lovely sea with its clean, fine sand and ever-moving, ever-living blue waters and blazing sunshine that scorches and burns but does not make you sweat. I had such a longing for the sea that I even dreamt about it at night; and as the bathing season drew near I used to go out every morning on the balcony to see what the sky looked like behind St Peter's. We were now at the end of May; and one Saturday I suggested to Ginetta, my fiancée, that we should go next day to Castelfusano for our first bathe of the year.

Rome rejoices in being near the sea if only for the times when a cooling breeze reaches the suffocating city. However, the beaches which stretch along the Lazio seaboard in the direction of Naples are really excellent and much less crowded than those nearer by at Ostia, Castelfusano and Civitavecchia, especially when just a little out of season. The big seaside holiday occurs for Romans, as for all other Italians, during the *Ferragosto*, the summer break that starts on the first Sunday of August until the *rientro* some three weeks later. At both the beginning and the end of this period the roads to, and then from, all points south and beachward are completely clogged with traffic. The Feast of the Assumption itself on August 15, standing as the religious peg to hang this holiday-making upon, was the traditional time to give tips to service providers in Rome. This greasing of the palms then went to furnish the little trip out that their city-dwelling families so desperately needed. Wealthier Romans would certainly leave the city for the whole of August and preferably longer, removing to their villas in the country. This noble tradition, followed both by emperors and popes and their attendant courts, has its scaled-down modern equivalent. Turning their backs on the medieval favorite resorts of Viterbo and Perugia, popes since Urban VIII have often spent their summers at Castel Gandolfo, high above Lago Albano, although it is said that John Paul II dislikes the baroque palace.

Almost immediately across the volcanic crater that forms the lake is an old Franciscan church, Our Lady of the Snows, and its attendant convent buildings, built upon the foundations of an ancient Roman villa belonging to the Scipio *gens*. Its name is Palazzola, and it is now the "villa" of the Venerable English College, which not only receives the annual six-week *villeggiatura* of the college students, but hosts guests and parish trips throughout the year. In the nineteenth and early twentieth centuries, the English and Welsh students who came to study at *Il Venerabile* stayed for a full six or seven years, not once returning home. The villa that gave them an escape from the summer heat of the city center was an absolute necessity, at least for continuing sanity, and today it is still a welcome resort to minds needing just a little rest before a reinvigorated return to the delights of the city.

The annual ordination of deacons from the college takes place at Palazzola in July, and some meetings of ARCIC (The Anglican/Roman Catholic International Commission) have been held there. It may have been on such an occasion that the then pope was heard to comment that he was quite aware of the location of the villa, a little higher up the slope than Castel Gandolfo, and on the opposite side of the lake: "this of course," he added, "enables you English to maintain your tradition of looking down on us." Wit, it seems, can be a happy companion to holiness.

Roman residents can still take themselves off to places further afield than the Colli Albani, the Alban Hills. Pliny the Younger devotes two of his letters to describing his country house in the upper valley of the Tiber. Some 125 miles north of Rome, at the border between modern Umbria and Tuscany, and on one of the routes to his family estates near Como, the villa was both farm and retreat after the pattern of the ancient Romans. The site of the villa has recently been excavated in a place that had long been traditionally associated with it, being known locally as Colle Plinio. Tiles and bricks from the extensive second-century structure firmly identify it as Pliny's Tibertine home, which he so lovingly describes:

The countryside is very beautiful. Picture to yourself a vast amphitheatre such as only could be the work of nature; the great spreading plain is ringed round by mountains, their summits crowned by ancient woods of tall trees... the meadows are bright with flowers, covered with trefoil and other delicate plants which always seem soft and fresh, for everything is fed by streams which never run dry... The river [Tiber] is navigable, so that all produce is conveyed to Rome by boat, but only in winter and spring—in summer its level falls and its bed has to give up the claim to the title of a great river until the following autumn... My house is on the lower slopes of a hill but commands as good a view as if it were higher up... It faces mainly South, and so from midday onwards in summer (a little earlier in winter) it seems to invite the sun into the colonnade. This is broad, and long in proportion, with several rooms opening out of it as well as the old-fashioned type of entrance hall... It is a great pleasure to look down on the countryside... for the view seems to be a painted scene of unusual beauty rather than a real landscape. (Letters, Book V, To Domitius Apollinaris, *Trans. Betty Radice*)

Jim Powrie and his wife Jill run an estate agency in Umbria not far from the site of Pliny's villa. Their own house has the Tiber at the bottom of its garden, and here in spring and late summer it has the quality of a limpid stream, the welcome water-playground of their two children and friends, with or without the assistance of a small boat. Even here, though, the Tiber can take on the yellow-brown hue reminiscent of cold tea, which earned it the epithet *flavus* (yellow) from the ancients. The Powries' clients, though mostly comprising their own British country-folk, represent the full gamut of European, Antipodean, and North American interest in the area. It is in the house that they sold me, high above the Tiber and looking down upon its curving path along the valley, identifiable by surrounding cypresses and oaks, that I have written the majority of this book. Far from Rome, we are yet imperceptibly but enduringly connected to it by the passage of countless gallons of water and by centuries of human traffic. High above the valley, Garibaldi's statue can still look down from Anghiari, a walled hill-town which disdains the description quaint (it's far too beautiful), as he looked down in person to descry the approaching Austrian armies in pursuit of him. His rallying cry *O Roma o Morte!*, Either Rome or death!, still has the power to move even when he seems to be pointing in the wrong direction. My own contemplation of the valley, rather more Pliny-like than Garibaldian, has been an inspiration.

So many people have traveled to Rome in search of education through the centuries (I'd count myself among them) that it can come as a surprise to recall that Romans have left home to study too. Waiting for my mother at Rome's Fiumicino airport, I was brought face to face with this realization by the arrival immediately before her plane of a horde of adolescents who had been to Britain for a month's English course. Before they started to stream in indissoluble bands through customs, their families, especially their parents, began to show the strain of the excitement that the coming reunion aroused. Middle-aged men and women paced up and down, chain-smoked and occasionally shared the odd sharp comment with their neighbors. Perhaps they had never been apart from their children before. Then, suddenly, there was running, hugging, kissing, leaping, shouting, and singing, as huge extended families burst into uncontrollable displays of emotion, awash with tears and relieved by laughter. Delight was sometimes tempered with a disbelieving, mock-disapproval as some kids came back with outrageously dyed hair, pierced features, and in one wonderfully comic variation, a whole class load of lads dressed in kilts. I remembered the language schools of my British university days, crammed with Italian youth at the time only notable for the mindless way they cycled and the nightly cries of "*Ciao; a domani, da Wimpy!*" as they rode off to their respectable digs. I won't say that it made me feel young again; it just reminded me that I still am.

Rome has a place for the young of all ages, perhaps because it is so old. I can't do better in ending this book than by quoting my own favorite close of an earlier and similar publication, Elizabeth Bowen's *A Time in Rome*. It also has the advantage of quoting from scripture, the Letter to the Hebrews, something which I have done little of; perhaps by this token you may at last believe that I am a vicar:

> *Two days later I left, taking the afternoon train to Paris. As before I had too much baggage to go by air. Such a day, when it does come, has nothing particular about it. Only from the train as it moved out did I look at Rome. Backs of houses I had not ever seen before wavered into mists, stinging my eyes. My darling, my darling, my darling! Here we have no abiding city.*

We ought all to leave Rome with too much baggage to go by air.

Chronology

1000-750BC	Prehistoric Rome. Iron age settlements on the Palatine
753BC	The traditional date for the foundation of Rome by Romulus and Remus; Year "0" in Roman calendar, the beginning of a line of seven kings
510BC	Expulsion of the Etruscan Tarquin family, the last kings. Foundation of the Republic, ruled by Consuls elected from the Senate
312BC	Appius Claudius acts as Censor and builds the first aqueduct and the Appian Way to points south of Rome
300sBC	Series of Social Wars in which the Republic defeats other local powers in mainland Italy
260s -202BC	Series of Punic Wars in which the Republic defeats its main international rival, the Phoenician colony of Carthage
90–31BC	Series of Civil Wars in which the Republic conquers foreign territories but becomes increasingly politically fragmented under the rule of various successful generals
48–44BC	Julius Caesar emerges as the dominant figure in the Roman world, but his unprecedented power is cut short by assassination
31BC	Octavian, Caesar's heir, emerges triumphant from the power struggle following his death, and as Augustus (27BC), becomes first Emperor
60sAD	SS. Peter and Paul traditionally thought to have been martyred during Nero's persecution of Christians
69	The Julio Claudian Family succeeded by the Flavian dynasty of Emperors. Vespasian builds the Colosseum
96–180	The "Pax Romana" reaches its greatest stability and extent under Trajan, Hadrian and their successors
180	Empire undergoes political instability after the death of Marcus Aurelius; spasmodic persecution of Christians continues
312	Constantine seizes power and recognizes Christianity as official religion; Byzantium refounded as Constantinople replaces Rome as capital
410	First Sack of Rome by Alaric and the Goths; St. Ambrose and St. Augustine writing; Barbarian rule in Italy
590	Pope St. Gregory the Great and the growth of Western monasticism
608	The Last Imperial monument erected in the Forum, marking a brief period of Byzantine influence in Rome
800	Charlemagne crowned as first Holy Roman Emperor as papacy looks westward for legitimacy and primacy
900s	The "Pornocracy of the Holy See" as the Senatrices Theodora I and II and Marusia control the city and the papacy
1075	Hildebrand (Pope St. Gregory VII) strengthens the papacy and founds its medieval ideology of superiority over secular authority
1095	Urban II preaches the First Crusade as Western political and theological interests turn East
1215	Innocent III holds the Fourth Lateran Council marking a high point for the medieval papacy

1300	Boniface VIII inaugurates the Jubilee
1305	The papacy removes to Avignon to receive direct French protection; noble Roman families fortify the Roman ruins
1378	The Great Schism begins in which two or three rival popes reign simultaneously, one definitively back in Rome
1417	Resolution of the Schism at the Council of Constance; Martin V, a Roman noble, inaugurates the Roman Renaissance
1444	Nicholas V founds the Vatican Library, invites Fra Angelico, Piero della Francesca and Massacio to Rome, and plans new St. Peter's
1492	Borgia ascendancy; Pinturicchio, Perugino and Fra Lippo Lippi in Rome
1503	Julius II re-establishes the credibility of the Papal States; Michelangelo and Raphael at work
1527	The Sack of Rome by Imperial troops as successive Medici popes fail to deal creatively with the Lutheran phenomenon
1544	The Counter Reformation is inaugurated with the Council of Trent
1585	Sixtus V, the most successful sixteenth-century pontiff, remodels the city and Vatican policy—Mannerism flourishes
1600	Giordano Bruno the last heretic to be burned at the stake by the Roman Inquisition; Roman Baroque flourishes under Bernini and Borromini
1660s	Queen Christina of Sweden is exiled in Rome; city of opera and early tourists
1690	The Stuart Court in exile arrives in Rome; the Grand Tour develops
1750	Building of the Trevi Fountain; political stagnation in Rome
1796	Napoleonic invasions and abduction of Pius VI; First Republic of Italy
1815	The Council Of Vienna re-establishes the integrity of the Papal States
1823	Keats dies in Rome; its role as a literary destination becomes increasingly established
1830	The First Year of Revolutions displaces Gregory XVI for a time; afterwards secret societies flourish
1848	The Second Year of Revolutions establishes the Roman Republic defended by Mazzini and Garibaldi
1860	The Kingdom of Italy founded without Rome
1870	The Rome of the Popes falls as the city is taken by Italian troops; Pius VII becomes the "Prisoner of the Vatican"
1880s	Building boom in Rome as the new capital develops
1892	Leo X publishes Rerum Novarum—rapprochement between papacy and modern world
1898	Foundation of La Rinascente; failure to build Metro on Parisian and London models
1900	Anarchist assassination of King Umberto I
1915	Entry of Italy into the First World War on Allied side
1922	Fascists come to power; Mussolini's March on Rome
1943	Rome the target of Allied bombing, then *città aperta*
1960	Rome Olympics; building of main stadium and completion of EUR
1991	Tangentopoli and the "Fall of the First Republic"
2000	Millennium celebrations and associated regeneration

Further Reading

Anderson, Robin, *Rome Churches of English Interest.* Rome: Vatican Polyglot Press, 1960.

Aston, Margaret, *The Fifteenth Century: The Prospect of Europe.* London: Thames and Hudson, 1968.

Barefoot, Brian, *The English Road to Rome.* Upton-Upon-Severn: Images, 1993.

Barzini, Luigi, *The Italians.* London: Hamish Hamilton, 1964.

—, *From Caesar to the Mafia: Sketches of Italian Life.* London: Hamish Hamilton, 1971.

Belloc, Hilaire, *The Path to Rome.* London: Nelson, 1942.

Boardman, John, ed., *The Oxford History of the Classical World.* Oxford: Oxford University Press, 1986.

Bowen, Elizabeth, *A Time in Rome.* London: Longman, 1960.

Carpanetto, Dino, *Italy in the Age of Reason 1685-1789.* London: Longman, 1987.

Claridge, Amanda, *Rome (Oxford Archaeological Guides).* Oxford: Oxford University Press, 1998.

Clark, Martin, *Modern Italy 1871-1982.* London: Longman, 1984.

Chandlery, P.J., *Pilgrim Walks in Rome.* London: Manresa Press, 1908.

Cochrane, Eric, *Italy 1530-1630.* London: Longman, 1988.

De Angelis, Bertolotti, *La Residenza Imperiale di Masenzio.* Rome: Fratelli Palombi Editori, 1988.

De Voragine, Jacobus, *The Golden Legend.* Princeton NJ: Princeton University Press, 1993.

Duffy, Eamon, *Saints and Sinners: A History of the Popes.* New Haven CT & London: Yale University Press, 1997.

Fallowell, Duncan, *To Noto or London to Sicily in a Ford.* London: Vintage, 1995.

Faure, Gabriel, *The Gardens of Rome.* London: Nicholas Kaye, 1960.

Frei, Matt, Italy, *The Unfinished Revolution.* London: Arrow, 1998.

Hare, Augustus. *Walks in Rome.* London: W. Ibister, 1874.

Hay, Denys, *Italy in the Age of the Renaissance.* London: Longman, 1989.

Hearder, Harry, *Italy in the Age of the Risorgimento 1790-1870.* London: Longman, 1983.

Heer, Friedrich, *The Holy Roman Empire.* London: Weidenfield and Nicholson, 1968.

Hutchinson, Robert, *When in Rome: An Unauthorised Guide to the Vatican.* London: Harper Collins, 1998.

Kelly, John, *The Oxford Dictionary of Popes.* Oxford: Oxford University Press, 1986.

Kininmonth, Christopher, *Rome Alive*. London: John Lehmann, 1951.

Lane Fox, Robin, *Pagans and Christians*. London: Viking, 1986.

Larner, John, *Italy in the Age of Dante and Petrarch*. London: Longman, 1980.

Lyall, Archibald, *Rome Sweet Rome*. London: Putnam, 1956.

Macadam, Alta, *Rome: Blue Guide*. London: A.& C. Black, 1994.

Mack Smith, Denis, *Mazzini*. New Haven CT & London: Yale University Press, 1994.

—, *Italy*. Ann Arbor: University of Michigan Press, 1969.

Mackinnon, Albert, *Things Seen in Rome*. London: Seeley, Service and Co., 1927.

Mertz, Barbara and Richard, *Two Thousand Years in Rome*. London: Dent, 1968.

Montanelli, Indro, *L'Italia del Novecento*. Milan: Superpocket, 1998.

Moravia, Alberto, *More Roman Tales*. London: Secker & Warburg, 1963.

Morton, H.V., *A Traveller in Rome*. London: Methuen, 1957.

—, *The Waters of Rome*. London: Connoisseur, 1966.

Motion, Andrew, *Keats: A Biography*. New York: Farrar, Straus & Giroux, 1998.

Pietrangeli, Carlo et al, *Guide Rionali di Roma*. Rome: Fratelli Palombi Editori, 1984.

Richardson, Jonathan (Senior and Junior), *An Account of Some of the Statues, Bas Reliefs, Drawings and Pictures in Italy, with Remarks*. London: 1722.

Roberts, Cecil, *And So To Rome*. London: Hodder & Stoughton, 1950.

Rodd, Rennell, *Rome of the Renaissance and Today*. London: Macmillan, 1932.

Ross Holloway, R., *The Archaeology of Early Rome and Latium*. London: Routledge, 1996.

Rowland, Ingrid D., *The Culture of the Late Renaissance*. Cambridge: Cambridge University Press, 1996.

Runciman, Steven, *The Fall of Constantinople*, 1453. Cambridge: Cambridge University Press, 1965.

Segala, Elisabetta, *Domus Aurea*. Rome: Electa, 1999.

Smith, Patrick, *A Desk in Rome*. London: Collins, 1974.

Story, William Wentmore, *Roba di Roma*. Boston Mass.: Houghton, Mifflin, 1893.

Trevelyan, George Macaulay, *Garibaldi's Defence of the Roman Republic*. London: Nelson, 1928.

Varriano, John, *Rome: A Literary Companion*. London: John Murray, 1991.

Index of Literary
& Historical Names

Index of Places